Leadership for Green Schools

D1552153

Leadership for Green Schools provides aspiring and practicing leaders with the tools they need to facilitate the design, leadership, and management of greener, more sustainable schools. Framed by theory and research, this text draws from the fields of sustainability science, built learning environment, and educational leadership to explain what green schools look like, what role school buildings play in advancing sustainable organizational and instructional practices, and why school leaders are "greening" their leadership. Sustainability can often seem like an unreachable, utopian set of goals, but this important resource uses illustrative examples of successful schools and leaders to show how establishing and managing green schools aligns with the work they are already doing to restore engaged learning within their schools and communities. *Leadership for Green Schools* is a unique and important resource to help leaders reduce the environmental impact of school buildings and immerse students in purposeful, meaningful learning for a sustainable, just future.

Special Features:

- ◆ Examples from award-winning schools and leaders—best-practices and illustrative examples throughout make whole school sustainability come to life and show how green leadership is a real possibility for the reader.
- ◆ Aligned with Professional Standards for Educational Leadership—provides the tools necessary for leaders to advance sustainability goals while at the same time fulfilling the core purposes of their job.
- ◆ End-of-chapter discussion questions—valuable pedagogical tools invite personal reflection and conversation.

Lisa A. W. Kensler is Associate Professor and Program Coordinator of Educational Leadership at Auburn University, USA.

Cynthia L. Uline is Professor Emeritus of Educational Leadership and Executive Director of the National Center for the 21st Century Schoolhouse, San Diego State University, USA.

Leadership for Green Schools

Sustainability for Our Children, Our Communities, and Our Planet

Lisa A. W. Kensler
Cynthia L. Uline

Routledge
Taylor & Francis Group

NEW YORK AND LONDON

First published 2017
by Routledge
711 Third Avenue, New York, NY 10017

and by Routledge
2 Park Square, Milton Park, Abingdon, Oxon, OX14 4RN

Routledge is an imprint of the Taylor & Francis Group, an informa business

Library of Congress Cataloging in Publication Data
Names: Kensler, Lisa A. W. | Uline, Cynthia L.
Title: Leadership for green schools : sustainability for our children, our
        communities, and our planet / by Lisa A.W. Kensler and Cynthia Uline.
Description: New York : Routledge, 2017. | Includes index.
Identifiers: LCCN 2016013525| ISBN 9780415715676 (hardback) |
        ISBN 9780415715683 (pbk.) | ISBN 9781315880525 (e-book) |
        ISBN 9781134737758 (mobipocket/kindle)
Subjects: LCSH: School buildings—Environmental aspects—United States. |
        Environmental education.
Classification: LCC LB3241.2 .K46 2017 | DDC 371.2—dc23
LC record available at http://lccn.loc.gov/2016013525

ISBN: 978-0-415-71567-6 (hbk)
ISBN: 978-0-415-71568-3 (pbk)
ISBN: 978-1-315-88052-5 (ebk)

Typeset in Palatino
by Swales & Willis, Exeter, Devon, UK

Printed and bound in the United States of America by Publishers Graphics,
LLC on sustainably sourced paper.

Dedication

From Lisa: For Mike, who is my best friend and inspiration.

From Cynthia: For Joe, who is my joy.

From us both: We dedicate this book to educational leaders and all who learn alongside them.

Contents

About the Authors

Lisa A. W. Kensler is an Associate Professor of Educational Leadership at Auburn University. She received her EdD in Educational Leadership from Lehigh University in 2008 and a Master's degree in biology from Old Dominion University in 1996. Prior to returning to her childhood stomping grounds in Pennsylvania to earn her doctorate, Lisa spent a decade serving as a secondary science teacher and teacher leader in Norfolk, VA, Annapolis, MD, and St. Louis, MO. She taught in public schools and an independent school. In all cases, she worked to create the sort of classrooms students would choose to attend, even if their attendance was not required. She empowered students to lead in the classroom and beyond. She and her students were active in Jane Goodall's Roots & Shoots program, designing and leading initiatives for making the world a better place. Prior to her work as an educator, Lisa was an ecologist. Early in her career she worked for the Smithsonian's National Museum of Natural History and the U.S. Fish and Wildlife Service studying coral reefs, Chesapeake Bay, and the Great Lakes.

Lisa's research is grounded in her lifelong love of nature and her experience as an ecologist and educator. She uses her understanding of living systems to inform her research related to green schools and the leadership and learning required for transforming schools into more socially just, ecologically healthy, and economically viable communities. She has published articles and book chapters on democratic community, trust, systems thinking, and sustainability. She also integrates sustainability into the educational leadership courses that she teaches. Lisa was the 2013 winner of the Emily & Gerald Leischuck Graduate Teaching Award, an award that recognizes "faculty members who have consistently shown evidence of superior teaching excellence. These individuals have gone above and beyond the call of duty by engaging their students in the classroom and instilling a love for life-long learning."

Cynthia L. Uline is a Professor Emeritus of Educational Leadership at San Diego State University. Cynthia received her PhD in Educational Administration from the Pennsylvania State University in 1995 and a Master's degree in Special Education from Syracuse University in 1979. Cynthia previously served on faculty at the Ohio State University, where she was an assistant and associate professor of Educational Administration from 1995 to 2005.

Cynthia also served as a classroom teacher, teacher leader, state education agency administrator, and an educational consultant working with school districts, community agencies, city governments, state agencies, and governors' offices, always seeking to facilitate meaningful partnerships on behalf of students and their families. Cynthia currently directs SDSU's National Center for the 21st Century Schoolhouse (http://go.sdsu.edu/education/schoolhouse/). The Center supports the planning and design of learner-centered schools through communication, research, and training. Over seven years, the Center delivered a fully online advanced certificate program in educational facility planning, with students representing 34 states and 5 countries. Developed in partnership with the Association for Learning Environments (formerly CEFPI), the Advanced Academy for Learning Spaces continues to provide training in the key knowledge and skills central to the design, construction, and maintenance of learner-centered school facilities.

Cynthia's research explores the influence of built learning environments on students' learning, as well as the roles leaders, teachers, and the public play in shaping these learning spaces. Her current research considers the potential of green schools as student-centered, ecologically responsive, and economically viable places for learning. She has published articles related to leadership for learning, leadership preparation, and the improvement of social and physical learning environments in journals such as *Educational Administration Quarterly, Teacher College Record, Journal of Educational Administration, Journal of School Leadership, International Journal of Leadership in Education, Leading and Managing, Journal of Research and Development in Education, Educational Leadership,* and *Educational Technology.* This is Cynthia's third co-authored book.

Preface

From Factories to Living Systems

The factory model of schooling is showing its age and limitations. This "was a model of school as something separate from daily life, something governed in an authoritarian manner, oriented above all else to producing, as efficiently as possible, a standardized product" (Senge, Cambron-McCabe, Lucas, Smith, & Dutton, 2012, p. 36). What was designed for the industrial era of the 19th and 20th centuries now fails to serve our children, our communities, and our planet in the 21st century. So much has changed. In light of new understandings regarding the science of learning, this factory model falls short in meeting the needs of most learners. In the wake of the industrial age, we also have a lot of cleaning up to do. The linear take–make–waste system of production, with its requisite focus on rampant consumerism, has stressed Earth's ecosystems (Leonard, 2010; Wijkman & Rockstrom, 2012). Environmental crises and social inequities threaten the resilience of local and global communities (Blewitt & Tilbury, 2013).

Traditional models of schooling simply do not prepare children to face the unprecedented environmental, social, and economic challenges of the 21st century. Whole school sustainability, practiced in green schools across the world, responds to these 21st-century needs, at the same time providing a comprehensive strategy for school improvement, addressing every aspect of education from school culture and climate to curriculum and facilities. This book steps beyond the traditional factory model of schooling to present a living system alternative, a model of schooling that better serves children's learning needs, as well as local and global environmental, social, and economic needs. In particular, we paint a picture of the promise and potential of whole school sustainability to restore vibrant, engaged learning within our schools and communities.

For Educational Leaders at Every Level

Our target audience for this book includes practicing and emerging educational leaders, as well as people like us, who prepare them. We include school administrators, teachers, staff, students, parents, community members, and policy makers as educational leaders. Transforming education, on the magnitude we present here, does not happen without deep engagement of leaders throughout our educational systems. We are particularly cognizant that school principals and central office administrators need this primer on green schools and whole school sustainability. Research repeatedly tells us of the critical role positional leaders play in facilitating change for sustainability (Buckler & Creech, 2014), and no other comprehensive introduction to sustainability, that we know of, speaks directly to this vitally important audience. Therefore, we utilize the Professional Standards for Educational Leaders as a backdrop for our writing. The Professional Standards did not drive our writing, but we were careful to keep the standards in mind. We will describe these standards and their relevance to whole school sustainability further in Chapter 1.

We expect you to find that whole school sustainability is about working differently rather than more. Sustainability has relevance to every aspect of school leadership. Fundamentally, changes will flow more naturally from thinking differently about your school, replacing factory model thinking with living system model thinking. Reflecting on their extensive international research into successful school leadership, Day and Leithwood (2007) noted that, "The work of our successful principals strongly suggests that they thought of their organizations as living systems, not machines" (p. 200). We don't know how many, if any, of these principals were involved with green schools or sustainability, as these details were not discussed explicitly in any of the book's featured cases. We do know that they effectively led schools that facilitated student learning. We increasingly learn from studies of effective leadership that command and control strategies, rooted in mechanistic thinking, do not work. In this book, we consider schools to be living systems. We step beyond metaphorical conversations and delve into the reality that, as humans, we are living systems, and we depend on the natural systems in which we live. By extension, we are wise to design, manage, and lead our schools with this understanding.

Understanding our human organizations, schools in particular, as living systems results in two primary benefits. First, we understand students, not as products of a 12-year assembly line, but as individual beings for whom the love of learning is an innate capacity. With this perspective, we stop demanding that learners perform as we direct. We stop blaming our students for disengaging. Rather, we realize that children and adults are voracious learners by nature and we design, manage, and lead for the conditions that allow this love of learning to flourish. Second, because our human communities are dependent on socio-ecological systems for life support, we accept responsibility for our actions. We realize that our daily actions contribute either to harming or enhancing Earth's social communities and ecological systems and we consciously seek to minimize negative and maximize positive socio-ecological impacts. Our aim in this book is to paint a vivid picture of possibility for our schools. Our schools can be vibrant centers of learning and socio-ecological responsibility. We think you will see that these are mutually reinforcing aims that provide powerful leverage for school improvement, as well as for the future of life on Earth.

Our picture of possibility is not simply imaginative or theoretical. It is supported by research across disciplines such as neuroscience, psychology, education, organizational studies, building sciences, ecology, and more. It is also grounded in our personal research that has taken us into green schools across the United States, as well as a few beyond our borders. We have met many trailblazing educators who are leading the way out of the factory model and into a new model of whole school sustainability. We hope that your imagination is sparked by reading this book and that you will see opportunities for leaving the factory model behind in order to better serve our children, our communities, and our planet.

To Encourage and Extend Learning

We organized this book with a focus on learning, whether formal classroom learning or less formal individual or group learning. Vibrant love of learning is a prerequisite for making progress towards a more resilient and sustainable future, as deep, transformative change comes only as a consequence of deeply engaged learning. Whole school sustainability offers restorative approaches for cultivating vibrant learning in our schools, as we detail throughout the book. For our readers' learning pleasure, we offer end of chapter discussion questions that invite reflection on your own practice and context while also challenging you to continuously expand your green school efforts. The book begins with an introductory chapter, "Leading Schools with a Green Frame of Mind." This chapter provides an overview of sustainability and its relevance to education and educational leadership. We describe the Professional Standards for Educational Leadership and provide a crosswalk between these standards and the chapters of this book. We also introduce two school leaders who represent composites of the many school leaders we have met during our visits to their green schools. These two leaders, Angela and Tom, will travel with us through the book and keep us grounded in real life practice of school leadership.

The following nine chapters are organized into three main sections inspired by Barr, Cross, and Dunbar's (2014) whole school sustainability framework. Their framework includes organizational culture, physical place, and educational program. Our three sections also address these common domains of schooling, although we approach some of the details differently. In the spirit of understanding schools as living systems, Part I describes the DNA of whole school sustainability. Part II describes healthy ecosystems for facilitating the love of learning. Part III delves deeply into meaningful, purposeful, and engaged learning and teaching.

Part I: The DNA of Whole School Sustainability

Chapters 2, 3, and 4 comprise Part I. The DNA of whole school sustainability includes the values, principles, vision and missions that we see in schools that practice whole school sustainability. Chapter 2, "In the Best Interests of Children," presents an argument that greener, more sustainable, schools are very much in the best interest of children, our communities, and our planet. We explore the purposes of schooling and our ethical responsibilities for meeting the needs of the 21st century. Chapter 3, "Design Principles for Whole School Sustainability," discusses the guiding principles underlying whole school sustainability. We frame the practice of whole school sustainability with both ecological and democratic principles. We make the case that healthy social systems, governed by democratic principles, are nested within ecological systems. Thus, we also consider ecological principles, those that govern healthy living systems, in the design, management, and leadership of schools. These guiding principles meet school leaders where they are and facilitate design for whole school sustainability from the inside out, the way living systems grow and develop. Chapter 4, "Greening Your School's Vision," illustrates the transformative power of sustainability-focused visions and missions for leading schools throughout the 21st century.

Part II: Healthy Ecosystems for Learning

Part II of this book (Chapters 5, 6, and 7) continues with a deep exploration of healthy learning ecosystems, including school buildings set within their broader socio-ecological communities. In Chapter 5, "Place, Community, and Partnerships," we describe how green schools are deeply rooted in, and intentionally engaged with, their glocal (global and local) communities. We consider the role of place and place-based learning in developing children's understanding of the complex interdependencies that exist between human and natural systems. The chapter examines the challenges associated with harnessing this deep knowledge of place in order to build a 21st-century, global community. Our focus narrows to the building as a place and source for learning in Chapter 6, "Green School Buildings as Dynamic Learning Environments." We examine the role school facilities play in supporting students' learning and overall well-being. The chapter builds a compelling case for providing high-quality, sustainable school facilities as a means for realizing children's current learning potential and for protecting their future quality of life. In Chapter 7, "Operations and Maintenance for Whole School Sustainability," we examine how green-minded principals, together with their facilities colleagues, manage healthy, safe, and sustainable learning environments in ways that reduce energy, conserve natural resources, and minimize waste. The chapter also explores how these green operation and maintenance routines provide opportunities for leveraging the facility as a three-dimensional textbook.

Part III: Meaningful, Purposeful, Engaged Learning

Part III of this book (Chapters 8, 9, and 10) takes a detailed look at learning in green schools: learning that is meaningful, purposeful, and engaged. Chapter 8 focuses on student learning and Chapter 9 on teacher learning. We see human learning as a valuable ecosystem service and explain what we mean by that in Chapter 8, "For the Love of Learning." This chapter provides an overview of mind, brain, and educational science and demonstrates its applicability to education for sustainability. We demonstrate the potential for green schools to maximize student learning while at the same time cultivating stronger, healthier local communities and reducing the school's ecological footprint. In Chapter 9, "Innovative Teaching in Green Schools," we turn to teacher learning and examine the ways teachers learn and model the sustainability-related behaviors, dispositions, and habits of mind they seek to develop in their students. The chapter considers how teachers acquire deep knowledge of the principles and constructs underlying education for sustainability. We also explore how green school principals develop and sustain professional communities among teachers, providing opportunities for teachers to reflect deeply and critically on their own and each other's teaching practice. Chapter 10, "Green School Networks, Recognition Programs, and Resources," ends our book with a detailed overview of U.S. Department of Education Green Ribbon School award winners. These schools are already leading the way into a greener, more sustainable future. You will also find an overview of resources for supporting your work towards whole school sustainability.

Finally, this book is fundamentally about redesigning schools to better serve children and adults' love of learning so that we might learn together how to live into a future characterized by healthy ecosystems, equitable societies, and prosperous economies.

The future can't be predicted, but it can be envisioned and brought lovingly into being. Systems can't be controlled, but they can be designed and redesigned. We can't surge forward with certainty into a world of no surprises, but we can expect surprises and learn from them and even profit from them. We can't impose our will upon a system. We can listen to what the system tells us, and discover how its properties and our values can work together to bring forth something much better than could ever be produced by our will alone. (Meadows & Wright, 2008, p. 169)

References

Barr, S. K., Cross, J. E., & Dunbar, B. H. (2014). *The whole-school sustainability framework: Guiding principles for integrating sustainability into all aspects of a school organization.* Retrieved from Washington, DC: http://centerforgreenschools.org/sites/default/files/resource-files/Whole-School_Sustainability_Framework.pdf

Blewitt, J., & Tilbury, D. (2013). *Searching for resilience in sustainable development: Learning journeys in conservation.* New York: Routledge.

Buckler, C., & Creech, H. (2014). *Shaping the future we want: UN Decade of Education for Sustainable Development (2005–2014) Final Report.* Retrieved from France: http://unesdoc.unesco.org/images/0023/002303/230302e.pdf

Day, C., & Leithwood, K. (Eds.). (2007). *Successful principal leadership in time of change: Qn international perspective.* Dordrecht, The Netherlands: Springer.

Leonard, A. (2010). *The story of stuff.* New York: Free Press.

Meadows, D. H., & Wright, D. (2008). *Thinking in systems: A primer.* White River Junction, VT: Chelsea Green Publishing.

Senge, P. M., Cambron-McCabe, N., Lucas, T., Smith, B., & Dutton, J. (2012). *Schools that learn (updated and revised): A fifth discipline fieldbook for educators, parents, and everyone who cares about education.* New York: Crown Business.

Wijkman, A., & Rockstrom, J. (2012). *Bankrupting nature: Denying our planetary boundaries.* New York: Routledge.

Acknowledgements

We wish to acknowledge the many school leaders across the United States who opened their schoolhouse doors to us. From Boston, MA to Lansdale and Bethlehem, PA, from Trenton, NJ to Munford, AL, from Virginia Beach, VA to Grand Rapids, MI, from Reynoldsburg and Cincinnati, OH to Denver, CO, from Portland, OR to San Diego and Sacramento, CA, and so many points in between, these green-minded school leaders welcomed us in and willingly shared their many challenges and triumphs in seeking to create more sustainable school communities. In particular, we thank Tim Cole from Virginia Beach City Public Schools for helping us find a great photo of a green school for our cover! We are honored to tell the story of outstanding administrators, teachers, students, facility professionals, designers, parents, and community members who work together to design, lead, and manage greener, more vibrant schools where students, along with their teachers, love to learn each day. We acknowledge their collective commitment to a sustainable future, one that is healthy, just, and prosperous for all living things.

We also acknowledge and appreciate the many individuals who have informed our research and writing, including scholars of educational leadership, sustainability, and green school design, upon whose shoulders we stand. As well, we acknowledge the many international, national, regional, and local leaders in the field of whole school sustainability and green schools who continue to teach us and engage our thinking. In particular, we wish to thank the inspiring group of individuals working in the Center for Green Schools at the U.S. Green Building Council for sharing their expertise, their energy, and their encouragement. We particularly acknowledge the Green School Fellows for allowing us to learn from their experiences in facilitating green habits of mind and practice in school districts and state departments across the United States. We thank Joseph Murphy for giving of his time at the early stages of our journey, sharing his best thinking and cheering us on. And, we especially thank our friend and colleague, Dr. Megan Tschannen-Moran, Professor of Educational Leadership at the College of William and Mary, who recognized the seeds of a powerful partnership, without which this book would not have been possible.

Finally, we acknowledge the strong support of San Diego State University and Auburn University and our respective Colleges of Education and Departments. We are honored to work with and learn from individuals who have committed themselves to supporting the work of educators across the country as they seek to improve schools on behalf of their students, their communities, and the wider world.

1

Introduction: Leading Schools with a Green Frame of Mind

Messages like "Think Green," "Go Green," and "Be Green" fill the marketing airwaves these days and draw attention to the growing sustainability movement; a movement focused on improving the well-being of our planet's ecological and social systems. What does it mean to Go Green in school? What does it look like to lead schools with a greener frame of mind? How might such leadership benefit students, teachers, parents, and the community at large? With all that leaders face each day as they work to improve teaching and learning for every student in their school and across their district, who among them has the time to consider green understandings and practices as a priority in school life? Imagine. Yet another responsibility laid at the schoolhouse steps, namely, the stewardship of our planet and global community. How might you as a school leader respond to such a charge? As you consider these questions, we invite you to get to know Angela and Tom, school leaders who are also living with these questions and learning their way towards whole school sustainability.

Tom and Angela represent composites of the many school leaders we have met during our research. They lead schools within a school district where improving achievement is the top priority and creating a more sustainability-oriented school community is a complementary goal. They each grapple with sustainability-related expectations, scrutinizing the ways a green frame of mind might extend and enhance their capacity as instructional leaders. Their stories will show up throughout the book as illustrations of the work already underway in schools around the world. Following our introduction of Tom and Angela, we will define sustainability and introduce its relevance to school leadership, with an overview of the Professional Standards for Educational Leadership (National Policy Board for Educational Administration, 2015).

Meet Tom, High School Principal

Tom is in his eighth year as principal of a large comprehensive high school. His school was built in the 1960s according to a design that leaves much to be desired in terms of energy efficiency. External hallways connect a warren of single and double classroom structures. As a consequence, any time doors open, they open to the outside, resulting in a loss of heating or cooling, depending upon the season. Old single-paned windows exacerbate the problem. With age, the windows have also taken on a glaze that restricts views in and out of classrooms.

As part of the science curriculum, students at Tom's school were given energy audit training sponsored by the district maintenance and operations department. They examined energy usage in ten classrooms on campus, focusing specifically on the efficiency of classroom windows. They compared the room temperature at the window site in these classrooms with the temperature in similarly sized classrooms at a newly renovated green high school on the other side of the district. Results of the audit revealed that temperatures near their classroom windows were 10 degrees colder during a winter month than the temperatures at the newly renovated school. Their presentation of findings to a group of community experts earned them resources from a recent district bond program to replace windows across their campus. In the context of an expansive campus renovation, new double-paned windows will also feature internal blinds that reduce dust and allergens and open views to the fields beyond their classrooms.

Tom's school has good space for a large learning garden. "At one time, this school was the district's agriculture school. These surrounding fields were all planted with alfalfa. We have a greenhouse and good outdoor space. We're trying to transition from an old 60s Ag school, with a traditional Future Farmers of America program, to a more modern environmental studies and business focused school. Students get engaged when the work is real to them." Tom says he is always looking for the value-added.

> How does it get structured into the fabric of what we're doing as opposed to a set-aside that distracts from the primary goal? Of course, it's financially beneficial if done well, but I don't want to convey that financial benefit is the only reason to develop greener states of minds.

Thinking green is a valuable lifelong habit. After all, public education has a role to play in developing productive citizens. It's part of this civic education.

Meet Angela, K–8 Principal

Angela is principal of the district's arts and sciences, Waldorf-inspired K–8 school. The school seeks to develop critical thinking and creative problem solving skills through an integrated and rigorous curriculum that integrates the arts and environmental stewardship. According to Angela, "The heart of the matter is sustainable lifestyle, sustainable human development, sustainable Earth." Angela was pleased when the district facility and maintenance department approved plans for school learning gardens. Garden agreements, signed by principals and the facilities department, include design specifications related to Americans with Disabilities Act (ADA) compliance, siting requirements that take account of mechanical and plumbing systems, and maintenance guidelines for upkeep. The school's expansive garden provides students daily opportunities to learn all aspects of gardening, irrigation, organic pest control, seed propagation, and construction. Angela also looks to these outdoor learning experiences as a source of literary and artistic inspiration, vocabulary learning, and foreign language development. And, the harvested vegetables promote healthy eating habits. "We put bowls of cherry tomatoes, sweet peas, carrots, or radishes in the cafeteria, our classrooms, and around our quad so, at break time, kids can eat healthy snacks. And, they do!"

In the first year of Angela's tenure at the school, she and her teachers sponsored school action days during which students took up shovels and pole diggers to plant trees. One day they planted 25. "They took ownership and wanted to add posts with their names at the base of the trees they planted. They said, 'We're coming back in five years to see how much our trees have grown.'" Angela was quick to make a point how these activities align with the district's priority for improving student learning and achievement.

> Students benefit from a rich, project-based curriculum. They conduct rigorous research on gardening, solar energy, water collection, and gray water. The students raise chickens on campus and have engineered a special system of ramps and pulleys that allow the eggs to gently roll out from under the hens and be caught and transported to avoid breakage. If it's simply a mandate for increased achievement, it becomes a chore that's really painful and counterproductive. We really try to make learning meaningful and alive.

With encouragement and support from district leadership, Tom and Angela are experimenting with green school leadership practices, rethinking curriculum, instruction, assessment, and management practices in light of an increasingly complex, connected, and challenged global environment. To manage change and meet these challenges, today's graduates require deep content knowledge, advanced technological skillfulness, the capacity for critical thinking and problem solving, the ability to integrate information across sources and disciplines, as well as a disposition toward creativity and innovation, collaboration, cultural competence, and global awareness (Autor, Levy, & Murnane, 2003; Schrader & Lawless, 2011; Suarez-Orozco, 2005). They also need models for how to live as responsible global citizens and environmental stewards. The likelihood that students graduate equipped with this knowledge, skill and inclination, rests in the capacity of school leaders to accomplish fundamental changes in attitude, instruction, and infrastructure aimed at producing authentic, relevant and integrated approaches to 21st-century teaching and learning. Future-focused school leaders see the value and importance of remaining awake to rapidly changing characteristics and needs of a global society on behalf of the students who will inherit this complex world.

Sustainability Defined

Generally speaking, sustainability captures the interface between human civilization and the natural world and emphasizes the degree to which human beings choose to live within the ecological carrying capacity of planet Earth, presently and into the future. Sustainability science examines planetary, social, and economic issues in holistic fashion. As a new field of study, sustainability crosses a vast array of disciplines including the life and physical sciences, engineering, economics, and social sciences (Bettencourt & Kaur, 2011), exploring the question of how humans might live on planet Earth in ways that are more ecologically healthy, socially just, and economically viable. The notion of sustainability first appeared in the public discourse in 1987 with the often cited Brundtland Commission report that defined sustainability as, "ensur[ing] that it [human activity and development] meet the needs of the present without compromising the ability of future generations to meet their own needs" (World Commission on Environment and Development (WCED), 1987, I.3.27). Sustainability, as a field of study and focal point for action, asks urgent questions. How do we endure on Earth? How do we take care of our planet, each other, and the resources we depend upon for our survival? How do we live responsibly so that those who come after us can live? Humanity has yet to fully answer these questions. School leaders have a critical role to play in developing more sustainable school practices, engaging students in these big questions and preparing them to discover and enact answers.

In relatively new fields, it is common for the field-specific language to evolve and change. This is currently true within the field of sustainability. A family of related terms has emerged as this field of study and practice has coalesced (Edwards, 2005; Gladwin, Kennelly, & Krause, 1995). These terms include sustainable development (UNESCO, 2005), ecological sustainability (Purser, Park, & Montuori, 1995), environmental sustainability (Goodland, 1995), ecocultural sustainability (Glasser, 2007), and others (Edwards, 2005). We will use the term sustainability to refer holistically to the necessary integration of environmental (planet), social (people), and economic (prosperity) systems and concerns.[1] "Green" has emerged as a term synonymous with sustainability, although some argue that the term conveys too narrow a conception, focusing primarily on the environmental aspects of sustainability and product development (Yanarella, Levine & Lancaster, 2009). In this book, we have chosen to utilize green and sustainability as equivalent terms, at the same time recognizing sustainability as a property of community rather than a property simply of individuals or products. As Capra (2009) explained:

> Sustainability, then, is not an individual property but a property of an entire web of relationships. It always involves a whole community. This is the profound lesson we need to learn from nature. The way to sustain life is to build and nurture community. A sustainable human community interacts with other communities—human and nonhuman—in ways that enable them to live and develop according to their nature. (p. 2)

Figure 1.1 depicts these community systems as nested—economic systems are nested within social systems and both are nested within ecological systems. This nestedness implies deep interdependence; economic and social systems are dependent on the health and capacity of ecological systems to nourish life with clean air, water, and food. Sustainability science recognizes the impossibility of separating economic, equity, and ecological issues from each other. Because both economic and social systems are dependent on ecological systems, they must be subject to the laws, limits, and processes of these life systems. Human well-being depends on our ability to understand and live in accord with nature's laws, limits, and processes. Sustainability calls for the intentional and intelligent integration of human and ecological systems. It is both a theoretical and practical field with a dramatic sense of urgency and relevance to all communities.

Figure 1.1 Sustainability Addresses Three Nested Systems

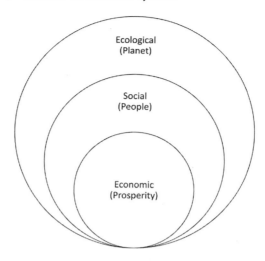

The urgent need for sustainability science to find answers and influence practice results from a long list of ecological, social, and economic challenges confronting humanity today. These challenges include climate change, natural disasters, biodiversity loss, population growth, social inequities, and economic crises, all of which have become common features in our daily news. Such challenges relate to individual behaviors as well as regional and global patterns of behavior, the results of which often transcend state, national, and even cultural borders. Addressing these profound challenges requires we shift our fundamental worldview from one that sees humankind as separate from and conquerors of nature, to one that sees humankind as integral with and dependent upon nature. Historically, this more unified and integrated perspective has not been without its champions (see, for example, work by Aldo Leopold (1949) and Rachel Carson (1962)). Nevertheless, western discourse about humankind's relationship to the natural world has more often been framed in the familiar dualism of man versus nature, resulting in a pervasive attitude of mastery and control over all that surrounds us. In the name of progress, personal investment, economic expansion, Manifest Destiny, human culture has imposed its will on nature. Now, faced with the consequences of these anthropocentric (human-centered) habits of mind and practice, many in the physical, natural, and social sciences sound a wake-up call and a call to action.

In combination, these local and global concerns demand new ways of living in the world, and evidence suggests there is hopeful movement. Research in the field of environmental psychology documents an emerging "new paradigm in which humans are viewed as an integral part of nature" (Schultz & Zelezny, 1999, p. 263). This more ecocentric (nature-centered) worldview appears across a broad array of disciplines, including the organizational sciences (Drengson, 2011; Gladwin et al., 1995; Kallio & Nordberg, 2006; Purser et al., 1995), business management (Christensen, Peirce, Hartman, Hoffman, & Carrier, 2007; Stubbs & Cocklin, 2008a, 2008b), and higher education (Corcoran & Wals, 2004). We have yet to reach agreement regarding the appropriate purposes and/or methods for educating people about these complex socio-ecological issues. Still, the discourse related to sustaining life on our planet grows ever more vibrant and active in scientific, governmental, for profit, not for profit and many educational enterprises around the world (Hawken, 2007; Hawken, Lovins, & Lovins, 1999; Senge, Smith, Kruschwitz, Laur, & Schley, 2008).

The Benefits of Green School Leadership

School leaders currently face unprecedented demands. National, state, and local accountability systems challenge school leaders to collect, record, interpret, and present objective evidence that all students are achieving desired outcomes. To be responsible within this highly charged policy context and, at the same time, responsive to the needs of increasing diverse school communities, school leaders rightfully sharpen their focus on the core functions of the enterprise, learning and teaching. They may understandably conclude that they have little time or resources left to think beyond this primary responsibility.

These same leaders are keenly aware that our increasingly complex global environment, with its corresponding international connectedness as well as competition, also challenges them to rethink curriculum, instruction, and assessment through the lens of the 21st century. A sustainability frame of reference provides educational leaders a clear logic for this work. In fact, a new generation of school leaders are leading with this sustainability-focused frame of mind or green leadership; with the clear understanding that human organizations, including schools, impact the health of local and global socio-ecological communities and vice versa. These sustainability-minded leaders recognize that school is the place where the next generations have the opportunity to develop learning capacity for creating a healthy and prosperous future. Here students learn the deep content knowledge, as well as the soft skills necessary for responsible global citizenship. Indeed, a rigorous and sustainability-relevant curriculum has potential to motivate students and engage them in the world outside the classroom walls.

As well, students learn from sustainability-minded, green school management practices, from high-performance, green designs to increased energy and water efficiency to improved indoor air quality to greener purchasing practices and the like. Formal K–12 education plays a critical role in the evolution of our social systems by both introducing content knowledge and modeling social habits and practices. In terms of the sustainability movement, greener schools advance a relevant and integrated curriculum (Henderson & Tilbury, 2004; Nolet, 2009) and model sustainable building design and management practices for students and the broader community (Edwards, 2006; Higgs & McMillan, 2006). And, green school leadership represents fiscally responsible practice, saving tax dollars while also saving the environment through reductions in energy use, water use, and waste production. In summary, green leadership improves the learning experience and capacity of students by cultivating healthier organizational conditions, modeling 21st-century practices, and redirecting funds away from operations and towards curriculum and teaching.

The Role of the School Building

The physical structure of a school building can introduce students to ideas and concerns outside the range of their experience, encouraging them to question familiar details of the built environment and the ways they, as students, function within it (Uline, 2000). Why is our schoolyard paved? How many ways does light enter our building? What sorts of materials comprise the walls and floors and ceilings of our classrooms, and why should we care? Where is the furnace and how efficiently does it do its job? What happens to the trash we produce in a day, across a week, throughout the year? We should not disregard the significance of school as a place to model the values and habits of responsible social, cultural, and environmental citizenship, for the students who attend and for the larger communities these students call home (Uline, Tshcannen-Moran, & Wolsey, 2009).

Across the United States, 85,530 traditional public, 4,480 public charter, and 26,230 private schools (NCES, 2013) present a significant opportunity for K–12 education to assist in creating more sustainable socio-ecological systems, locally and globally. As we work to green existing school facilities, and apply green principles to the design and construction of new schools, we articulate and advance sustainability goals and purposes. Likewise, when we utilize these green schools as teaching tools, we extend our capacity to model socio-ecologically aware norms and practices. Beyond conserving energy, decreasing stress on natural resources, preserving surrounding habitats, and reducing waste, we improve the ecological literacy of our students, teachers, administrators, and community members.

In the United States prominent calls for greener schools are relatively new. However, growing numbers of U.S. school leaders are engaging in sustainability-related efforts and are part of a growing international green schools movement (Mathar, 2006; Wals, 2009). Although there is no one directory of school leaders engaging in greening their schools, there are some data points worth highlighting. The U.S. Green Building Council (USGBC) tracks and publishes a list of school projects that register for LEED programs, both new and retrofit buildings. LEED certification standards include a broad array of green building practices that increase energy and water efficiency, reduce carbon footprints, improve indoor air quality, and guide greener purchasing practices. As of February 2016, 3,904 school projects were registered with the USGBC's LEED certification program (USGBC, 2016). Of these, only 1,732 school projects have obtained some level of LEED certification, a number representing just over 1% of all K–12 schools in the United States. Certainly LEED certification is only one indicator of involvement in sustainability related efforts. Another indicator is the 735 Eco-Schools across 45 of the United States, plus the District of Columbia (NWF, 2016). We will discuss additional trends in our final chapter. Might it be possible that the best way to learn environmental citizenship will be to practice environmental citizenship in greener schools? In Bernstein's (2003) extensive review of "innovative and ambitious policies, programs, and practices" for changing the development of school buildings, she noted that, "In the best cases, the buildings themselves are interactive tools for learning" (p. vii).

As early as 1848, when school facilities were just beginning to assume the status of publicly supported civic buildings, Henry Barnard, then Education Commissioner for Rhode Island, launched a personal crusade for enhancing the quality of America's school buildings, advocating for "schoolhouse[s] . . . well adapted to all the various ends which should be sought, such as the convenience, comfort, and health of pupils, convenience for supervision and conduct of the school, and facilities for the most successful prosecution of study" (Barnard, 1970, pp. 45–46). Barnard stands prominent among educators who combined knowledge of school design with the intentions of pedagogical reform. In fact, Bernard spoke directly to classroom instruction and knowledge acquisition. He suggested that the "cardinal points accurately ascertained by the compass" be painted on the ceiling and that classrooms be equipped with "plans of the school-house, playground, village green, district, town and county . . . a globe, tellurion, orrery, and similar apparatus [in order to] lead children to an accurate conception of states, continents, the earth, and the system of which it forms a part" (p. 76). More than 150 years later, as green school buildings make energy management systems visible to the building occupants, provide water-reuse demonstration areas, support wildlife habitats, incorporate green roofs and daylight compensation systems, students learn their place within the interdependent, socio-ecological networks that influences our planet, our people, and our shared prosperity across the globe.

New Jersey was the first to require that all new school designs adhere to the green building standards of LEED guidelines (Muse & Plaut, 2006). According to the Environmental Law Institute, other states have initiated similar requirements; Arizona in 2005; Washington and Hawaii in 2006; Illinois, Colorado, Ohio, and Rhode Island in 2007; the District of Columbia, Connecticut, Maryland, and Florida in 2008; Kentucky in 2009; and California in 2011. A few states, Pennsylvania, New Hampshire, California, New Mexico, and Kentucky, provide some form of financial incentive for greening schools (Bernstein, 2010). These emerging state policies provide substantial evidence that the policy climate for some school leaders has changed and for others will likely be changing.

And, as green school leaders move in the direction of whole school and whole systems approaches to sustainability, they not only teach about sustainability via the curriculum, but the school community becomes a vibrant place for learning together how to live more sustainably (Birney & Reed, 2009; Rauch, 2002; Stone & Barlow, 2005). Processes such as designing, building, and managing healthy, high-performance facilities (Bernstein, 2003; Gordon, 2010), purchasing, reusing, and recycling ecologically intelligent materials (Goleman, 2009), and growing and serving more local, organic food (Morgan & Sonnino, 2008) become engaging learning resources and opportunities for adults and children. Labels for these schools commonly include eco-schools, enviroschools, green schools (Henderson & Tilbury, 2004), and sustainable schools (Birney & Reed, 2009; Gough, 2005). School leaders and leadership are crucial to these whole school/system transformations (Higgs & McMillan, 2006; Schelly, Cross, Franzen, Hall, & Reeve, 2010).

Green School Practices Embedded within School Leadership Concepts and Ideals

School leadership presents powerful opportunities and immense responsibilities. Today, school leaders engage in preparing young people for a world we cannot now imagine. As adults, we need only summon images of rotary phones and bound encyclopedias to be reminded of the speed and trajectory of change in our lifetimes. The very nature of this fast paced world begs continuous revisiting of the standards, that is, the concepts and ideals directing educational leadership practice in the 21st century. Contemporary efforts to reform educational leadership practice and preparation span almost three decades. Beginning with the 1987 National Commission of Excellence in Educational Administration papers and the 1989 National Policy Board for Educational Administration (NPBEA) report, educational leadership professional organizations, the larger policy community, and scholars of the field acknowledged the need to reform educational leadership as a profession, spurring close scrutiny of more traditional approaches to leadership preparation (Griffiths, Stout, & Forsyth, 1988; Murphy, 1992).

In 1994, The Council of Chief State School Officers (CCSSO), in partnership with the NPBEA, convened the Interstate School Leadership Licensure Consortium (ISLLC). The Consortium set out to develop a framework of leadership standards to inform the preparation, assessment, and continued professional development of school leaders (ISLLC, 1996). These standards, first published in 1996 and modestly updated in 2008, aimed to enhance the quality of educational leadership, transitioning educational administrators from organizational managers to instructional leaders. The ISLLC initiative was a highly collaborative effort supported by numerous nongovernmental organizations and foundations, including the Pew Charitable Trust and the Danforth Foundation.[2]

The ISLLC Standards provided "a framework for policy creation, training program performance, life-long career development, and system support" focused on producing "effective instructional leadership that positively impacts student achievement" (CCSSO, 2008, p. 13). In the United States, all 50 states developed school leadership standards that reflect the influence of the ISLLC standards (Roach, Smith, & Boutin, 2011).

With an eye toward the significant challenges educational leaders currently face, and will face in the future, the ISLLC Standards have recently undergone substantial review and revision, informed by empirical research, input from scholars in the field, and feedback from more than 1,000 school and district leaders. These latest revisions seek to better align the professional leadership standards with the daily work of educational leaders and the ever-growing leadership demands of the 21st century.

The 2015 Standards, now named the Professional Standards for Educational Leaders (PSEL), "have been recast with a stronger, clearer emphasis on students and student learning, outlining foundational principles of leadership to help ensure that each child is well-educated and prepared for the 21st century" (National Policy Board for Educational Administration, 2015, p. 2). The 2015 Standards adopt a future-focused orientation, acknowledging the changing world within which educational leaders practice. The 2015 Standards reflect interdependent domains, qualities, and values of leadership integral to students' academic success and well-being, including the following ten interdependent areas of concern:

1. Mission, Vision, and Core Values
2. Ethics and Professional Norms
3. Equity and Cultural Responsiveness
4. Curriculum, Instruction and Assessment
5. Community of Care and Support for Students
6. Professional Capacity of School Personnel
7. Professional Community for Teachers and Staff
8. Meaningful Engagement of Families and Community
9. Operations and Management
10. School Improvement

Close examination of these, most recent standards, reveal new opportunities for identifying and clarifying the knowledge, disposition, and skills central to green school leadership practices. Recalling Tom's concerns about structuring greener frames of mind into the "fabric of what we're doing as opposed to a set-aside that distracts from the primary goal," consider the following three examples as introduction to more detailed discussions found in later chapters of this book.

The leader functions included under Standard 9, "Effective educational leaders manage school operations and resources to promote *each* student's academic success and well-being," could include expectations for actions consistent with more sustainable or green school practices. Emerging research on healthy, high-performing schools (schools built and managed for socio-ecological sustainability) suggest they are healthier places for students and teachers, more environmentally responsible, and less expensive to operate (Bernstein, 2003; Edwards, 2006; Gordon, 2010). Additionally, promoting the welfare of students and staff could certainly include purchasing and serving healthier and more sustainable food choices (Stone & Barlow, 2005).

Standard 3 highlights the importance of equity and social justice. There are strong arguments already made by others for understanding that true social justice cannot occur outside the realm of ecological justice, or eco-justice (Furman & Gruenewald, 2004).

Finally, Standard 10 states, "Effective educational leaders act as agents of continuous improvement to promote *each* student's academic success and well-being." Clearly, this standard calls for school leaders to "Assess and develop the capacity of staff to assess the value and applicability of emerging educational trends and the findings of research for the school and its improvement" (Element F of Standard 10, National Policy Board for Educational Administration, 2015, p. 18). Socio-ecological sustainability and education for sustainability are critically important present and future trends (Marx, 2006) to which educational leaders must attend. Emerging trends in U.S. state and local policy suggest increasing policy expectations for building healthy, high-performing schools, also referred to as green schools (Bernstein, 2003, 2010; Gordon, 2010).

Across chapters in this book we will explore how these sustainability-focused leadership roles and functions align with and advance the leadership concepts and ideals we have embraced nationally as central to effective instructional leadership that positively influences student learning and achievement. Further, we will explore these leadership concepts and ideals within a 21st-century school context, exploring which expectations and

Table 1.1 Crosswalk between the Professional Standards for Educational Leadership and Chapters 2–10 of This Book

	DNA of Whole School Sustainability			Healthy Learning Ecosystems			Meaningful, Purposeful, Engaged Learning		
	Ch2	Ch3	Ch4	Ch5	Ch6	Ch7	Ch8	Ch9	Ch10
PSEL 1: Mission, Vision, and Core Values	✔	✔	✔						✔
PSEL 2: Ethics and Professional Norms	✔	✔	✔						✔
PSEL 3: Equity and Cultural Responsiveness		✔		✔	✔	✔	✔	✔	✔
PSEL 4: Curriculum, Instruction, and Assessment		✔			✔	✔	✔	✔	✔
PSEL 5: Community of Care and Support for Students		✔		✔			✔		✔
PSEL 6: Professional Capacity of School Personnel		✔						✔	✔
PSEL 7: Professional Community for Teachers and Staff	✔	✔	✔					✔	✔
PSEL 8: Meaningful Engagement of Families and Community		✔		✔					✔
PSEL 9: Operations and Management	✔	✔			✔	✔			✔
PSEL 10: School Improvement	✔	✔	✔	✔	✔	✔	✔	✔	✔

indicators might necessitate more emphasis in light of today's challenges and tomorrow's needs. Table 1.1 provides a crosswalk between Professional Standards for Educational Leadership and this book's chapters. Although we did not explicitly write the chapters to the standards, you will find the chapter content reflective of the standards concepts and ideals.

Learning from the Stories of Green School Leaders

Whole school approaches to sustainability, or green schools, are a relatively new phenomenon in K–12 education. This book tells the story of green school leaders like Tom and Angela, as well as other superintendents, principals, teachers, and students who are leading according to continuously developing educational leadership policy and standards in ways that reduce the environmental impact of school buildings and engage students in purposeful, meaningful learning for a sustainable future. These leaders seem to be re-inventing school to be part of the solution rather than the problem (Orr, 1992). They are designing and leading new ecocentric models of school that not only serve the learning needs of students but also intentionally attend to the needs of local and global socio-ecological systems. Through their stories you will gain deeper understanding of how you, as a leader, can facilitate the design, leadership, and management of greener, more vibrant schools, identifying your own opportunities to contribute to a sustainable future, one that is healthy, just, and prosperous for all living things.

Notes

1 Others have detailed the history of the sustainability movement and you may want to refer to Edwards (2005) and Hawken (2007) for additional information.
2 Representatives from the following professional organizations participated in the development of the standards: American Association of Colleges for Teacher Education, American Association of School Administrators, Association for Supervision and Curriculum Development, Association of Teacher Educators, National Association of Elementary School Principals, National Association of Secondary School Principals, National Association of State Boards of Education, National Conference of Professors of Educational Administration, National Policy Board for Educational Administration, National School Boards Association, University Council of Educational Administration (Interstate School Leadership Licensure Consortium, 1996).

References

Autor, D., Levy, F., & Murnane, R. (2003). The skill content of recent technological change: An empirical exploration. *Quarterly Journal of Economics, 118,* 1279–1333.

Barnard, H. (1970). *School architecture or contributions to the improvement of school-houses in the United States.* New York: Teachers College Press.

Bernstein, T. (2003). *Building healthy, high performance schools.* Washington, DC: Environmental Law Institute. Retrieved from Environmental Law Institute website: http://www.elistore.org/reports_detail.asp?ID=10925

Bernstein, T. (2010, Nov. 2010). *Healthy, high performance school facilities: Developments in state policy.* Retrieved from Environmental Law Institute website: http://www.eli.org/Program_Areas/Healthy_Schools/index.cfm

Bettencourt, L. M. A., & Kaur, J. (2011). Evolution and structure of sustainability science. *PNAS, 108*(49), 19540–19545. doi:10.1073/pnas.1102712108/-/DC Supplemental

Birney, A., & Reed, J. (2009). *Sustainability and renewal: Findings from the leading sustainable schools research project.* Nottingham: National College for Leadership of Schools and Children's Services. Retrieved from Institute of Education, University of London website: http://dera.ioe.ac.uk/2061/

Capra, F. (2009). *The new facts of life. Center for Ecoliteracy.* Retrieved from Center for Ecoliteracy website: http://www.ecoliteracy.org/essays/new-facts-life

Carson, R. (1962). *Silent spring.* New York: Houghton Mifflin Company.

CCSSO. (2008). *Educational leadership policy standards: ISLLC 2008 as adopted by the National Policy Board for Educational Administration.* Washington, DC: Council of Chief State School Officers.

Christensen, L. J., Peirce, E., Hartman, L. P., Hoffman, W. M., & Carrier, J. (2007). Ethics, CSR, and sustainability education in the Financial Times top 50 global business schools: Baseline data and future research directions. *Journal of Business Ethics, 73,* 347–368.

Corcoran, P. B., & Wals, A. E. J. (Eds.). (2004). *Higher education and the challenge of sustainability: Problematics, promise, and practice.* Norwell, MA: Kluwer Academic Publishers.

Drengson, A. (2011). Shifting paradigms: From technocrat to planetary person. *Anthropology of Consciousness, 22*(1), 9–32.

Edwards, A. R. (2005). *The sustainability revolution: Portrait of a paradigm shift.* Gabriola Island, BC, Canada: New Society Publishers.

Edwards, B. W. (2006). Environmental design and educational performance. *Research in Education, 76,* 14–32.

Furman, G. C., & Gruenewald, D. A. (2004). Expanding the landscape of social justice: A critical ecological analysis. *Educational Administration Quarterly, 40*(1), 47–76.

Gladwin, T. N., Kennelly, J. J., & Krause, T.-S. (1995). Shifting paradigms for sustainable development: Implications for management theory and research. *Academy of Management Review, 20*(4), 874–907.

Glasser, H. (2007). Minding the gap in social learning. In A. E. J. Wals (Ed.), *Social learning towards a sustainable world*. Wageningen, The Netherlands: Wageningen Academic.

Goleman, D. (2009). *Ecological intelligence: How knowing the hidden impacts of what we buy can change everything*. New York: Broadway Books.

Goodland, R. (1995). The concept of environmental sustainability. *Annual Review of Ecology and Systematics, 26*, 1–24.

Gordon, D. E. (2010). *Green schools as high performance learning facilities*. Washington, DC: National Clearinghouse for Educational Facilities, National Institute of Building Sciences.

Gough, A. (2005). Sustainable schools: Renovating educational processes. *Applied Environmental Education and Communication, 4*(4), 339–351.

Griffiths, D. E., Stout, R. T., & Forsyth, P. B. (Eds.). (1988). *Leaders for America's schools: The report and papers of the National Commission on Excellence in Educational Administration*. Berkeley, CA: McCutchan Publishing Company.

Gump, P. V. (1987). School and classroom environments. In D. Stokols, & I. Altman (Eds.), *Handbook of environmental psychology* (pp. 691–732). Wiley-Interscience Publication, New York.

Hawken, P. (2007). *Blessed Unrest: How the largest movement in the world came into being and why no one saw it coming*. New York: Penguin Group.

Hawken, P., Lovins, A. B., & Lovins, L. H. (1999). *Natural capitalism: The next industrial revolution*. London: Earthscan.

Henderson, K., & Tilbury, D. (2004). *Whole-school approaches to sustainability: An international review of whole-school sustainability programs*. Canberra, Australia: Australian Research Institute in Education for Sustainability.

Higgs, A., & McMillan, V. (2006). Teaching through modeling: Four schools' experiences in sustainability education. *The Journal of Environmental Education, 38*(1), 39–53.

ISLLC. (1996). *Standards for school leaders*. Washington, DC: Council of Chief State School Officers.

Kallio, T. J., & Nordberg, P. (2006). The evolution of organizations and natural environment discourse. *Organization & Environment, 19*(4), 439–457. doi:10.1177/108 6026606294955

Leopold, A. (1949). *A sand county almanac and sketches here and there*. New York: Oxford University Press.

Marx, G. (2006). *Future-focused leadership: Preparing schools, students, and communities for tomorrow's realities*. Alexandria, VA: Association for Supervision and Curriculum Development.

Mathar, R. (2006). Eco-schools and green schools. In J. C.-K. Lee & M. Williams (Eds.), *Environmental and geographic education for sustainability: Cultural contexts* (pp. 139–153). New York: Nova Science Publishers.

Morgan, K., & Sonnino, R. (2008). *The school food revolution: Public food and the challenge of sustainable development*. London: Earthscan.

Murphy, J. (1992). *The landscape of leadership preparation: Reframing the education of school administrators*. Newbury Park, CA: Corwin Press.

Muse, A., & Plaut, J. (2006). An inside look at LEED: Experienced practitioners reveal the inner workings of LEED. *Journal of Green Building, 1*(1), 1–8. doi:10.3992/jgb.1.1.1

National Policy Board for Educational Administration (2015). *Professional Standards for Educational Leaders* Retrieved from Reston, VA: http://www.ccsso.org/Documents/2015/ProfessionalStandardsforEducationalLeaders2015forNPBEAFINAL.pdf

NCES. (2013). *Fast facts.* Retrieved from the NCES website: https://nces.ed.gov/fastfacts/display.asp?id=55

Nolet, V. (2009). Preparing sustainability-literate teachers. *Teachers College Record, 111*(2), 409–442.

NWF. (2016). *Calling all eco-schools.* Retrieved from the NWF website: http://www.nwf.org/Eco-Schools-USA.aspx

Orr, D. W. (1992). *Ecological literacy: Education and the transition to a postmodern world.* Albany: State University of New York Press.

Purser, R. E., Park, C., & Montuori, A. (1995). Limits to anthropocentrism: Toward an ecocentric organization paradigm? *Academy of Management Review, 20*(4), 1053–1089.

Rauch, F. (2002). The potential of education for sustainable development for reform in schools. *Environmental Education Research, 8*(1), 43–51.

Roach, V., Smith, L., & Boutin, J. (2011). School leadership policy trends and developments: Policy expediency or policy excellence? *Educational Administration Quarterly, 47*(1), 71–113. doi:10.1177/0011000010378611

Schelly, C., Cross, J., Franzen, W., Hall, P., & Reeve, S. (2010). Reducing energy consumption and creating a conservation culture in organizations: A case study of one public school district. *Environment and Behavior, XX*(X), 1–28.

Schrader, P.G. & Lawless, K.A. (2011). Research in immersive environments and 21st century skills: An introduction to the special issue. *Journal of Educational Computing Research, 44*, 385–390.

Schultz, P. W., & Zelezny, L. (1999). Values as predictors of environmental attitudes: Evidence for consistency across 14 countries. *Journal of Environmental Psychology, 19*, 255–265.

Senge, P. M., Smith, B., Kruschwitz, N., Laur, J., & Schley, S. (2008). *The necessary revolution: How individuals and organizations are working together to create a sustainable world.* New York: Doubleday.

Stone, M. K., & Barlow, Z. (Eds.). (2005). *Ecological literacy: Educating our children for a sustainable world.* San Francisco: Sierra Club Books.

Stubbs, W., & Cocklin, C. (2008a). Conceptualizing a "sustainability business model." *Organization & Environment, 21*(2), 103.

Stubbs, W., & Cocklin, C. (2008b). Teaching sustainability to business students: Shifting mindsets. *International Journal of Sustainability in Higher Education, 9*(3), 206–221.

Suarez-Orozco, M. M. (2005). Rethinking education in the global era. *Phi Delta Kappan, 87*(3), 209–212.

Uline, C. (2000). Decent facilities and learning: Thirman L. Milner Elementary School and beyond. *Teacher College Record, 102*, 444–462.

Uline, C. Tschannen-Moran, M. & Wolsey, T.D. (2009). The walls still speak: The stories occupants tell. *Journal of Educational Administration, 47*(3), 400–426. doi:10.1108/09578230910955818

UNESCO. (2005). UN Decade of education for sustainable development (2005–2014): The DESD at a glance. Paris, France: UNESCO.

USGBC. (2010). Data retrieved December 2010 from USGBC website: http://www.centerforgreenschools.org/leed-for-schools.aspx

USGBC. (2016). Personal communication.

Wals, A. E. J. (2009). *Review of contexts and structures for education for sustainable development 2009: Learning for a sustainable world*. Paris, France: UNESCO.

WCED. (1987). *Our Common Future.* Oxford: Oxford University Press.

Yanarella, E. J., Levine, R. S., & Lancaster, R. W. (2009). Green versus sustainability: From semantics to enlightenment. *Sustainability, 2*(5), 296–302. doi:10.1089/SUS.2009.9838

Yates, J. J. (2012). Abundance on trial: The cultural significance of "sustainability." *The Hedgehog Review* (Summer), 8–25.

Part I

The DNA of Whole School Sustainability

2

In the Best Interests of Children

[V]alues constitute the essential problem of leadership and the educational institution is special because it both forms and is formed by values.

(Hodgkinson, 1991, p. 11)

Tom and Angela just left a district leadership team meeting about the upcoming accreditation processes. At the top of the agenda is revisiting their district mission and vision statements. They find themselves in a parking lot conversation about the purpose of schooling and the best interest of children. They are challenged by the tendency of a few of their colleagues to prefer "rubber stamping" their mission, vision, and goals rather than revisiting, refreshing, and renewing a system-wide commitment to serving their students in today's interconnected and interdependent world. They wonder if raising student test scores is a deep enough purpose for their work. They also wonder if a fairly narrow focus on math and reading achievement is enough to fully engage their students in learning. They leave work that day asking, "What does the world need from PK–12 education today? What does our local community need from our school? What do our students need? How should we live, learn, and teach in order to meet these needs?" They agree to work together to explore these deeper questions of purpose, 21st-century needs, best interests of children, and ethics. After some research and reflection, they plan to engage their colleagues in meaningful conversations about what it means to be an ethical educator and leader during these times of rapid social, economic, and environmental change.

Purpose of Schooling Yesterday and Today

Conversations about the deeper purposes of schooling are rare among practicing teachers and administrators (Pekarsky, 2007). In an interview, Tony Wagner recently explained:

> Too often, I think the teaching profession is kind of heads down, get the job done, you know, focus on the kids in front of you, do what's required, without having the time to sort of look around and reflect, how is the world changing, how is what I'm teaching today different from what I taught 10 or 20 years ago, how does it need to be different? (PBS Newshour, 2014, n.p.)

Teachers' days are filled with urgent and important tasks, the primary one being leading learning among classrooms full of students. Teachers are engaged directly with students most of their day. During this time they are fully present with students, inquiring, listening, responding, and reflecting. In the little time that teachers have without students, they are planning lessons, preparing activities, grading, tracking student progress, and performing assigned duties (*Status of the American public school teacher 2005–2006*, 2010). Administrators' days are filled with different, but equally all consuming, tasks. Their day may begin before dawn with answering last night's flurry of parent emails. They then greet students entering school and kick the day off with announcements. Meetings with parents, students, and teachers fill their daily calendars. As frequently as possible, they spend time observing, coaching, and celebrating the teaching and learning going on in their building (Grissom, Loeb, & Mitani, 2015). The reality of teaching and learning in schools simply does not often allow for educators to step back and reflect on challenging questions like the purpose of schooling.

In the United States, individual state departments of education set statewide goals for school performance. Thus, it may not be surprising that school district mission statements appear to vary somewhat by state (Stemler, Bebell, & Sonnabend, 2011), but not systematically at the intrastate or more local levels (Schafft & Biddle, 2013). If state level educators and bureaucrats are setting the direction for their state's schools in terms of student achievement goals and related outcomes, educators at the school level may become so focused on meeting these ends that they lose sight of deeper, more meaningful reasons for teaching and learning. School-based educators may find themselves mindlessly perpetuating purposes, values, and missions from a time gone by. When outdated and unexamined purposes are governing at deep levels, schools become disconnected from the real needs of their communities and the learning feels irrelevant and unengaging to students. With this in mind, it certainly seems less surprising that students would be leaving schools at high rates. A 2006 study that surveyed and interviewed high school dropouts from across the United States found that "most dropouts are students who could have, and believe they could have, succeeded in school" (Bridgeland, Dilulio Jr., & Morison, 2006, p. iii). As reported by dropouts, the most common reasons for leaving schools early were that school was boring and they did not feel inspired or motivated to stay. When asked what schools might do to help them graduate, 81% of dropouts wanted school to be more relevant and engaging; they wanted opportunities for real world and experiential learning.

So many of our schools today are not deeply connected to, or informed by, society's current local and global needs. Students can't help but feel the inherent disconnect. Even those students that persist may graduate with a cynical disregard for learning (Barth, 2001). Intentional connection to meaningful, purposeful work in schools comes through high-quality dialogue among school community members about the deeper aims of education and how these aims serve current local and global needs (Bezzina, 2012; Starratt, 2007). Tom and Angela are making time to clarify and invigorate their sense of purpose for getting up and heading to school each day. They will eventually engage their colleagues in this effort as well. Angela and Tom decide to investigate historical purposes of school, as well as more current views. Ultimately, they want to know what has stayed the same, what has changed, and what, if anything, is missing from today's conversation.

Following his historical review of educational aims, Hodgkinson (1991) classified the purposes, or ends, of education into three main interrelated and interdependent strands: aesthetic, economic, and ideological. According to Hodgkinson, aesthetic purposes of education address individuals' "self-fulfillment and the enjoyment of life" (p. 23). Economic purposes of education improve the capacity of individuals to financially support themselves. Finally, ideological purposes seek to develop citizenship and moral education. Bebell and Stemler (2012) presented a thorough review of modern perspectives on the purpose of schooling, including academic, legislative, legal, and business perspectives. Table 2.1 summarizes their presentation with the addition of educational purposes from Wagner (2008) and Marx (2014).

Table 2.1 demonstrates that modern perspectives on the purposes of schooling still tend to fit Hodgkinson's (1991) classification scheme of aesthetic,

Table 2.1 Summary of Bebell and Stemler's (2012) Review of Modern Perspectives on the Purpose of Schooling

Perspective or Discipline	Purpose of Education (page numbers indicate reference location within Bebell and Stemler (2012), unless otherwise noted)	Classification according to Hodgkinson's (1991) three purposes for education: aesthetic, economic, ideological
Philosophy	Teach students how to live pragmatically and immediately in their current environment (p. 4)	aesthetic
	Teach students how to live as members of a society (p. 4)	aesthetic, economic, ideological
	Develop students to be (1) citizens; (2) capable of self-improvement; (3) prepared for occupations (p. 4)	ideological, aesthetic, economic
History	Tied to social and economic needs (p. 4)	ideological, economic
Sociology	Practical credentialing (p. 4)	economic
	Develop skills associated with (1) reading and math; (2) political participation; (3) job/career preparation; (4) social and moral responsibility (p. 4)	aesthetic, ideological, economic
Legislative	State constitutions vary in their articulation of the purpose of education and in whether education is considered a fundamental right (p. 5)	
Legal	Kentucky's Supreme Court identified seven elements defining adequate education that have been widely cited as precedent. These include attention to the cognitive, civic, emotional, physical, artistic, and vocational aspects of a whole person (p. 6)	aesthetic, ideological, economic
Business	Develop teamwork, social skills, critical thinking, integrity, honesty (p. 7)	aesthetic, economic
	Develop ethics, integrity, communication, soft skills, teamwork, continuous learning, global understanding (p. 7)	aesthetic, ideological, economic
	Develop skills associated with critical thinking/ problem-solving; collaboration/leadership; agility/ adaptability; initiative/entrepreneurialism; effective oral/written communication; accessing/analyzing information; curiosity/imagination (Wagner, 2008)	aesthetic, ideological, economic
Future needs	Citizenship, employability, interesting lives, releasing ingenuity, stimulating imagination, creativity, inventiveness (Marx, 2014)	aesthetic, ideological, economic

ideological, and economic purposes for schooling. However, as time marches on from earlier times, educators must consider how best to meet these core purposes of schooling. For example, Pink (2006) presented a clear argument for business needs changing over time. Workers need different capacities to "survive and thrive" in each age, from the agricultural age of the 18th century to the industrial age of the 19th century to the information age of the 20th century and now into the conceptual age of the 21st century. Pink says, "In short, we've progressed from a society of farmers to a society of factory workers, to a society of knowledge workers. And now we're progressing yet again—to a society of creators and empathizers, of pattern recognizers and meaning makers" (p. 50). The major strands of educational purpose may not change through time, but the means for meeting those ends certainly need to change with the times; it is in the children's best interest to match their education to the needs of the time. As many have said before, "Educators are preparing students for a world that does not yet exist." In fact, a rule of thumb used by some futurists is that "60% of jobs ten years from now haven't been created yet" (Frey, 2011, as quoted in Marx, 2014, p. 171). Educators have an ethical responsibility to be watching the future as it approaches and to do their best to align students' educational opportunities with current and future needs.

As Tom and Angela considered the needs of the 21st century, they wondered if their schools have yet moved out of the 19th and 20th centuries. Here they are nearly two decades into the 21st century, and they wondered how well they were developing their students' capacity to live, learn, and eventually work within the context of a century characterized by exponential change. This question left them feeling a deep moral and ethical responsibility they had not consciously considered in a very long time. The future was walking through their building's entryway each and every school day. In so many ways, the purpose of education is to help create our common future. Hodgkinson (1991) argued that education is a moral endeavor, because its purposes are fundamentally related to all aspects of the human condition:

> Here the aim is to create from the plastic raw material of developing human minds the qualities and characters that will populate and determine the future of our kind—art not for the sake of art but for the sake of humanity. What higher art form can there be than this; the moral art of educational leadership? (p. 142)

Angela and Tom decided to carefully consider the needs of the 21st century, in particular those needs that seem particularly different than the needs of the 20th century.

Identifying Critical Needs of the 21st Century

We hear news reports daily that detail challenging needs at all levels of society, locally, regionally, and globally. These needs are deeply interrelated and interdependent. It truly is "a small world after all." As our first chapter presented, our schools are nested within ecological, social, and economic systems, from local to regional to global scales. Marx (2014) detailed 21 trends that are critically relevant to our collective future; they have direct implications for education and they certainly reflect the needs of the 21st century. He classified the trends into the following spheres: demographic, technology, economic, energy and environment, international/global, education and learning, public and personal leadership, and well-being. Most of these trends relate directly to the nested conception of sustainability that we presented in Chapter 1, ecological, social, and economic systems. Figure 2.1 reorganizes Marx's 21 trends into the ecological, social, and economic spheres of sustainability. Some of the trends specifically address issues at the individual scale, and so the figure includes a sphere for the individual scale as well. AtKisson (1999) defined sustainability in terms of individual well-being, nature, society, and economy.

We will next provide an overview of the needs within each domain of sustainability, as indicated by Marx's trends. We will not discuss each trend in detail. Marx has already done that for you in his 2014 book, *Twenty-One Trends for the 21st Century: Out of the Trenches and Into the Future.* These trends and related needs present direct implications for educational practice. The sustainability movement challenges the status quo in every arena of our lives. Fundamentally, education for sustainability, through the hidden and written curricula, presents a response to 21st-century needs and represents a transition away from industrial age values of unrestrained growth and rampant consumption towards more sufficient prosperity and intelligent consumption. Educators have the opportunity to engage fully in the sustainability movement, modeling new ways of living in the world through both the hidden curriculum and the written curriculum. We take a broad view of the hidden curriculum here. In addition to perpetuating social relationships and structures (Giroux & Penna, 1979; Kentli, 2009), the hidden curriculum also informs human–Earth relationships. The management of waste, the use of energy and water, the time spent in nature (or not) all teach students about their relationship with, and responsibility for, planet Earth and each other.

The following trends, although not included in the figure, certainly relate to each sphere: Depth, Breadth, and Purpose of Education; International/ Global; Continuous Improvement; Polarization; and Authority. See Marx for complete discussion of these trends.

Figure 2.1 Marx's (2014) Trends for the 21st Century, as They Relate to Four Spheres of Sustainability

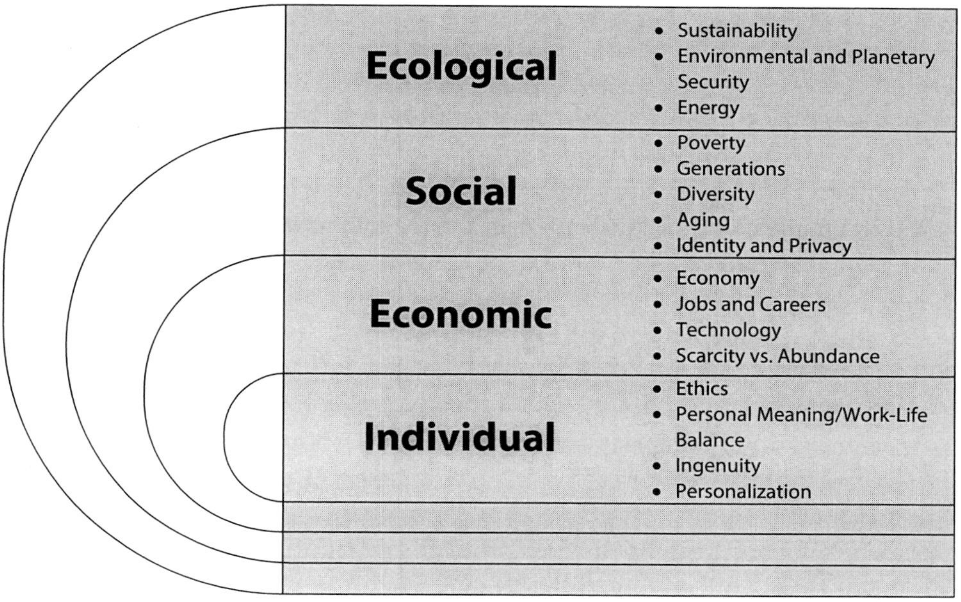

The Ecological Sphere of Sustainability

Table 2.2 Summary of Marx's (2014) Trends Most Related to Earth's Ecological Systems, as Summarized on September 9, 2015 in Education Week (http://www.edweek.org/ew/marketplace/books/sneak-peek-21-trends-for-the-21st-century-gary-marx.html)

Sustainability	Sustainability will depend on adaptability and resilience in a fast-changing, at-risk world.
Environmental and Planetary Security	Common opportunities and threats will intensify a worldwide demand for planetary security.
Energy	The need to develop new sources of affordable and accessible energy will lead to intensified scientific invention and political tension.

Three of Marx's (2104) trends relate directly to the ecological sphere of sustainability—sustainability itself, environmental and planetary security, and energy (Table 2.2). Developments in scientific understanding about our planetary systems and their interdependency among social and economic systems are primary drivers of the sustainability movement. In particular, the growing global population of 7 billion people, seeking increasing levels of material consumption, over stresses our planet's ecological systems, upon which humans depend. In their book *Bankrupting Nature: Denying Our Planetary Boundaries*, Wijkman and Rockstrom (2012) explain:

> We want to communicate that humanity is facing a critical reality. An abundance of scientific reports clearly point out that we are very close to a saturation point, where the biosphere cannot handle additional stress. We are already witnessing the hard impact that global environmental change has on both regional and local economies . . . Every day our production and consumption systems result in growing impact on the environment, through pollution, by displacing and eradicating countless species and ecosystems, and by disrupting the climate balance. This endangers the very basis of humanity's future development and prosperity. (p. 1)

If we, as educators, take the scientific warnings about the many interrelated crises facing our planet seriously then we likely feel a deep responsibility for cultivating educational conditions that serve a solution orientation. The challenges are so big and so interrelated that simple solutions are not to be found. Rather, we must collectively cultivate the conditions in which we co-create a new future where solutions naturally emerge from now unfamiliar ways of thinking and living in the world. First, we must imagine the possibility of a vibrant, prosperous future that restores and sustains Earth's ecological systems, rather than degrades and destroys them. Schools can assist children in developing their creative capacity to see and work for such a future (Robinson, 2015). Schools influence students on a daily basis through both the hidden curriculum and the written curriculum. This influence can cultivate deep awareness and understanding of the interrelated nature of the planet's needs and human's place within Earth, or it can perpetuate industrial age thinking and acting that situates humans as separate from and dominant over Earth. Developing ecological consciousness and responsible environmental behaviors in ourselves and in our students is a primary challenge facing educators for sustainability.

Christopher Uhl (2013) describes ecological consciousness as seeing "ourselves, not as *apart from* Earth (as we now tend to do), but instead, as *a part* of Earth—literally *a part of* the body of Earth!" (p. xi, emphasis in the original). This shift in mental models is a dramatic one, as each model leads to entirely different ways of being in the world; each determines what we value, what we notice, the questions that we ask, the choices that we make, and how we act (Table 2.3). It would be too simplistic to suggest that any one of us holds entirely one mental model or the other. We are in an age of transition and most of us have many mental models influencing the way we live day to day. School leaders have opportunity to intentionally create the conditions in which we cultivate more and more behavior flowing from an understanding of our deep interdependence with

Table 2.3 Contrast between Two Mental Models Relative to Human–Earth Relationships

	Mental Models about Human–Earth Relationship	
	Industrial Age Thinking—Humans Separate from and Dominant over Earth	Ecological Consciousness—Humans Integral and Interdependent in Earth
We are likely to value . . .	Status and wealth as indicated by the things we own and the clothes we wear	High-quality personal relationships, natural beauty, outdoor experiences over things
We are likely to notice . . .	A continuous flow of material things that we want, but don't have	New ways of reducing our ecological footprint through reduced consumption and creativity
We are likely to ask . . .	How can I earn enough money to purchase the next greatest thing (outfit, shoes, technology, gadget, vehicle, etc.)?	How can I use my purchasing dollars to reflect my values and positively impact other people, the planet, and future generations?
We are likely to choose . . .	Consumption (purchasing more and more things) over experiences; earning power over meaningful, purposeful work	Experiences over consumption; meaningful, purposeful work over earning power alone
We are likely to act . . .	As if Earth belongs to humans	As if humans belong to Earth

planet Earth. They do this through (1) modeling mindful attention to reducing the school's ecological footprint and (2) teaching students to understand the science of sustainability and how to work for positive change.

What Are We Modeling for Our Students?

Students are watching us closely. They notice the school yard and whether it is cared for thoughtfully. They notice what we do with our trash. Do we put it in the recycle bin that may be more than a few steps away or in the closest trash can? They notice if we mindlessly leave the lights on in rooms as we leave. They notice whether we use paper as if it was an infinite resource. They notice their teachers' and administrators' personal actions. They also notice the school's systems and procedures. School building designs and adults' practices within these four walls tell our students what we value. They also notice whether or not they are invited to join in responsible behaviors and whether they have opportunities for taking meaningful action beyond the school walls (Chawla & Cushing, 2007). Students report that they need and want to learn these behaviors in school through instruction as well as through participating in environmentally responsible behaviors (de Leeuw, Valois, & Seixas, 2014; Zsóka, Szerényi, Széchy, & Kocsis, 2013).

Part II of this book will provide detailed descriptions of how adults model environmentally responsible practices through building design and management. However, let's consider waste as a brief example. In living ecosystems, waste is recycled throughout the system. Coral reefs do not have a place in the reef where they send all of their waste; one organism's waste is another's food. The industrial age produced a continuous flow of waste that we have accumulated in landfills. This practice is unsustainable and inconsistent with how nature works. One way students can learn to align their thinking and acting with ecological principles, to operate from ecological consciousness, is through engaging in recycling efforts. Schools exist along a continuum from having no recycling programs to approaching zero waste production through recycling everything from paper to food waste. Assuming at least some recycling is taking place, schools also vary in the degree to which students are involved in these efforts. It may be that students are simply taught where to place their recyclables, with little attention paid to whether they actually follow through correctly. Or, students may actually lead the recycling efforts in their school and promote recycling community wide. Students who have the opportunity to lead environmentally responsible behaviors in their school, and promote positive change in their communities, are more likely to continue such efforts into adulthood (Chawla & Cushing, 2007). Modeling efforts for reducing our ecological footprint, while at the same time building student capacity to model the efforts themselves, constitute the most effective means for meeting the ecological needs of the 21st century.

How Do Lessons about Ecology Show Up in Our Written Curriculum?

Of course ecology lessons already exist in in the school's written curriculum. Learning about nature's animals and plants is a long time mainstay in any school curriculum. However, developing the capacity for, and an understanding of, ecological consciousness is not necessarily the typical educational approach. It is far more in line with what Smith and Williams (1999) call ecological education. They explain:

> For us, ecological education connotes an emphasis on the inescapable embeddedness of human beings in natural systems. Rather than seeing nature as other—a set of phenomena capable of being manipulated like parts of a machine—the practice of ecological education requires viewing human beings as one part of the natural world and human cultures as an outgrowth of interactions between our species and particular places. (p. 3)

In ecological education and education for sustainability, children learn to see themselves as integral to the web of life. They have formative experiences in

Table 2.4 Summary of Marx's (2014) Trends Most Related to Earth's Social Systems, as Summarized on September 9, 2015 in *Education Week* (http://www.edweek.org/ew/marketplace/books/sneak-peek-21-trends-for-the-21st-century-gary-marx.html)

Poverty	Understanding will grow that sustained poverty is expensive, debilitating, and unsettling.
Generations	Millennials will insist on solutions to accumulated problems and injustices and will profoundly impact leadership and lifestyles.
Diversity	In a series of tipping points, majorities will become minorities, creating ongoing challenges for social cohesion. Worldwide: Growing numbers of people and nations will discover that if we manage our diversity well, it will enrich us. If we don't manage our diversity well, it will divide us.
Aging	In developed nations, the old will generally outnumber the young. In developing nations, the young will generally outnumber the old.
Identity and Privacy	Identity and privacy issues will lead to an array of new and often urgent concerns and a demand that they be resolved.

nature that include time for play and recreation (Louv, 2008), deep study of their local ecological systems, and service learning that influences positive change in their communities (Chawla, 1998; Chawla & Cushing, 2007).

The Social Sphere of Sustainability

Marx's trends that most directly relate to the social sphere of sustainability (Table 2.4) indicate dramatic demographic changes taking place across human communities worldwide. In particular, awareness of the growing gap between those living in extreme poverty and those living in extreme wealth presents another major driver for the sustainability movement. The industrial age has left us with deep inequities within our human family. Developing empathy in ourselves and our students appears, in the social sphere of sustainability, as a key challenge for sustainability educators. Empathy initiates our caring for fellow humans (Goleman & Senge, 2014). Schools that cultivate empathy, care, and trust become places where creativity, responsible risk taking, and innovation thrive (Robinson, 2015). They also become central learning hubs for the community, as we discuss further in Chapter 5. These vibrant learning communities (Tschannen-Moran & Gareis, 2015) provide the social context necessary for developing the next generation of leaders who will address growing social inequities and related challenges among the 9 billion people expected by 2050.

Children entering kindergarten in 2020 will emerge as leaders in 2050. Looking ahead, Wijkman and Rockstrom (2012) see that, "[t]he only way to avoid rising tensions and, indeed, conflicts around access to increasingly scarce natural resources and environmental space will be through policies anchored in principles of equity and justice" (p. 179). As today's teachers engage children in learning principles of equity and justice, they prepare them to lead from these core values and principles as adults. Equity and justice are core principles of democratic practice and we will see them applied to classroom practice in Chapters 8 and 9.

What Are We Modeling for Our Students?

It is critical to remember that our social systems are embedded within our ecological systems. Democracy is not just about human social practices. So many of the world's social needs, locally and globally, are rooted in deeply hierarchical thinking—industrial age thinking—that positions humans above nature, as well as above other human beings. Thus social justice issues are often inseparable from ecological issues, referred to by many as ecojustice or environmental justice (C. A. Bowers, 2010; Furman & Gruenewald, 2004; Lowenstein, 2010). For example, consider that school facility disrepair is more typical in communities that serve primarily minority and low-income students. Significant health risks exist for these children due to these building conditions (A. J. Bowers & Urick, 2011). Students whose health is compromised by attending school have increased absences due to illness, as the school building literally pushes them out of school. It is not a far leap to suppose that the phenomenon of high school dropouts may have some roots in schools' ecological health. We could provide many more examples (e.g., Boone & Fragkias, 2012; Martusewicz, Edmundson, & Lupinacci, 2014; Turner, 2015). In short, the quality and state of school facility repair communicates the degree to which communities value and care for their next generation. Students notice these messages as they relate to themselves and their peers across town.

How Do Lessons about Democracy and Social/Ecojustice Show Up in Our Written Curriculum?

Just as students develop ecological consciousness through meaningful learning experiences in nature, they develop an understanding of democracy and social/ecojustice through meaningful participation in democratic processes. Many have written about the benefits of democratic schools and classrooms, from Dewey (1916) on. Most recently and relevant here are works related to caring school communities (Battistich, Solomon, Watson, & Schaps, 2010), youth participatory action research (Kornbluh, Ozer, Allen, & Kirshner, 2015; Ozer & Wright, 2012), and ecojustice (Martusewicz et al., 2014; Turner, 2015). In all of these cases, democratic school contexts that are caring by nature nurture student engagement in learning and meaningful action for improved social and ecological conditions. In a recent, large-scale study of Chicago youth, Kahne and Sporte (2008) found that:

> experiences that focus directly on civic and political issues and ways to act (e.g., undertaking service learning projects, following current events, discussing problems in the community and ways to respond, providing students with a classroom in which open dialog about controversial issues is common and where students study topics that matter to them, and exposure to civic role models) are highly efficacious means of fostering commitments to civic participation. (p. 754)

We will be better prepared to meet the needs of the 21st century if our classrooms develop empathic students with the capacity to identify and act on opportunities for social action and community improvement. Such democratic engagement of students, through strategies like youth participatory action research, aligns well with the new Common Core and Next Generation Science standards (Kornbluh et al., 2015). And, these strategies have proven particularly effective for students traditionally underserved in schools (Kahne & Sporte, 2008). In Chapter 3, we will discuss the principles of democratic practice in greater detail and we will apply them to learning and teaching in Chapters 8 and 9. For now, consider that democracy, as practiced in schools, provides a powerful means for engaging students in deep learning that can lead to change for a more sustainable future.

The Economic Sphere of Sustainability

Table 2.5 Summary of Marx's (2014) Trends Most Related to Earth's Economic Systems, as Summarized on September 9, 2015 in *Education Week* (http://www.edweek.org/ew/marketplace/books/sneak-peek-21-trends-for-the-21st-century-gary-marx.html)

Economy	An economy for a new era will demand restoration and reinvention of physical, social, technological, educational, and policy infrastructure.
Jobs and Careers	Pressure will grow for society to prepare people for jobs and careers that may not currently exist.
Technology	Ubiquitous, interactive technologies will shape how we live, how we learn, how we see ourselves, and how we relate to the world.
Scarcity vs. Abundance	Scarcity will help us rethink our view of abundance.

Four of Marx's (2014) trends relate directly to the economic sphere of sustainability (Table 2.5). Economic systems are tightly embedded in ecological and social systems. However, the economic systems of the industrial age operated as if resources were infinite and people disposable. Taking, making, and wasting along a linear trajectory was the norm, as Leonard (2010) detailed and explained in her book, *The Story of Stuff*. She quoted Victor Lebow, a retailing analyst from the mid-1940s:

> Our enormously productive economy . . . demands that we make consumption our way of life, that we convert the buying and use of goods into rituals, that we seek our spiritual satisfaction, our ego satisfaction, in consumption . . . we need things consumed, burned up, replaced and discarded at an ever-accelerating rate. (p. 160)

Resources were, and continue to be, harvested at astonishing rates and products produced with little attention to social and environmental costs. Industrial age thinking, thinking that situates Earth as an infinite resource for human consumption, is rapidly becoming outdated and dangerous. A common measure of our over consumption suggests it would take three to four more planets to support the Earth's population at the United States' current standard of living.

Growing awareness of the unsustainability of industrialized capitalism is leading towards a more "conscious capitalism," an expression of capitalism that relies on "the wisdom of enlightened self-interest" (Aburdene, 2007, p. xxii). The world's needs and society's values are informing and changing how business gets done. In fact, Aburdene (2007) documents that profits flow increasingly towards those companies that are socially and environmentally responsible, "The global movement to enforce higher labor, environmental and economic standards is not going away" (p. 173). As an example, Ray Anderson (with White 2011), in his book *Business Lessons from a Radical Industrialist*, detailed his personal story of transformation from an unaware and unconcerned CEO to a leader who accepted responsibility for the environmental and social impacts of producing carpet. He's been quoted as saying, "At the end of the day, the role of business is to generate prosperity and a better quality of life for everyone. So, we should never operate at the expense of the earth or societies or future generations." Although Anderson died in 2011, Interface's (carpet company) Mission Zero continues and aims to not only reduce all negative environmental and social impacts of carpet production to zero, but to "become a restorative company, giving back more than we take" (Interface, 2016). The take–make–waste model of production and consumption are yielding to innovations more reflective of ecological consciousness.

Our economy is changing. The world of business is changing. Employment opportunities and expectations are changing. To what extent are the children of today learning about the world's needs, their own capacity to lead change, and their ability to navigate this transition into a new economy?

As Angela and Tom reflected on what they were learning, they realized that they rarely thought much about their school's engagement with the economy; at least not beyond the fact that their budgets were forever too small. They saw an opportunity to prepare students to understand and thrive in a new economy built on values for a more enlightened age. Once again, they considered student learning opportunities through two primary lenses: (1) the hidden curriculum comprised of their day-to-day leadership and management practices and (2) the written curriculum with which teachers and students engage each day.

What Are We Modeling for Students?

Tom and Angela had an opportunity to deepen their clarity about the values they wanted to model in their school. They wanted to align their professional practice with consciousness of, and thoughtful participation in, the larger economy. They brainstormed some possible areas for further exploration and study:

◆ **School budgets.** What values inform our school budget process and allocation? How might we use our funds creatively to grow more sustainable practices within our school and district? Green revolving funds are a relatively new strategy for tracking saved funds from energy conservation programs and then reinvesting these funds into new projects that continue to provide returns on the investment. Green school leaders across the country are leading the way with these innovative practices (Indvik, Orlowski, & Foley, 2013).

◆ **Purchasing.** How intentional are we about aligning our values with our purchasing decisions? Is it enough to purchase the lowest priced items? Might it be possible to be fiscally responsible and consider environmental, social, and health impacts of our purchasing practices? Green school leaders are increasingly asking these questions and finding it possible to be fiscally conservative as well as environmentally and socially responsible. The Responsible Purchasing Network provides extensive information and guidance for schools and many other organizations (www. responsiblepurchasing.org).

◆ **Fundraisers.** What companies do we align ourselves with when it comes to our school fundraisers? What values are we promoting? Have we ever considered the environmental, social, and individual wellness impacts of the products we sell? What activity-based fundraisers might raise money, but not depend on consumption of more things? For responsible purchasing, companies that practice more conscious capitalism are available to help you raise money for your school. Organizations like Green America make finding your next responsible fundraiser easy (http://www.greenamerica.org/livinggreen/fundraisers.cfm).

How Do Lessons about the Economy Show Up in Our Written Curriculum?

Angela and Tom sought to more explicitly teach their students about growing trends towards a more conscious capitalism, raising their awareness of an individual's opportunity to help accelerate this economic shift through his/her purchasing power and leadership. This would be a long-term project and would necessarily involve faculty-wide conversations. Angela and Tom knew they had a lot to learn about the take–make–waste habits of the Industrial Age, as well as the emerging economy built on values serving the planet, people, and prosperity in preparation for such discussions. Green school leaders might consider a book group to discuss the book *Affluenza* by de Graaf, Wann, and Naylor (2104). In its third edition since 2001, *Affluenza* points the way toward "a society based on not *more* but *better*, not selfishness but sharing, not competition but community" (preface by Annie Leonard). De Graaf et al. (2014) define affluenza as "a painful, contagious, socially transmitted condition of overload, debt, anxiety, and waste resulting from the dogged pursuit of more" (p. 1). Learning to cultivate the capacity of our students to fight affluenza would go a long way towards shifting our economy into more conscious capitalism. It will also help them develop a deeper sense of individual wellness, the last sphere of sustainability in our discussion here.

The Individual Sphere of Sustainability

The individual sphere is not always explicitly included in the spheres of sustainability. We do so here because at least four of Marx's 21 trends seemed particularly relevant to individuals (Table 2.6). In addition, AtKisson (2008) identified human well-being as a fourth indicator of sustainability. He explains the four points of his Compass of Sustainability, "Nature supports the Economy, which supports Society, which supports human Wellbeing" (p. 143). Schools have a critical role to play in cultivating individual well-being among students. Sir Ken Robinson in his popular book, *Creative Schools: The Grassroots Revolution That's Transforming Education* ties together the four trends highlighted here, ingenuity, personalization, personal meaning, and ethics. First, he calls for our schools to be centers

Table 2.6 Summary of Marx's (2014) Trends Most Related to Individual Experience, as Summarized on September 9, 2015 in *Education Week* (http://www.edweek.org/ew/marketplace/books/sneak-peek-21-trends-for-the-21st-century-gary-marx.html)

Ingenuity	Releasing ingenuity and stimulating creativity will become primary responsibilities of education and society.
Personalization	In a world of diverse talents and aspirations, we will increasingly discover and accept that one size does not fit all.
Personal Meaning and Work–Life Balance	More of us will seek personal meaning in our lives in response to an intense, high tech, always on, fast-moving society.
Ethics	Scientific discoveries and societal realities will force widespread ethical choices.

of ingenuity and creativity, a dramatic departure from more familiar industrial models of education. Robinson notes that personalization in education is the strategy for keeping students engaged in learning; it is "most urgently needed in education" (Robinson, 2015, p. 83).

Personalization is not simply sitting students in front of computer programs that track their individual progress and feed them the next most appropriate problem. It is "essential that as they grow, students should be able to focus more on some disciplines than others as their interests start to become more focused" (Robinson, 2015, p. 156). Students who graduate from high school, clear about who they are and what they love, will be far more likely to find meaningful career paths. I have said many times that in the spirit of well-roundedness, we graduate students who have no idea who they are or what they love; they spend their adult lives purchasing self-help books on finding their purpose in life. Our world desperately needs purpose driven, engaged high school graduates. Lastly, Robinson's book is an ethical rallying cry for the type of education that our children and world need, "The stakes have never been higher, and the outcomes could hardly matter more" (p. 257). Green school leaders challenge themselves to confront Marx's 21 megatrends, thinking deeply about the needs they present for education in the 21st century. It's in the best interest of today's children to do so. It's in the best interest of tomorrow's children to do so. And it's in the best interest of planet Earth to do so.

In the Best Interests

"It's about the kids" is a common mantra in schools. Educators often ask "What is in the best interest of students?" as they consider day-to-day decision making, leading change and continuous improvement (Frick, 2011; Walker, 2012). Some administrators may even lead faculty meetings with an empty student chair present in the room, a constant reminder that their work ought to be focused on meeting student needs. Shapiro and Stefkovich (2010) argued that serving the best interest of the student was the central imperative for school administrators, and in doing so, they would be serving the best interest of all students. Their framework called for considering student rights, responsibilities, and respect. However, not every educator will necessarily understand, interpret, and enact "What's best for students" in the same way.

> Indeed, the term "best interest" is often used to support a point being made by an author with no clear definition of what specifically is in the best interests of the student and no specific guidance as to what action/decisions are consonant with a student's best interests. (Stefkovich & Begley, 2007, p. 214)

For as frequently as educators invoke "best interests" arguments, either for an individual child or all children, Walker (2012) observed a lack of critical explanation or interpretation of the concept. Scholars of educational leadership have only recently presented definitions of this core educational concept (Begley & Stefkovich, 2007; Stefkovich & O'Brien, 2004) and explored school leaders' understanding of "best interests" (Frick, 2011; Stefkovich & Begley, 2007; Stefkovich & O'Brien, 2004; Walker, 2012). Their work continues to suggest that practicing principals' understanding and application of "best interests" varies from theory and by individual principal (Frick, 2011).

As we engage in thinking about the best interests of children, we also notice what has not been discussed in the literature thus far. The scholars and practitioners cited above appear to have bound their "best interests" frameworks in space and time. In other words, the ethical frameworks address the best interests of students in a school here and now. First, the "here" is bound by the school walls, as if disconnected from broader social and ecological needs, both locally and globally. Although the importance of student's social communities is acknowledged, little to no attention recognizes the ecological contexts in which and on which human systems depend. The "best interests" literature is anthropocentric or human centered, rather than ecocentric or nature centered. Second, the students for whom the ethical frameworks apply are today's students who appear on the school's enrollment lists. Little to no discussion appears to address the reality that administrators' decision making has impacts on contemporaries beyond the school walls and the environment, as well as future generations.

These definitions remain too narrow for the challenges we face in the 21st century; they leave out critical opportunities for school leaders like Angela and Tom to consider and discuss their ethical responsibility for making wise decisions relative to local and global ecological, social, and economic needs, as well as these same needs for future generations. In other words, these popular ethical frameworks served educators well in the 20th century, but require updating and expanding if they are to adequately address 21st-century needs (Furman & Gruenewald, 2004). Bottery (2014) poses this critical question to educational leaders:

> If we have not inherited the world from our ancestors but, rather, have borrowed if from all life to come, in what condition will we return it? Perhaps, then, this is the critical ethical issue with which educational leaders should be concerned and from which their ethical leadership should be developed. (p. 91)

In our ethical decision making we must consider future generations and nature in addition to our contemporaries (Becker, 2011). Becker's sustainability ethics provides a clear approach for expanding current educational leadership ethical frameworks. Becker notes that:

> sustainability is a normative and evaluative concept. Sustainability has an inherent ethical dimension and denotes a fundamental ethical issue . . . Sustainability asks for a paradigm shift, for a replacement of the established ideal of the human being as an autonomous and independent individual with a new ideal of the human being as a fundamentally dependent and related being—fundamentally related to contemporaries, future generations, and nature. (p. 1)

Practicing a sustainability ethic is not an add-on; it is a new lens through which to consider all decisions. Through this lens, decisions that appeared mundane take on new ethical importance. The chemicals used to clean the tables and floors influences your students' health via indoor air quality and impacts the watershed in which the school sits. The t-shirts you sell for building school spirit exploited or honored the people who made them; their manufacturing process was environmentally destructive or restorative. The food you serve has many student and environmental health implications. The list goes on and on; the implications critical.

School leaders have the opportunity to integrate sustainability ethics into their practice and thus facilitate students learning how to live in more sustainable ways. This is how we will fundamentally fulfill the purpose of education and meet the needs of the 21st century. We hope that you are leaving this chapter with a deeper understanding and commitment to your ethical responsibility for considering your daily decisions through the lens of sustainability—considering our local and global contemporaries, our future generations, and our Earth upon which we all depend. This book will continue to explore in depth what a sustainability ethic looks like in action. The next chapter explores the underlying principles that guide the work of designing, leading, and managing a green school.

Conclusion

School leadership is a moral art (Hodgkinson, 1991). It demands that school leaders strive for clarity around their core values, the purpose of schooling, and the best interests of students. We began here because your answers to these questions inform your perspective, your motivation, and your practice. This chapter asked readers to examine future trends in terms of needs facing the 21st century. We propose that the purpose of school is to help meet these needs, both through present management practices and through educating our students to understand and respond intelligently to these needs. School leaders who lead with a primary focus on test scores and other narrow measures of achievement may be missing an opportunity to truly engage students and teachers in meaningful, purposeful learning. Brenden Freeman (2016), a high school drop out, shared a passionate call for meaningful education that should resonate with communities everywhere:

> The only way to overcome this crisis of curriculum is for all of us—parents, school staff, former graduates and dropouts—to band together to let our students know they are NOT lost causes. That they are NOT in this all alone. That there is a REASON for what they are doing and their community cares about their emotional and educational well-being. We are falling far behind in all of these areas, but if we refuse to let these appalling graduation rates stay where they are at and constantly commit to bettering our future youth, we can make a permanent difference.

Green schools and this book are very much about bringing education into the 21st century to meet our students' needs, our communities' needs, and our planet's needs. Whole school sustainability is a high leverage solution for many social, economic, and environmental challenges facing us today. It is the type of education in which we all want to be a part.

Questions for Discussion

1. What are your core values? What is the purpose of school from your perspective? How do you define the best interests of children? How should education meet the needs of the 21st century? Our students? Our communities? Our planet?

2. How many planets would it take to support the planet's population living *your* lifestyle? The Global Footprint Network has a Personal Footprint Calculator to help you find out: http://www.footprintnetwork.org/en/index.php/GFN/page/personal_footprint/. What opportunities do you have for reducing your footprint? Are you willing? Why or why not?

3. Read Glen Thomas' poem, "Tomorrow's Child". What opportunities do you see in your school for considering tomorrow's children as well as today's children? What ethical responsibilities do you have to do so? What actions will you take? Visit the Ray C. Anderson Foundation (www.raycanderson foundation.org) to see what they continue to do for tomorrow's children.

Tomorrow's Child

© Glenn C. Thomas 1996
Used with Permission

Without a name; an unseen face
and knowing not your time nor place
Tomorrow's Child, though yet unborn,
I met you first last Tuesday morn.

A wise friend introduced us two,
and through his shining point of view
I saw a day that you would see;
a day for you, but not for me.

Knowing you has changed my thinking,
for I never had an inkling
That perhaps the things I do
might someday, somehow, threaten you.

Tomorrow's Child, my daughter/son
I'm afraid I've just begun
To think of you and of your good,
though always having known I should.

Begin I will to weigh the cost
of what I squander; what is lost
If ever I forget that you
will someday come to live here too.

References

Aburdene, P. (2007). *Megatrends 2010: The rise of conscious capitalism*. Charlottesville, VA: Hampton Roads Publishing.

Anderson, R. C., & White, R. A. (2011). *Business lessons from a radical industrialist*. Toronto, Ontario: McClelland & Stewart Ltd.

AtKisson, A. (1999). *Believing Cassandra: An optimist looks at a pessimist's world*. New York: Chelsea Green Publishing Company.

AtKisson, A. (2008). *The ISIS agreement: How sustainability can improve organizational performance and transform the world*. Sterling, VA: Earthscan.

Barth, R. S. (2001). *Learning by heart*. San Francisco: Jossey-Bass.

Battistich, V., Solomon, D., Watson, M., & Schaps, E. (2010). Caring school communities. *Educational Psychologist, 32*(3), 137–151. doi:10.1207/s15326985ep3203_1

Bebell, D., & Stemler, S. (2012). *The school mission statement: Values, goals, and identities in American education*. New York: Routledge.

Becker, C. (2011). *Sustainability ethics and sustainability research*. New York: Springer Science & Business Media.

Begley, P. T., & Stefkovich, J. (2007). Integrating values and ethics into post secondary teaching for leadership development. *Journal of Educational Administration, 45*(4), 398–412. doi:10.1108/09578230710762427

Bezzina, M. (2012). Paying attention to moral purpose in leading learning: Lessons from the leaders transforming learning and learners project. *Educational Management Administration & Leadership, 40*(2), 248–271. doi:10.1177/1741143211427979

Boone, C. G., & Fragkias, M. (2012). *Urbanization and sustainability: Linking urban ecology, environmental justice and global environmental change* (Vol. 3). New York: Springer Science & Business Media.

Bottery, M. (2014). Leadership, sustainability, and ethics. In C. M. Branson & S. J. Gross (Eds.), *Handbook of ethical educational leadership* (pp. 81–92). New York: Routledge.

Bowers, A. J., & Urick, A. (2011). Does high school facility quality affect student achievement: A two-level hierarchical linear model. *Journal of Education Finance, 37*(1), 72–94.

Bowers, C. A. (2010). Educational reforms that foster ecological intelligence. *Teacher Education Quarterly*, Fall, 9–31.

Bridgeland, J. M., Dilulio Jr., J. J., & Morison, K. B. (2006). *The silent epidemic*. Retrieved from Washington, DC: http://www.civicenterprises.net/MediaLibrary/Docs/the_silent_epidemic.pdf

Chawla, L. (1998). Significant life experiences revisited: A review of research. *Journal of Environmental Education, 29*(3), 11–30.

Chawla, L., & Cushing, D. F. (2007). Education for strategic environmental behavior. *Environmental Education Research, 13*(4), 437–452. doi:10.1080/13504620701581539

de Graaf, J., Wann, D., & Naylor, T. H. (2104). *Affluenza: How overconsumption is killing us—and how we can fight back*. San Francisco: Berrett-Koehler Publishers, Inc.

de Leeuw, A., Valois, P., & Seixas, R. (2014). Understanding high school students' attitude, social norm, perceived control and beliefs to develop educational interventions on sustainable development. *Procedia—Social and Behavioral Sciences, 143,* 1200–1209. doi:10.1016/j.sbspro.2014.08.160

Dewey, J. (1916). *Democracy and education.* New York The Free Press.

Freeman, B. (2016, February 17). "I wasn't supposed to drop out." *The Times: Apalachicola & Carabelle.* Retrieved from http://www.apalachtimes.com/news/20160217/i-wasnt-supposed-to-drop-out

Frick, W. C. (2011). Practicing a professional ethic: Leading for students' best interests. *American Journal of Education* (August), 527–562. doi:0195-6744/2011/11704-0004

Furman, G. C., & Gruenewald, D. A. (2004). Expanding the landscape of social justice: A critical ecological analysis. *Educational Administration Quarterly, 40*(1), 47–76.

Giroux, H. A., & Penna, A. N. (1979). Social education in the classroom: The dynamics of the hidden curriculum. *Theory and Research in Social Education, VII*(1), 21–42.

Goleman, D., & Senge, P. M. (2014). *The triple focus: A new approach to education.* Florence, MA: More Than Sound, LLC.

Grissom, J. A., Loeb, S., & Mitani, H. (2015). Principal time management skills. *Journal of Educational Administration, 53*(6), 773–793. doi:10.1108/jea-09-2014-0117

Hodgkinson, C. (1991). *Educational leadership: The moral art.* Albany, NY: SUNY.

Indvik, J., Orlowski, M., & Foley, R. (2013). *Green revolving funds: A guide to implementation & management.* Retrieved from Cambridge, MA: http://www.centerfor greenschools.org/sites/default/files/resource-files/GRF_Full_Implementation_Guide.pdf

Interface. (2016). Our sustainability journey—Mission Zero. Retrieved from http://www.interfaceglobal.com/Sustainability/Interface-Story.aspx

Kahne, J. E., & Sporte, S. E. (2008). Developing citizens: The impact of civic learning opportunities on students' commitment to civic participation. *American Educational Research Journal, 45*(3), 738–766. doi:10.3102/0002831208316951

Kentli, F. D. (2009). Comparison of hidden curriculum theories. *European Journal of Educational Studies, 1*(2), 83–88.

Kornbluh, M., Ozer, E. J., Allen, C. D., & Kirshner, B. (2015). Youth participatory action research as an approach to sociopolitical development and the new academic standards: considerations for educators. *The Urban Review.* doi:10.1007/s11256-015-0337-6

Leonard, A. (2010). *The story of stuff.* New York: Free Press.

Louv, R. (2008). *Last child in the woods: Saving our children from nature deficit disorder.* Chapel Hill, NC: Algonquin Books of Chapel Hill.

Lowenstein, E., Martusewicz, R., & Voelker, L. (2010). Developing teachers' capacity for ecojustice education and community-based learning. *Teacher Education Quarterly* (Fall), 99–118.

Martusewicz, R. A., Edmundson, J., & Lupinacci, J. (2014). *Ecojustice education: Toward diverse, democratic, and sustainable communities.* New York: Routledge.

Marx, G. E. (2014). *Twenty-one trends for the 21st century: Out of the trenches and into the future.* Bethesda, MD: Education Week Press.

Ozer, E. J., & Wright, D. (2012). Beyond school spirit: The effects of youth-led participatory action research in two urban high schools. *Journal of Research on Adolescence, 22*(2), 267–283. doi:10.1111/j.1532-7795.2012.00780.x

PBS Newshour. (2014, August 18). Would greater independence for teachers result in higher student performance? Retrieved from http://www.pbs.org/newshour/bb/greater-independence-teachers-result-higher-student-performance/

Pekarsky, D. (2007). Vision and education: Arguments, counterarguments, rejoinders. *American Journal of Education, 113*, 423–450.

Pink, D. H. (2006). *A whole new mind.* New York: Riverhead Books.

Robinson, K. (2015). *Creative schools: The grassroots revolution that's transforming education.* New York: Viking.

Schafft, K. A., & Biddle, C. (2013). Place and purpose in public education: School district mission statements and educational (dis)embeddedness. *American Journal of Education, 120*(1), 55–76.

Shapiro, J. P., & Stefkovich, J. A. (2010). *Ethical leadership and decision making in education: Applying theoretical perspectives to complex dilemmas* (3rd ed.). New York: Routledge.

Smith, G. A., & Williams, D. R. (1999). *Ecological education in action: On weaving education, culture, and the environment.* Albany, NY: SUNY Press.

Starratt, R. J. (2007). Leading a community of learners: Learning to be moral by engaging the morality of learning. *Educational Management Administration & Leadership, 35*(2), 165–183. doi:10.1177/1741143207075387

Status of the American public school teacher 2005–2006. (2010). Retrieved from Washington, DC: http://eric.ed.gov/?id=ED521866

Stefkovich, J. A., & Begley, P. T. (2007). Ethical school leadership: Defining the best interests of students. *Educational Management Administration & Leadership, 35*(2), 205–224. doi:10.1177/1741143207075389

Stefkovich, J. A., & O'Brien, M. G. (2004). Best interests of the student: An ethical model. *Journal of Educational Administration, 42*(2), 197–214.

Stemler, S. E., Bebell, D., & Sonnabend, L. A. (2011). Using school mission statements for reflection and research. *Educational Administration Quarterly, 47*(2), 383–420. doi:10.1177/0013161X10387590

Tschannen-Moran, M., & Gareis, C. (2015). Principals, trust, and cultivating vibrant schools. *Societies, 5*(2), 256–276. doi:10.3390/soc5020256

Turner, R. J. (2015). *Teaching for ecojustice: Curriculum and lessons for secondary and college classrooms.* New York: Routledge.

Uhl, C. (2013). *Developing ecological consciousness: The end of separation* (2nd ed.). New York: Rowman & Littlefield Publishers, Inc.

Wagner, T. (2008). *The global achievement gap.* New York: Perseus Book Group.

Walker, K. (2012). The principle of best interests of students in the principalship. *Journal of Educational Administration and Foundations, 22*(2), 27–60.

Wijkman, A., & Rockstrom, J. (2012). *Bankrupting nature: Denying our planetary boundaries.* New York: Routledge.

Zsóka, Á., Szerényi, Z. M., Széchy, A., & Kocsis, T. (2013). Greening due to environmental education? Environmental knowledge, attitudes, consumer behavior and everyday pro-environmental activities of Hungarian high school and university students. *Journal of Cleaner Production, 48*, 126–138. doi:10.1016/j.jclepro.2012.11.030

3

Design Principles for Whole School Sustainability

As you read the last chapter you may have thought to yourself, "Our school is so far from a green school, I don't even know where to begin. This type of transformative change is just too big for us to take on right now. We have curriculum initiatives, classroom management initiatives, intervention initiatives, and more. There just is not time for one more thing!" Leadership for whole school sustainability does not need to take more time; it simply requires seeing and seizing opportunities for doing the work of school differently. Keeping a set of fundamental principles in mind will reveal new opportunities for green school leadership. You will soon be designing, leading, and managing a greener school—a school community where learning thrives in healthier conditions.

Green schools are education's contribution to the sustainability movement. As we described in the introduction (Chapter 1), the sustainability movement is very much about better aligning human ways of living on this planet with the laws of nature so that humans and nature might thrive into the future. Fundamentally, the human race depends on healthy ecological systems for our own health and well-being. As you will see throughout this book, whole school sustainability offers a systemic solution to many of the challenges facing education today, challenges deeply rooted in the factory model of school. Unfortunately, most schools today still operate on mechanical assumptions and principles of the factory model (Capra & Luigi, 2014; Senge, Cambron-McCabe, Lucas, Smith, & Dutton, 2012). Therefore, leading schools for sustainability (green schools) requires intentionally and systematically redesigning our educational systems and processes from the inside out.

Simply imposing new, greener practices on an industrial model will not result in deep transformation of our educational system. The guiding principles presented here inspire new questions, new observations, and new practices and facilitate leading and learning for greener schools.

This chapter will present a principle-based model for designing, leading, and managing green schools. Once you understand these core principles, you will begin seeing opportunities for redesigning your school from the inside-out; this is principle based design. Principles meet us where we are. They are not a prescribed program, dictating what should be done and when. Rather, you are free to use your professional judgment alongside your deep understanding of your unique context. We will begin with an overview of our model and then follow with an in-depth examination of each core principle. By the end of the chapter we hope you see practical and doable opportunities for continuing the work of transforming your school from the inside-out.

Ecological Principles + Democratic Principles = Green Schools

Wheatley (1999) inspired our approach,

> If nature uses certain principles to create her infinite diversity and her well-organized systems, it is highly probable that those principles apply to human life and organizations as well. There is no reason to think we'd be the exception. Nature's predisposition toward self-similarity gives me confidence that she can provide genuine guidance for the dilemmas of our time . . . For several decades now, there has been a growing chorus of research and practice that sings the praises of participative management. In reaction to this chorus, there are many critiques that describe the problems and shortcomings of participation. How can we know whom to believe? Is participation a fad that, like so many others, we can wait out, knowing it will pass? Is it based on democratic principles and is therefore non-transferable to other cultures? . . . For me, new science answers those questions definitively. I believe in my bones that the movement towards participation is rooted in our changing perceptions of the organizing principles of life . . . All life participates in the creation of itself, insisting on the freedom to self-determine. (pp. 162–163)

Our framework (Figure 3.1) integrates ecological principles and democratic principles—honoring our deep interdependence with all life and our inherent need for participation. Foundational to our framework are the following two assertions: (1) ecological principles govern healthy and sustainable life systems, the systems in which our social systems exist and upon which they depend (Capra, 1996, 2002; Wheatley, 1999; Wheatley & Kellner-Rogers, 1996) and (2) democratic principles govern socially just (Furman & Gruenewald, 2004; Furman & Starratt, 2002) and continuously learning social systems (Kensler, Caskie, Barber, & White, 2009; Slater & Bennis, 1964).

The practice of democracy in organizations (Cloke & Goldsmith, 2002; Fenton, 2002; Slater & Bennis, 1964; Stohl & Cheney, 2001) and schools (Allen & Glickman, 1998; Dewey, 1916; Koopman, Miel, & Minsner, 1943; Woods, 2005) has a long history and retains an active presence in current educational leadership literature (Cate, Vaughn, & O'Hair, 2006; Davies, 1999; Woods & Kensler, 2012). More democratic forms of leadership are consistent with school leadership models (shared leadership, distributed leadership, etc.) associated with improved student performance (Leithwood, Louis, Anderson, & Wahlstrom, 2004). Historically, the educational leadership literature has not considered the school as nested within or interdependent with ecological systems; the role and importance of ecological principles have been invisible to many school leaders and leadership development

Figure 3.1 Theoretical Framework Integrating Ecological and Democratic Principles

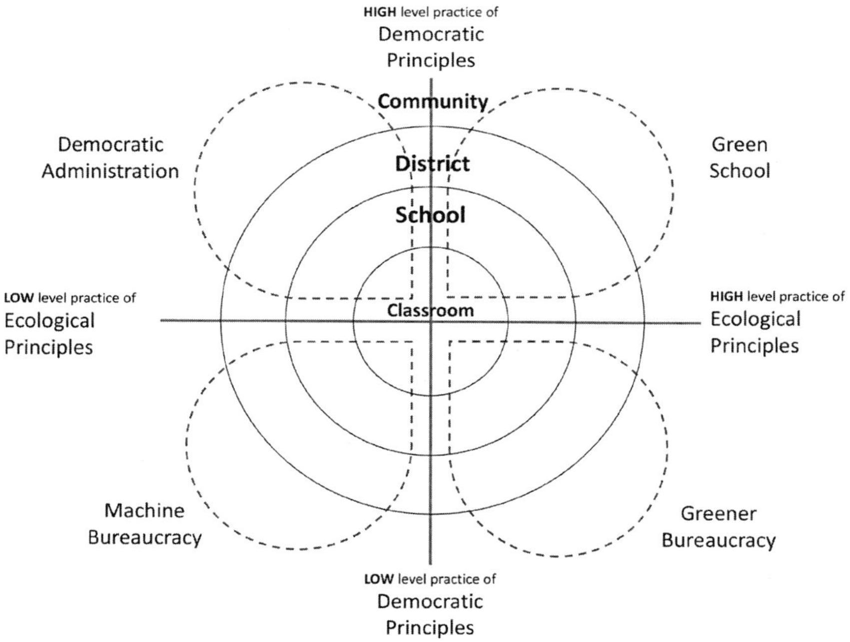

The dotted lines emphasize the indistinct nature of the four categories of schools: Machine Bureaucracy, Democratic Administration, Green Bureaucracy, and Green School. (Originally published in Kensler (2012a). Reprinted here with permission.)

programs. However, green school leaders are leading the way by bringing both ecological and democratic principles to the forefront of their practice. The greenest schools reflect both ecological and democratic principles.

Figure 3.1 illustrates four general categories of school organizations defined by the degree to which they intentionally practice both democratic principles and ecological principles:

◆ Machine bureaucracy (low level practice of democratic and ecological principles)
◆ Greener bureaucracy (low level practice of democratic principles and higher level practice of ecological principles)
◆ Democratic administration (higher level practice of democratic principles and low level practice of ecological principles)
◆ Green school (high level practice of both democratic and ecological principles).

Although practicing democracy in schools has a long history, the intentional practice of ecological principles is quite new to educational conversations. Ecological principles are important, because our social systems, including our schools, are nested within and interdependent with local and global ecological systems. We depend on healthy ecological systems for clean air, water, food, and many other ecological services and our human activities have direct effects on these ecological systems, upon which we depend. Integrating the practice of ecological principles into school leadership facilitates shifting away from more industrial/bureaucratic models and better aligns with how nature works. When we introduce ecological principles into the design, management, and leadership of schools, school communities come to life. Our school systems transform more naturally from the inside out. They become vibrant places that engage their members in local, relevant, and transformative learning.

Ecological + Democratic Principles

We will present the set of ecological and democratic principles as a nested set of principles. The ecological principles are foundational. They govern healthy life systems. Democratic principles extend from ecological principles to govern healthy social systems. In fact, scientists have found evidence that consensus decision making (an aspect of democratic practice) is present in non-human social groups such as insects, birds, and mammals (Conradt & Roper, 2005, 2007; Seeley, 2010). This emerging evidence of democratic practice within non-human social systems lends additional credibility to the

Slater and Bennis (1964) claim that democracy is a "functional necessity whenever a social system is competing for survival under conditions of chronic change" (p. 53). The changing community, political, economic, technological conditions facing education require continuous learning within schools. Healthy human social systems where learning thrives are associated with democratic practice and high levels of trust (Kensler et al., 2009; Meier, 2002). Shifting from factory model practices towards practices more consistent with how nature works requires deep learning. Ecological and democratic principles help facilitate and sustain this adaptive and transformative learning.

Table 3.1 presents an overview of this nested set of principles. Our discussion will continue with a section for each ecological principle. In each section, we will briefly define the ecological principle and the associated democratic principle/s. We will also highlight their relevance to designing, managing, and leading green schools by previewing material to be discussed in future chapters. The definitions for the principles have also been discussed in previously published research (Fenton, 2002; Kensler, 2010, 2012a; Kensler et al., 2009).

Nested Systems

Nested Systems: *Every living system is itself an integrated whole and at the same time, part of a larger system; change at one level affects the other levels.*

Individual and Collective: *When individuals understand the unique contribution they make toward achieving collective goals.*

Table 3.1 A Nested System of Ecological and Democratic Principles

Ecological Principles	Democratic Principles
Nested Systems	Individual and Collective
Networks, Partnership, and Diversity	Fairness and Dignity
	Decentralization
Self-Organization and Emergence	Purpose and Vision
	Integrity
	Choice
Matter Cycles and Energy Flows	Transparency
Dynamic Balance and Feedback	Reflection and Evaluation
	Dialogue and Listening
	Accountability

Living systems are nested systems (Capra, 1996, 2002). Consider your own body as an example. Your body is made up of many trillions of individual cells nested within tissues that are nested within organs that are nested within organ systems, all nested within your body. Beyond individuals, organisms (not just humans!) live within communities nested within larger systems, including the universe and beyond. This nestedness suggests interdependence within and among the different levels of organization. Individually we are dependent on our organ systems functioning properly and they are dependent on our caring for them properly. Beyond individual body systems, individual living things depend on other living things for food, shelter, procreation, and companionship. Local communities and regional governments are interdependent and so on. You get the idea.

Nestedness also means that we can focus our attention at different levels of any given system. For example, we can consider a classroom or a school as a complete unit, bounded by its walls. Unfortunately, if we consciously or unconsciously consider that the classroom or school is disconnected from the larger systems in which they exist, then we miss important relationships and influences that come from these different levels of the nested systems. Educators immediately understand that family dynamics as well as school climate and culture influence student performance in the classroom. Community financial support of schools in many cases dictates a school's financial situation. Less frequently considered by educators are the ecological interdependencies between school buildings and the local and global environment. School schedules, budgets and sometimes the actual buildings are affected by extreme weather events—snow, cold, heat, tornadoes, and hurricanes (Buchanan, Casbergue, & Baumgartner, 2009; Evans & Oehler-Stinnett, 2006). School carbon emissions contribute to atmospheric carbon dioxide concentrations and efforts to conserve energy not only save money, but also reduce carbon emissions (Kneifel, 2010). Disposing of left-over pharmaceuticals in the trash, down the drain, or toilet contaminate local drinking water and waterways (Council on School, 2009; Ruhoy & Daughton, 2008; Tong, Peake, & Braund, 2011). Schools sit within larger social, economic, and ecological systems with which they are interdependent. A green school leader keeps these local to global interdependencies in mind when making decisions and encourages others to do the same. This ecological principle will show up frequently throughout this book.

Individual and Collective

When we focus on our social systems within schools, the democratic principle of *Individual and Collective* calls us to keep in mind both individuals and the whole. Many organizational leadership challenges relate to balancing the needs of individuals with the needs of the whole. Individuals should be aware of and understand their unique contributions to the whole. Their individual sense of purpose and vision need to align with the overall organization's purpose and vision, as we will discuss further in the next chapter. As organizations make collective progress towards shared goals, individuals need to be acknowledged and celebrated, in small ways such as private conversations or thoughtful notes, in addition to more formal public expressions of appreciation such as student or teacher of the month programs. Collective celebrations of success are also critical to promoting change and continuous improvement. These energizing celebrations help to remind everyone of common aims and provide evidence of progress toward these aims. In all living systems, individuals comprise the broader community and within this collective there are diverse and complex networks of relationships, our next ecological principle.

Networks, Partnership, and Diversity

> **Networks, Partnership, and Diversity:** *All living things are connected directly and/or indirectly; dense, diverse networks and partnerships provide resilience.*

> **Fairness and Dignity:** *When each person is treated justly and regarded impartially.*

> **Decentralization:** *When power is appropriately shared among people at all levels of the organization.*

Competition for resources certainly plays an important role in living systems. Individual creatures often have to compete for space, food, and mates. However, the most resilient and successful living systems are diverse communities with a plethora of partnerships set within dense networks of relationship (Capra, 1996, 2002). Ecologists have documented that communities with greater species diversity, partnerships, and networks are better able to withstand and recover from major disturbances (Peterson, Allen, & Holling, 1998). For example, if a forest is comprised of just one or two species of trees and a pest successfully attacked the trees, killing all or most of them, then that forest will be much harder hit and have a much more difficult time recovering. In addition, the other species dependent on the trees would also suffer and/or be displaced. Whereas in a diverse forest some or even many of the tree species may be resistant to the pest, fewer trees would die off, fewer other species displaced, and the damage would be less and recovery would likely be faster. This principle shows up in many ways for green school leaders.

For example, it has relevance for selecting sites for new school build-ings, design and maintenance of school grounds, and developing partner-ships with other organizations. Jacobs (1961) documented in her classic book, *The Death and Life of Great American Cities*, that successful cities reflected this ecological principle. Thriving city blocks and neighborhoods included schools, businesses, homes, and recreational spaces all together; they did not provide for only single use. This diversity of services meant that people were actively present in the community throughout all times of day; there were not long periods of time when trouble could fester unnoticed. The design and maintenance of school grounds matters too. Diverse local vegetation planted on school grounds contributes to the ecological health of the area by attracting and supporting insects and birds. These school yard habitats also serve as outstanding educational resources for children to learn about their local ecologies (Rivkin, 1997). Emerging research is also demonstrating strong connections between green school yards and children's well-being and resilience (Chawla, Keena, Pevec, & Stanley, 2014). You will read more about school yard hab-itats in Chapter 6 and their connection to student well-being and learning in Chapter 8. As school leaders and community planners consider build-ing new schools, site selection and design contribute to the community's overall well-being and sustainability (Erwin, Beighle, Carson, & Castelli, 2013; Vincent, 2014)

This ecological principle of *Networks, Partnership, and Diversity* relates directly to our social systems as well. Diverse partnerships with outside organizations strengthen a school's capacity to innovate for sustainability. For example, consider Sandy Grove Middle School in North Carolina. This school is on the cutting edge of sustainable design, producing more energy than it uses over a year's time, as well as many other exciting features. In addition, it is the result of an innovative partnership between the school dis-trict and developer. The developer leases the land from the school district, owns the building, and leases the building back to the school district, making the project financially feasible for all concerned (Pritchard, 2014). Another inspiring example of partnerships in action is that of Broughal Middle School in Pennsylvania. This green building and community school relies on active partnerships to provide a wide selection of after school programs, com-munity health services, family support services, and social services. It, like other community schools, is truly a central hub of resources, education, and learning (Blank, Jacobson, & Melaville, 2012; Heers, Van Klaveren, Groot, & Maassen van den Brink, 2016; Reina et al., 2014; Satullo, 2012). Two dem-ocratic principles flow directly from this ecological principle and support developing healthy, diverse partnerships and networks: *Fairness and Dignity*; and *Decentralization*.

Fairness and Dignity

Diversity within social systems includes a vast array of differences. Most basically, individual perspectives and past experiences will differ, and both of these relate to other forms of difference such as gender, class, race, ethnicity, religion, sexual orientation, and so on. When practiced, the democratic principle of *Fairness and Dignity* addresses two sides to the same coin. On the one side, fairness means that rules, policies, and guidelines are applied consistently across different individuals and groups; one is not privileged over another. On the other side, dignity means that people are treated with deep respect; they feel valued. Both fairness and dignity create the conditions for each individual to fully express their unique individuality without fear of undue criticism, harassment, or bullying. Schools and districts characterized by less fear have more positive school climates where vibrant learning and continuous improvement are more likely (Louis, 2007; Tschannen-Moran, 2004; Tschannen-Moran & Gareis, 2015). In these educational organizations, trust is more likely to flourish and allow for more decentralized leadership and broad participation in change initiatives.

Decentralization

Decentralization is the sharing of power. Those in positional power or administrative positions have the choice to share their power or not. They can view power as a limited commodity, hoard it, and strive to keep control. This classic style of authoritarian leadership leads to strong, less flexible hierarchies and bureaucracies. This centralized leadership expresses very little trust in followers and typically, followers reflect the same low trust in their leaders. Social systems like these are unhealthy, less productive, and not characterized by continuous learning or improvement; their social networks are more rigid and less resilient (Daly, 2009, 2010; Daly, Liou, Tran, Cornelissen, & Park, 2013). Where decentralization is practiced, positional leaders share or distribute their power by empowering others to engage more fully in leading and governing. Active networks of relationships purposefully form and dissipate as needed, in order to accomplish necessary work (Wheatley, 1999). Leaders of consistently improving schools maximize the learning capacity of vibrant networks.

> This strategy capitalizes on the fact that key insights often emerge in unusual places. By working through organized networks, the likelihood increases that these ideas may surface, be systematically examined, and if promising, moved rapidly into testing and refinement. In addition, promising practices emerging in the network are likely to diffuse more rapidly and are further tested and refined as others take them up. (Bryk, Gomez, Grunow, & LeMahieu, 2015, p. 11)

Networks of green school leaders and schools are actively engaged in the work of learning to implement whole school sustainability strategies. You can read more about these networks and opportunities for joining them in Chapter 10.

Self-organization and Emergence

Self-organization and Emergence: *All life changes and evolves over time; change in living systems is natural and continuous within individuals, communities, and populations.*

Purpose and Vision: *When an organization and the individual know their reason for existing and have a sense of intentional direction.*

Integrity: *When each person steadfastly adheres to high moral principles and consistently practices the organization's core values.*

Choice: *When each person is encouraged to exercise their right to choose between a diversity of possibilities.*

Living systems have been self-organizing since the beginning of life itself. Although we may not fully understand how life began on planet Earth, scientists have learned a lot about how living systems organize, grow, and change. Self-organization leads to the emergence of novelty and adaptation (Capra, 1996, 2002). Capra (2010) explained,

Living systems generally remain in a stable state, even though energy and matter flow through them and their structures are continually changing. But every now and then such an open system will encounter a point of instability, where there is either a breakdown or, more frequently, a spontaneous emergence of new forms of order.

This spontaneous emergence of order at critical points of instability, which is often referred to simply as "emergence," is one of the hallmarks of life. It has been recognized as the dynamic origin of development, learning, and evolution. In other words, creativity—the generation of new forms—is a key property of all living systems. (n.p.)

Living systems are open and closed systems. As Capra explained they are open to their environment and use energy and matter to maintain their structure. However, they are operationally closed, meaning they contain the information that they need to be and reproduce themselves. He described this fundamental characteristic of life as "self-maintenance via a mechanism of self-regeneration from within. Life is a factory that makes itself from within" (Capra & Luigi, 2014, p. 131). As environmental conditions change, life responds creatively.

Understanding this principle can help inform how we think about change within our organizations. Rather than imposing change from positional power atop the organizational chart, leaders with a living systems perspective cultivate the conditions in which change happens and novelty emerges. These conditions include principles that we have already discussed—diverse networks characterized by high levels of trust and power sharing—and those we turn to next. Three democratic principles extend directly from the ecological principle of self-organization: *Purpose and Vision*, *Integrity*, and *Choice*. Recall, living systems are both closed and open. In terms of being closed, their defining information exists within them. In individuals, this defining information takes the form of DNA. In our organizations, this defining information may or may not be particularly clear to the organizational members. However, we know that a clear, shared vision is a common finding across all studies of effective schools (Murphy & Torre, 2014) and our next chapter discusses this in depth.

Purpose and Vision

What is the purpose of your school? What and how clear is your school's vision? How explicitly and intentionally does your school community explore these questions? In social systems, purpose and vision serve as the guiding information around which organizations may self-organize. In human social systems such as educational organizations, purpose is fundamental to the system's design and implementation. "Vision guided institutions are institutions organized around conceptions of what they are most fundamentally about, conceptions that give meaning and direction to the activities of the participants and to the enterprise as a whole" (Pekarsky, 2007, p. 426). We discussed the power of purposefully meeting the needs of the 21st century in Chapter 2. Mission and vision statements typically communicate, both internally and externally, a school's sense of purpose. The degree to which this sense of purpose is shared, understood, and practiced may vary broadly from school to school (Stemler, Bebell, & Sonnabend, 2011). Where the purpose, vision, and mission appear to be clear, understood, and shared, schools perform more effectively (Hawley & Rollie, 2002; Pekarsky, 2007; Sammons, Hillman, & Mortimore, 1995).

In recent studies of school mission statements across the United States (Bebell & Stemler, 2012; Stemler et al., 2011), concepts specifically related to green schools such as ecological, social, and/or economic sustainability, have not yet emerged as common themes. However, trailblazing schools are beginning to explicitly identify sustainability-related topics as a core component of their mission and vision. For example, Pine Jog Elementary School, a Green Ribbon School in the School District of Palm Beach County, Florida, posts this mission statement on their website:

> Our mission is to develop a community of environmentally conscious learners who value and respect themselves, others and the world we share through integrating science, technology, nature and art. This mission is accomplished through collaborative efforts between our school, Pine Jog Environmental Education Center and Florida Atlantic University. (Pine Jog, 2016)

In a recent study of U.S. Department of Education Green Ribbon School award winners, Warner and Elser (2014) found that the schools with the highest degree of sustainability project interconnectedness (presumably closer to practicing whole school sustainability) were those schools that were envisioned and designed to be green schools or they were "small private or charter schools with strong leadership" (p. 16). In essence, their DNA includes a commitment to sustainability. We discuss purpose and vision in more detail in the next chapter. The degree to which a community is true to their purpose and vision is determined by their *Integrity*, our next democratic principle.

Integrity

The integrity with which individuals and organizations align with the organization's purpose, mission, and vision determine, in large part, the degree to which the purpose and vision are fully lived and realized. Individuals with integrity adhere to high moral principles. They practice what Sergiovanni (2005) and Fullan (2003) have referred to as moral leadership. Integrity also refers to wholeness and may apply to individuals as well as organizations. Within individuals, a narrow "saying–doing" gap indicates integrity; one behaves consistently with his or her espoused beliefs (Argyris, 1992). Within organizations that reflect high levels of integrity there is alignment across individuals' core values and the organization's purpose, mission, and vision. In other words, everyone is "on the same page" or "rowing in the same direction." Just as closing the saying–doing gap at the individual level requires continuous reflection, deep organizational integrity requires reflective conversations among organizational members. Collective learning depends on these reflective conversations (Senge et al., 2012). We return to these collective experiences in Chapter 9 with discussions of teacher learning for whole school sustainability. Although individual and collective integrity call for alignment of core values and practice, this does not mean that each individual expression will be identical; having some freedom of choice is another principle practiced in more democratic social systems.

Choice

Capra and Luigi (2014) make the important point that the behavior of living systems is constrained by environmental conditions, but determined by their self-organizing structure. For example, a bean plant develops from seed to plant according to the interaction between the directions for growth embedded in its DNA and the environmental conditions in which it finds itself. Its growth behavior may be constrained by nutrient availability, but these conditions cannot drive behavior in ways that vary from its guiding internal structure. Human social systems, designed by us, are driven by choice. We have the freedom to choose what we notice, what we find meaningful, what we find disturbing, what we find inspiring, and so forth (Wheatley, 1999). As we make choices and act on them, we live in patterned ways that collectively form our organizational networks that also drive what we experience as our organizational culture. As Wheatley explained,

> The new science keeps reminding us that in this participative universe, nothing living lives alone. Everything comes into form because of relationship. We are constantly called to be in relationship—to information, people, events, ideas, life. Even reality is created through our participation in relationships. We choose what to notice; we relate to things and ignore others. Through these chosen relationships, we co-create our world. (1999, p. 145)

Matter Cycles and Energy Flows

Matter Cycles and Energy Flows: *Matter cycles through all living systems (e.g., water, geochemical) without producing a steady stream of unused waste; one's waste is another's food; local cycles interact with regional and global cycles. The sun fuels most ecological systems on Earth; every transfer of energy results in some energy loss, thus energy needs are ongoing.*

Transparency: *When ideas flow freely and information is openly and responsibly shared.*

In all living systems on Earth, matter cycles and energy flows (Capra, 1996, 2002). The Earth is comprised of material elements and molecules, some of which serve as the building blocks of life. These molecules move between living and non-living systems through biogeochemical cycles (e.g., water cycle, carbon cycle, nitrogen cycle, etc.). If there were not biogeochemical cycles—in other words, if these material elements simply "went away" after one use—then we would eventually run out of the materials needed for living systems to exist. Living systems depend on the constant re-use of matter's basic building blocks. Within a forest, when a tree dies the nutrients that make it up become food for other organisms and eventually return to the soil for use within new generations of trees and other organisms. Nothing is wasted in nature. Everything is recycled. One organism's waste is another's food. Energy drives these natural cycles. It takes energy for living systems to break down food and use the building blocks for their growth and development. The sun serves as the ultimate source of energy for most living systems on Earth. Energy flows through the system, it is not recycled. Activating this principle, *Matter Cycles and Energy Flows*, in schools results in economic, environmental, and educational benefits for schools.

Schools use energy and matter every day. They could not remain open without energy and matter. The way a school's occupants (students, teachers, staff, and administration) think about and use energy and matter has economic, environmental, and social consequences within and beyond the school walls. The efficient use of energy and resources can save a school a significant amount of money. In fact, the United States Environmental Protection Agency (EPA) estimates that at least 25% energy savings are readily possible across U.S. public schools. Since energy expenses are second only to personnel expenses in most schools, these savings amount to a very large annual sum of $2 billion that can be redirected towards teaching and learning (*Energy Efficiency Programs in K–12 Schools: A Guide to Developing and Implementing Greenhouse Gas Reduction Programs*, 2011). As of early in 2015, there were seven K–12 schools verified as zero energy buildings and nearly 20 more working towards this goal (NBI, 2015). These innovative buildings use net zero energy over the course of a year; some even contribute more energy to the grid than they use. Reducing energy usage also has a positive effect on the environment through reducing a school's carbon footprint—the amount of carbon released to the atmosphere through the burning of fossil fuels (e.g., oil, natural gas, coal). Reducing our carbon footprint is seen as a key lever for slowing global warming and related climate change effects (Kagawa & Selby, 2010). Practicing the ecological principle of *Matter Cycles and Energy Flows* means maximizing the efficiency of energy flowing through your school. We will further discuss energy use and conservation in Chapters 6 and 7. We turn now to discuss the other half of this principle, *Matter Cycles*, and its relevance for schools.

In healthy ecosystems, everything is recycled and nothing is wasted. There is no "away" for things to be thrown. This is far from the reality in our take–make–waste systems of production (Leonard, 2010), as we have already discussed in our second chapter. We throw so much away that our landfills are filling up and communities are seeking creative solutions. Reducing the waste that we send off to landfills is a high leverage solution to this challenge. Schools can be community leaders in this waste reduction effort by following five key rules—reduce (reduce purchasing where possible, purchase products with less packaging), reuse (repurpose used materials as often as possible), recycle (participate in recycling programs, provide opportunities for community members to recycle), compost (collect food waste, compost it, and use the soil), and purchase recycled materials (develop and follow purchasing guidelines that prioritize purchasing products made from recycled materials). Similar to the benefits of energy efficiency, following these five rules of waste reduction leads to economic, environmental, and educational benefits for schools. According to a recent waste stream analysis study conducted in Minnesota, only 15% of the waste generated in schools is true garbage, meaning that it actually needs to head to the landfill (Cioci & Farnan, 2010). This suggests that those schools that have not already focused on waste reduction could reduce the amount of waste hauled to landfills by 85%, saving themselves hauling fees as well. We will further discuss the reduction and management of waste in Chapters 6 and 7. Information flows through our social systems like energy (Wheatley, 1999). Transparency frees the flow of information to fuel learning.

Transparency

The democratic principle, *Transparency*, relates directly to the flow of information throughout an organization's social system. This information may flow formally or informally. Formal leaders may share information freely or keep information close. Individuals may also share information in an inclusive and open way or restrict information flow via tight cliques and exclusive networks. We have all experienced the grapevine effect; news that we care about, good and bad, can travel quite quickly through our social networks! The free and responsible flow of information through a school community energizes the system, fueling learning and innovation. Where the information flow is restricted or hoarded individuals feel uninformed, alienated, and often frustrated. Leading change for sustainability will require sharing relevant and meaningful information in timely and responsible ways. As Wheatley explains,

> Anything that supports reflective conversations among new and different parts of the organization is important . . . Through these processes, new information is spawned, new meanings develop, and the organization grows intelligence. (1999, p. 108)

Dynamic Balance and Feedback

Dynamic Balance and Feedback: *Feedback loops help maintain a relatively steady state with continuous fluctuations between upper and lower boundaries.*

Reflection and Evaluation: *When there is careful and thorough consideration and feedback regarding previous actions, events, or decisions.*

Dialogue and Listening: *When we listen and engage in conversation in a way that brings out new levels of meaning and connection.*

Accountability: *When each person and the organization as a whole is responsible to each other and their community for their actions.*

Living systems are continuously responding to stimuli, changing, growing, and adapting. Only dead living systems appear to stop altogether and even then they don't really stop changing, as decomposition takes over (Capra, 1996, 2002; Capra & Luigi, 2014). Although constant change characterizes living systems, the changes take place within a set of boundaries. Feedback loops work to keep living systems in dynamic balance and these feedback loops exist at all levels of life's nested systems, from cells on up. For example, fitness tracking devices like the popular Fitbit provide real-time feedback to their users about progress towards user-defined goals. With information in hand, fitness buffs can better regulate their activity levels. This is similar to the dashboards featured in some green buildings that provide users with data related to energy and water usage. The information these dashboards convey serves to close the loop between building users and the demands they place on building systems. Feedback such as this can help encourage more sustainable choices and behaviors (Chen, Taylor, & Wei, 2012; Pierce, Odom, & Blevis, 2008).

As another example, Kensler (2012b) wrote about work–life balance, not as a perfect steady state for which to discover the secret, but as a dynamic balance between intolerable extremes. In her case, she described the extremes as ranging from no work and, thus, no income to meaningful work that filled every waking moment and left little time for other endeavors. As she described, maintaining equilibrium is an energy intensive endeavor and involves continuous adjustment to feedback from family members, friends, co-workers, as well as personal reflection. As educators, we are deeply aware of the critical role feedback and reflection plays in learning. Teachers who provide high quality feedback to students in a timely manner can ignite students' love of learning, while others, whose feedback is absent or cruel, may shut down learning. Teacher evaluation systems work in similar ways. Processes and strategies for providing feedback fuel or dampen learning. Three democratic principles help guide productive feedback in social systems, *Reflection and Evaluation*, *Dialogue and Listening*, and *Accountability*.

Reflection and Evaluation

One of the assumptions of democracy is a continuous drive towards perfectibility (Kensler, 2010). This tension between the current state, the way things are, and a more perfect state, the way we want things to be, fuels progress and motivates purposeful learning (Senge et al., 2012). Green school leaders understand that sustainability, much like democracy, is an ideal aim more than a defined destination. Therefore, enacting whole school sustainability requires frequent pauses for reflection and evaluation. Where are our practices consistent with the aims of whole school sustainability and where do they fall short? What are our measures of success and how might they continue to stretch us beyond our current practice? The work of reflection and evaluation takes time and skill (Osterman & Kottkamp, 2004). Effective school leaders design the time into their schedules and provide the professional development support to build capacity for this important work (Lambert et al., 2002).

Dialogue and Listening

Learning is very much a social endeavor; we learn through conversation (Bransford, Brown, & Cocking, 2000). However, carrying on effective learning conversations requires artful facilitation and skill (Ellinor & Gerard, 1998). People need support and practice in listening deeply to differing perspectives and finding common ground upon which to build (Uline, Tschannen-Moran, & Perez, 2003). Whole school sustainability presents many opportunities for dramatically changing the way educational work gets done. From greening building maintenance to school curriculum, whole school sustainability touches every aspect of work in schools. These changes will not take root and grow if people are not engaged in powerful conversations about what sustainability means to them, their personal values, beliefs, and practices. School leaders hold the positional power to invite these conversations and build collective capacity for learning. Deep change will occur over time, as people learn together how to live and work differently.

Accountability

That for which individuals and the group are accountable defines the boundaries within which dynamic balance fluctuates. These upper and lower boundaries may come in the form of formal local, state, and federal policies or they may be more informal. We also have personal, peer, supervisor, and organizational expectations that hold us accountable for our performance, some formal and some informal. Regardless, there are thresholds that, when crossed, result in consequences. These consequences provide concrete feedback that aims to push activity and performance back within the defined boundaries. Educators are all too familiar with high stakes accountability policies, their related testing protocols, and punitive consequences for low performance. We don't need convincing that accountability systems and processes can be destructive. However, educators may also design their own accountability systems for their school communities. In what ways are individuals in your school community held accountable for living the system's core values, purpose, mission, and vision? Do these ideals sit on shelves and walls or are they vibrantly active within the school community? Systems and processes that encourage individual and collective reflection, evaluation, dialogue, and listening are forms of accountability that encourage learning towards a more consistent expression of one's core values, purpose, mission, and vision, a discussion we take into the next chapter.

Conclusion

The factory model of schooling reinforces anthropocentric and mechanical thinking. It has a long track record of lackluster results. As we discussed in Chapter 2, this industrial model drives the perception that humans are separate from and dominant over Earth rather than integral and interdependent with Earth. Structuring education in the image of factories designed for efficient mass production may very well be at the root of student and teacher disengagement, a fundamental problem for so many schools today. Our children, our communities, our planet need a redesigned educational system. Ecological and democratic principles offer a way to approach this work locally and from the inside out, rather than through top-down, mandated changes. These principles help guide a process of realignment with how nature and healthy, learning social systems actually work. Once we have consciously committed to break away from old, familiar models, then ecological and democratic principles help us see many opportunities for intentionally improving our schools.

> The potent force that shapes behavior in these organizations and in all natural systems is the combination of simply expressed expectations of purpose, intent, and values, and the freedom for responsible individuals to make sense of these in their own way. Organizations with integrity have truly learned that there is no choice but to walk their talk. Their values are truthful representations of how they want to conduct themselves, and everyone feels deeply accountable to them . . . When each person is trusted to work freely with those principles, to interpret them, learn from them, talk about them, then through many iterations a pattern of ethical behavior emerges. It is recognizable in everyone, no matter where they sit or what they do. (Wheatley, 1999, p. 129)

Questions for Discussion

1. Where on Figure 3.1 would you plot your classroom, school, and/or district? In other words, how would you describe the current operation of ecological and democratic principles in these systems? Where do you see opportunities for expanding the operation of these principles?

2. Choose one principle that seems particularly active in your system (classroom, school, or district) and describe it. How does it operate? What are the effects?

3. Choose one principle that seems particularly absent or restricted in your system (classroom, school, or district) and develop a plan for putting it to work. For example, if your school generates a stream of waste with no effort to recycle, then the ecological principle of matter cycles/energy flows is not freely operating in your system. How could you begin to practice this principle in small ways first, by consciously reducing the generation of waste, while eventually working towards a zero waste system?

References

Allen, L., & Glickman, C. D. (1998). Restructuring and renewal: Capturing the power of democracy. In A. Hargreaves, A. Lieberman, M. Fullan, & D. Hopkins (Eds.), *International handbook of educational change* (pp. 505–528). Boston, MA: Kluwer Academic Publishers.

Argyris, C. (1992). *On organizational learning*. Cambridge, MA: Blackwell Publishers.

Bebell, D., & Stemler, S. (2012). *The school mission statement: Values, goals, and identities in American education*. New York: Routledge.

Blank, M. J., Jacobson, R., & Melaville, A. (2012). *Achieving results through community school partnerships: How district and community leaders are building effective, sustainable relationships*. Retrieved from Washington, DC: https://www.americanprogress.org/issues/education/report/2012/01/18/10987/achieving-results-through-community-school-partnerships/

Bransford, J., Brown, A. L., & Cocking, R. R. (Eds.). (2000). *How people learn: Brain, mind, experience, and school*. Washington, DC: National Academy Press.

Bryk, A. S., Gomez, L. M., Grunow, A., & LeMahieu, P. G. (2015). *Learning to improve: How America's schools can get better at getting better*. Boston, MA: Harvard Education Press.

Buchanan, T. K., Casbergue, R. M., & Baumgartner, J. (2009). Consequences for classroom environments and school personnel: Evaluating Katrina's effect on schools and system response. In R. P. Kilmer (Ed.), *Helping families and communities recover from disaster: Lessons learned from Hurricane Katrina and its aftermath* (pp. 117–139). Washington, DC: American Psychological Association.

Capra, F. (1996). *The web of life*. New York: Anchor Books.

Capra, F. (2002). *Hidden connections*. New York: Doubleday.

Capra, F. (2010). *Life and leadership for a sustainable community*. Retrieved from: http://www.ecoliteracy.org/article/life-and-leadership-sustainable-community

Capra, F., & Luigi, L. P. (2014). *The systems view of life: A unifying vision*. Cambridge: Cambridge University Press.

Cate, J. M., Vaughn, A., & O'Hair, M. J. (2006). A seventeen-year case study of an elementary school's journey: From traditional school to learning community to democratic school community. *Journal of School Leadership, 16*, 86–111.

Chawla, L., Keena, K., Pevec, I., & Stanley, E. (2014). Green schoolyards as havens from stress and resources for resilience in childhood and adolescence. *Health Place, 28,* 1–13. doi:10.1016/j.healthplace.2014.03.001

Chen, J., Taylor, J. E., & Wei, H.-H. (2012). Modeling building occupant network energy consumption decision-making: The interplay between network structure and conservation. *Energy and Buildings, 47,* 515–524. doi:10.1016/j.enbuild.2011.12.026

Cioci, M., & Farnan, T. (2010). *Digging deep through school trash: A waste composition analysis of trash, recycling and organic material discarded at public schools in Minnesota.* Retrieved from: https://www.pca.state.mn.us/sites/default/files/p-p2s6-14.pdf

Cloke, K., & Goldsmith, J. (2002). *The end of management and the rise of organizational democracy.* San Francisco, CA: Jossey-Bass.

Conradt, L., & Roper, T. J. (2005). Consensus decision making in animals. *Trends in Ecology and Evolution, 20*(8), 449–456. doi:10.1016/j.tree.2005.05.008

Conradt, L., & Roper, T. J. (2007). Democracy in animals: The evolution of shared group decisions. *Proceedings of the Royal Society Biology, 274*(1623), 2317–2326. doi:10.1098/rspb.2007.0186

Council on School, H. (2009). Policy statement—guidance for the administration of medication in school. *Pediatrics, 124*(4), 1244–1251. doi:10.1542/peds.2009–1953

Daly, A. J. (2009). Rigid response in an age of accountability. *Educational Administration Quarterly, 45*(2), 168–216.

Daly, A. J. (Ed.). (2010). *Social network theory and educational change.* Boston, MA: Harvard Education Press.

Daly, A. J., Liou, Y. H., Tran, N. A., Cornelissen, F., & Park, V. (2013). The rise of neurotics: Social networks, leadership, and efficacy in district reform. *Educational Administration Quarterly, 50*(2), 233–278. doi:10.1177/0013161x13492795

Davies, L. (1999). Comparing definitions of democracy in education. *Compare, 29*(2), 127–140.

Dewey, J. (1916). *Democracy and education.* New York The Free Press.

Ellinor, L., & Gerard, G. (1998). *Dialogue: Rediscovering the transforming power of conversation.* New York: John Wiley & Sons, Inc.

Energy efficiency programs in K–12 schools: A guide to developing and implementing greenhouse gas reduction programs. (2011). Retrieved from: http://www3.epa.gov/statelocalclimate/documents/pdf/k-12_guide.pdf

Erwin, H., Beighle, A., Carson, R. L., & Castelli, D. M. (2013). Comprehensive school-based physical activity promotion: A review. *New Quest, 65*(4), 412–428. doi:10.1 080/00336297.2013.791872

Evans, L., & Oehler-Stinnett, J. (2006). Children and natural disasters a primer for school psychologists. *School Psychology International, 27*(1), 33–55.

Fenton, T. (2002). *The democratic company.* Retrieved from Washington, DC: http://library.uniteddiversity.coop/Decision_Making_and_Democracy/Democratic_Company.pdf

Fullan, M. (2003). *The moral imperative of school leadership.* New York: Corwin Press.

Furman, G. C., & Gruenewald, D. A. (2004). Expanding the landscape of social justice: A critical ecological analysis. *Educational Administration Quarterly, 40*(1), 47–76.

Furman, G. C., & Starratt, R. J. (2002). Leadership for democratic community in schools. In J. Murphy (Ed.), *The educational leadership challenge: Redefining leadership for the 21st century*. Chicago, IL: The University of Chicago Press.

Hawley, W. D., & Rollie, D. L. (Eds.). (2002). *The keys to effective schools: Educational reform as continuous improvement*. Thousand Oaks, CA: Corwin Press.

Heers, M., Van Klaveren, C., Groot, W., & Maassen van den Brink, H. (2016). Community schools: What we know and what we need to know. *Review of Educational Research, online first* (X), 1–36. doi:10.3102/0034654315627365

Jacobs, J. (1961). *The death and life of great American cities*. New York: Vintage.

Kagawa, F., & Selby, D. (2010). *Education and climate change*. New York: Routledge.

Kensler, L. A. W. (2010). Designing democratic community for social justice. *International Journal of Urban Educational Leadership, 4*(1), 1–21. Retrieved from: https://docs.google.com/viewer?url=http://www.uc.edu/urbanleadership/abstract_pdf/IJUEL-1-Kensler.pdf

Kensler, L. A. W. (2012a). Ecology, democracy, and green schools: An integrated framework. *Journal of School Leadership, 22*(4), 789–814.

Kensler, L. A. W. (2012b). One family, different perspectives on work–life balance. In J. M. Marshall, J. S. Brooks, K. M. Brown, L. H. Bussey, B. Fusarelli, M. A. Gooden, … G. Theoharis (Eds.), *Juggline flaming chain saws* (pp. 105–112). Charlotte, NC: Information Age Publishing.

Kensler, L. A. W., Caskie, G. I. L., Barber, M. E., & White, G. P. (2009). The ecology of democratic learning communities: Faculty trust and continuous learning in public middle schools. *Journal of School Leadership, 19*(6), 697–734.

Kneifel, J. (2010). Life-cycle carbon and cost analysis of energy efficiency measures in new commercial buildings. *Energy and Buildings, 42*(3), 333–340. doi:10.1016/j.enbuild.2009.09.011

Koopman, G. R., Miel, A., & Minsner, P. J. (1943). *Democracy in school administration*. New York: D. Appleton-Century Company.

Lambert, L., Walker, D., Zimmerman, D. P., Cooper, J. E., Lambert, M. D., Gardner, M. E., & Szabo, M. (2002). *The constructivist leader*. New York: Teachers College Press.

Leithwood, K., Louis, K. S., Anderson, S., & Wahlstrom, K. (2004). *Review of research: How leadership influences student learning*. Retrieved from New York: http://www.wallacefoundation.org/knowledge-center/Pages/How-Leadership-Influences-Student-Learning.aspx

Leonard, A. (2010). *The story of stuff*. New York: Free Press.

Louis, K. S. (2007). Trust and improvement in schools. *Journal of Educational Change, 8*, 1–24.

Meier, D. (2002). *In schools we trust*. Boston, MA: Beacon Press.

Murphy, J., & Torre, D. (2014). Vision: Essential scaffolding. *Educational Management Administration & Leadership, 43*(2), 177–197. doi:10.1177/1741143214523017

NBI. (2015). 2015 *List of zero energy buildings*. Retrieved from: http://newbuildings. org/resource/2015-list-zero-energy-buildings/

Osterman, K. F., & Kottkamp, R. B. (2004). *Reflective practice for educators: Professional development to improve student learning* (2nd ed.). Thousand Oaks, CA: Corwin Press.

Pekarsky, D. (2007). Vision and education: Arguments, counterarguments, rejoinders. *American Journal of Education, 113*, 423–450.

Peterson, G., Allen, C. R., & Holling, C. S. (1998). Ecological resilience, biodiversity, and scale. *Ecosystems, 1*(1), 6–18.

Pierce, J., Odom, W., & Blevis, E. (2008, December 8–12). *Energy aware dwelling: A critical survey of interaction design for eco-visualizations*. Paper presented at the Proceedings of the 20th Australasian Conference on Computer–Human Interaction: Designing for Habitus and Habitat, Cairns, Australia.

Pine Jog. (2016). Pine Jog Elementary School home page. Retrieved from: http:// www.edline.net/pages/pine_jog_elementary_school.

Pritchard, C. (2014, February 17). Solar-powered Sandy Grove Middle School singled out as "Best of the Best" in current issue of Engineering News and Record. Retrieved from: http://www.fayobserver.com/news/local/ solar-powered-sandy-grove-middle-school-singled-out-as-best/article_ d7317960-0d29-54f7-92ba-545239e46998.html

Reina, V. R., Buffel, T., Kindekens, A., De Backer, F., Peeters, J., & Lombaerts, K. (2014). Enhancing engagement through a community school approach as the key to increase academic achievement. *Procedia—Social and Behavioral Sciences, 116*, 2078–2084. doi:10.1016/j.sbspro.2014.01.523

Rivkin, M. (1997). The schoolyard habitat movement: What it is and why children need it. *Early Childhood Education Journal, 25*(1), 61–66. doi:1082-3301/97/0900-0061

Ruhoy, I. S., & Daughton, C. G. (2008). Beyond the medicine cabinet: An analysis of where and why medications accumulate. *Environment International, 34*(8), 1157–1169. doi:10.1016/j.envint.2008.05.002

Sammons, P., Hillman, J., & Mortimore, P. (1995). *Key characteristics of effective schools: A review of school effectiveness research*. Retrieved from: http://files.eric.ed.gov/ fulltext/ED389826.pdf

Satullo, S. K. (2012, January 26). Broughal middle school's after-school programs thriving. Retrieved from: http://www.lehighvalleylive.com/bethlehem/index. ssf/2012/01/post_187.html

Seeley, T. D. (2010). *Honeybee democracy*. Princeton, NJ: Princeton University Press.

Senge, P. M., Cambron-McCabe, N., Lucas, T., Smith, B., & Dutton, J. (2012). *Schools that learn (updated and revised): A fifth discipline fieldbook for educators, parents, and everyone who cares about education*. New York: Crown Business.

Sergiovanni, T. J. (2005). *Strengthening the heartbeat*. San Francisco, CA: Jossey-Bass.

Slater, P., & Bennis, W. (1964). Democracy is inevitable. *Harvard Business Reveiw, 68*(5), 167–176.

Stemler, S. E., Bebell, D., & Sonnabend, L. A. (2011). Using school mission statements for reflection and research. *Educational Administration Quarterly, 47*(2), 383–420. doi:10.1177/0013161X10387590

Stohl, C., & Cheney, G. (2001). Participatory processes/paradoxical practices: Communication and the dilemmas of organizational democracy. *Management Communication Quarterly, 14*(3), 349–407.

Tong, A. Y., Peake, B. M., & Braund, R. (2011). Disposal practices for unused medications around the world. *Environment International, 37*(1), 292–298. doi:10.1016/j. envint.2010.10.002

Tschannen-Moran, M. (2004). *Trust matters.* San Francisco, CA: Jossey-Bass.

Tschannen-Moran, M., & Gareis, C. (2015). Principals, trust, and cultivating vibrant schools. *Societies, 5*(2), 256–276. doi:10.3390/soc5020256

Uline, C. L., Tschannen-Moran, M., & Perez, L. (2003). Constructive conflict: How controversy contributes to school improvement. *Teacher College Record, 105,* 782–816.

Vincent, J. M. (2014). Joint use of public schools: A framework for promoting healthy communities. *Journal of Planning Education and Research, 34*(2), 153–168. doi:10.1177/0739456x13513615

Warner, B. P., & Elser, M. (2014). How do sustainable schools integrate sustainability education? An assessment of Certified Sustainable K–12 schools in the United States. *The Journal of Environmental Education, 46*(1), 1–22. doi:10.1080/00958964. 2014.953020

Wheatley, M. J. (1999). *Leadership and the new science: Discovering order in a chaotic world* (3rd ed.). San Francisco: Berrett-Koehler.

Wheatley, M. J., & Kellner-Rogers, M. (1996). *A simpler way.* San Francisco: Berrett-Koehler.

Woods, P. A. (2005). *Democratic leadership in education.* Thousand Oaks, CA: Sage.

Woods, P. A., & Kensler, L. A. W. (2012). A nested view of democratic leadership and community. *Journal of School Leadership, 22*(4), 702–706.

4

Greening Your School's Vision

You need a vision so big it will require all the individual visions to accomplish it. You'll never evoke people's best efforts with your current vision, and you aren't even going to evoke your own best work.

(Waugh & Forrest, 2001, p. 100)

Angela and Tom have been preparing to co-create their school visions with their faculties over the coming weeks. Their work is prompted by their district's accreditation process, but they are committed to developing an authentic, ongoing process that engages their faculty, staff, students, and community. You may recall that Tom is principal of a large comprehensive high school and Angela is a principal of a Waldorf inspired K–8 school. Angela has been promoting, "Sustainable lifestyle, sustainable human development, and sustainable Earth" for the past few years and there is a lot of green-oriented, project-based learning taking place in her school. However, she is certain that they need to deepen their collective understanding of sustainability, their practice, and their vision. Tom's faculty is recently energized by a bond-funded building improvement project that their students researched and proposed. They are open to seeing more possibilities than ever before, and he wants to capitalize on this potential energy.

Effective leaders have vision and they intentionally cultivate shared vision. Whether you read personal accounts of successful individuals or academic texts related to organizational leadership, you will not be surprised to find that vision plays a central role. Since the earliest days of school effectiveness research (Edmonds, 1979) through today (Leithwood & Seashore-Louis, 2011; Murphy & Torre, 2014), scholars tell us about the critical role vision plays in high-performing schools. The former Interstate School Leaders Licensure Consortium (ISLLC) standards, now the Professional Standards of Educational Leaders (PSEL), have consistently featured vision as the first standard: "Effective educational leaders develop, advocate, and enact a shared mission, vision, and core values of high-quality education and academic success and well-being of *each* student" (NBEA, 2015). Vibrant shared visions are considered strong motivating forces in schools (Leithwood, Harris, & Hopkins, 2008; Murphy & Torre, 2014). More specifically, many studies on school leadership show that shared vision is strongly associated with teachers' reported job satisfaction, commitment, and perceptions of their leader's effectiveness (Leithwood & Sun, 2012) as well as engagement in organizational learning practices (Kurland, Peretz, & Hertz-Lazarowitz, 2010). A recent study showed that teachers' internalization of school goals into personal goals explained the positive relationship between school leadership practices (such as building shared vision) and teachers' engagement in professional learning activities (Thoonen, Sleegers, Oort, Peetsma, & Geijsel, 2011). We revisit this well-established connection between shared vision and teacher learning in Chapter 9. When school community members are involved in cultivating a shared vision for their school, they are more engaged in their work. This is really not news.

We know that powerfully shared visions predict teacher engagement and school success. We also know that school vision statements appear front and center on most web pages and hang in most hallways and classrooms. However, even with all of this focus on vision, there is a serious teacher engagement problem. Gallup recently painted a dreary picture of teacher engagement across the United States. Based on nationally representative teacher responses, 70% of teachers reported not being engaged, involved with, enthusiastic about, and committed to their work (Gallup, 2014). Stress related to standardized tests, punitive accountability, and poor administrative leadership were offered as explanations grounded in Gallup's survey responses. Mulford (2010) pointed out similar problems among teachers and students internationally, especially in countries with strong national approaches to school improvement such as common standards and curriculum. Strike (2004) expressed concerns about the standards-based reform over a decade ago,

> My central concern with standards-based reform, however, is that its ethos is that of the bank. It expresses no shared conception of a good

> education beyond the idea that higher test scores are better. There is
> no consensus and little discussion as to what ends higher scores serve
> beyond economic aspirations. (p. 228)

We suggest that this low teacher engagement challenge is, at its core, an indicator of a vision problem in schools. In this standards-driven era, school mission and vision statements are often driven by state mandates and developed in order to check off an accrediting body's to-do list (Bebell & Stemler, 2012; Gurley, Peters, Collins, & Fifolt, 2014). These aims and methods are just not enough to be motivating for most educators who entered the field with a deep desire to make a positive difference in the world (Palmer, 1998). These test score visions end up feeling small; they don't draw educators and students out of bed each morning with enthusiasm. Tom and Angela are feeling this tension in their district. They want to develop an authentic process, but they know that takes time, lots of time. They are torn between their desire to re-invigorate their visions for the 21st century and the pressure to get the vision-box checked off their to-do lists.

In this chapter we will build on the prior chapters' discussion of ethics and foundational principles for green schools through descriptive examples of schools where these principles are vibrantly practiced. These exemplar schools model the potential of transformative visions for learning and they present a palate of possibilities for sparking imagination and collective conversations about how schools might better meet the learning needs of 21st-century students. Following these examples, we rejoin Angela and Tom as they grapple with designing inclusive processes for cultivating shared vision within their school communities and we explore what we know and are still learning about developing powerful visions for whole school sustainability.

Envisioning Green Schools

The Center for Green Schools at the U.S. Green Building Council (the Center) holds a School Sustainability Leaders' Summit each year. The new sustainability director in Tom and Angela's school district recently attended a Summit and shared the Center's vision with them: "Green schools for all in this generation" (www.centerforgreenschools.org). The Center's vision is so big that it calls for dynamic and strategic engagement from every team member. Not only that, it draws engagement from supporters all over the world. It will take everyone and more to realize this vision of "green schools for all in this generation." Why this vision? Why do the Center staff and its supporters walk into work each morning with this aim on their minds? Because green schools provide the possibility of a dramatic transformation of the living system we know as school.

Green schools are deeply rooted in their own place, ecologically and socially; they grow out of their unique context. Visions for green schools emerge from collective, collaborative efforts. Leaders of green schools are charting new territory and this effort requires active learning along the way. Visions that are big enough to inspire long-term investment and commitment don't become realities overnight. They take time to evolve and grow. They begin with clarity of purpose. As we discussed in Chapter 2, the purpose of school ought to be more than facilitating student achievement for achievement's sake. We see the purpose of school as meeting the needs of the 21st century through attending to the best interests of today's children, tomorrow's children, and nature. The many green schools that Angela and Tom are learning about serve a purpose beyond student achievement alone. They seek to make the world a better place through their collective efforts. They aim to develop the learning capacity of their members—teachers, students, community members—to serve local and global needs. When people are able to connect their daily work to meaningful, purposeful aims, motivation soars. They feel passionate about their contribution to their vision for a healthy, flourishing community. This is the feeling Tom and Angela want to see grow throughout their school communities.

As was detailed in Chapter 3, we understand school systems to be living systems, comprised of living beings who are deeply interdependent and embedded in local and global socio-ecological systems. The principles we discussed govern healthy ecological and social systems. The challenge has been that the industrial age has left many humans unaware of their interdependence with all life. Mechanical systems and metaphors have influenced the design and management of our schools and organizations for more than a century (Senge, Cambron-McCabe, Lucas, Smith, & Dutton, 2012). This means that most of the adults in schools today grew up in schools that were far more reflective of the factory model than not. Our current generation is the fourth or fifth to be growing up within industrialized models. Thus, the factory model is primarily what we've known for generations, until we see new possibilities. We have the opportunity to imagine, design, and lead our way into a healthier system of learning that is better aligned with how nature works and humans learn. Rather than reform of a mechanistic system, green schools present the opportunity for more restorative solutions for the many social, economic, and environmental challenges of the 21st century.

Green schools strive to be healthy socio-ecological systems that engage deep individual and collective learning. Ideally, they are places that people of all ages would choose to attend, even if they were not required by either policy or checkbook. They are a transformative, systemic solution to many of our most pressing social and ecological challenges. Green school facilities dramatically reduce their environmental impacts while engaging their occupants in learning about these efforts. Students and teachers can experience the school building as a 3-D textbook (Kong, Rao, Abdul-Rahman, & Wang, 2014). The most exciting work is going on in schools where the facilities teams work in concert with the curriculum teams; they inform and enrich each other's work to help occupants live more consciously and responsibly in their buildings. Green school leaders build bridges between the historically divided curriculum and facilities' sides of the academic house. In Tom and Angela's district this work is under way, as a district leader describes, "The best way for us to accomplish this work of greening our schools and our curriculum is to bring together our facilities and operations personnel with our curriculum personnel. We have to make this one initiative." Imagine schools of the future as the center of community learning; a gathering place for learning how to live and learn in new, more sustainable ways. These centers of learning honor both their local ecology, culture, economy and their connections to these same systems on regional and global scales.

As we shift away from factory models of schooling, we discover that school buildings don't have to look, feel and act like factories. They can invite, inspire, and transform learning. The Living Building Challenge, a building certification program, invites us to

> Imagine a building designed and constructed to function as elegantly and efficiently as a flower: a building informed by its bioregion's characteristics, that generates all of its own energy with renewable resources, captures and treats all of its water, and that operates efficiently and for maximum beauty. (*Living Building Challenge 3.0: A Visionary Path to a Regenerative Future*, 2014, p. 2)

This vision of possibility has already come to life in some places; buildings like this exist today. These trailblazing buildings are breaking free of the industrial, take–make–waste systems, and are demonstrating that we can design, build, and maintain buildings that integrate recycled materials; use net zero energy; capture, treat, and reuse water; compost waste; grow produce; and serve as beautiful sun-filled spaces for learning 21st-century skills and dispositions. Children growing up in these spaces become sustainability natives, people who will live their lives with much deeper understanding of whole systems, including their ecological, social, economic interdependencies. Although the examples that follow are not all part of the Living Building Challenge, they all challenge traditional models of schooling and spark our imaginations.

Green School of Bali, Indonesia

You may be wondering where schools like this exist, as they seem too ideal-istic to be possible. The Green School in Bali, Indonesia, is one very inspir-ing example. The Center for Green Schools awarded Green School the 2012 Greenest School on Earth award. Their vision, mission, and values sit prom-inently on their website (www.greenschool.org), "Our vision is of a natural, holistic, student-centered learning environment that empowers and inspires our students to be creative, innovative, green leaders." Their mission, "con-tributes to [their] Vision by educating young leaders in global citizenship. Our purpose is to champion a new model of learning that connects the timeless lessons from nature to a relevant and effective preparation for a fast-chang-ing future." Finally, their values ground their mission, vision, and day-to-day work:

> We believe in three simple rules underlying every decision: be local; let your environment be your guide; and envisage how your grand-children will be affected by your actions. The eight Green School iRespect Values that guide us are: Integrity; Responsibility; Empathy; Sustainability; Peace; Equality; Community; Trust.

The videos, website, and research articles documenting Green School's work suggest a tight alignment between their espoused values and actual practices. The founders of Green School, John and Cynthia Hardy, explain,

> We are building Green School to create a new paradigm for learning. We want children to cultivate physical sensibilities that will enable them to adapt and be capable in the world. We want children to develop spiritual awareness and emotional intuition, and to encour-age them to be in awe of life's possibilities. (http://www.greenschool. org/general/green-school-history-and-founders/)

Their Heart of School building (administration and central gathering place) is a magnificent, open air, fully bamboo building that was built following traditional Indonesian practices. The classrooms, each a separate building, are also constructed according to traditional Indonesian practices and are open air, merging seamlessly with the surrounding rainforest. Green School students, faculty and staff grow and eat local food, prepared by traditional culinary practices. Their curriculum, although a standard Cambridge IGCSE model, is adapted to their context and tightly embedded in their local ecology and culture. In an early study of the school, just two years old at the time, authors Hazzard, Hazzard, and Erickson (2011) asked teachers whether a Green School would be possible in other places. Here is one teacher's response:

> we're trying to make something happen where the kids are really developing a connection with nature. Of course this can happen in inner cities—Chicago, New York—but it's going to require a lot more work, a lot more commitment and devotion on everyone's part, whereas here it just comes naturally. Just like any other place, it really depends on the teacher's influence. If you have good teachers showing the kids these influences, it's going to make it more powerful. *I think this place can happen anywhere where people really want it to happen. It takes the community to want it. It takes people . . . see[ing] how big an effect this is having.* You just have to embrace it. (p. 70, italics added for emphasis)

Although a bamboo Heart of School building may not be practical in other non-tropical regions of the world, the desire to create school buildings that reflect the Living Building Challenge of beauty and efficiency are possible and they do exist, as you will see in our next example. Like Green School, other schools also value the strengths of their local community enough to partner with them in extraordinary ways.

Hood River Middle School of Hood River, Oregon

Hood River Middle School's Music and Science building, in Hood River, Oregon, is another inspiring example of how a community committed to sustainability can transform the educational experience for their students. This middle school serves just under 550 students in grades 6–8, 31% of whom are Hispanic and 65% White. Forty-nine percent of the students qualify for free or reduced lunch. This community built a net zero, 21st-century building next to their 1927 main building in 2010. As a net zero building, this facility uses net zero energy over each full year. The building project will have paid for itself within a 20-year period, depending on the rate at which energy prices increase (a faster increase in energy prices translates into a faster return on their investment).

Students at Hood River use their building and surrounding landscape as a living laboratory to learn about STEAM (science, technology, engineering, art, and math) concepts in practical, project and problem based ways. The building's structural and mechanical systems are visible to the students and their teachers integrate lessons about these systems into their coursework. For example, students participated in solar panel and water filtration system installation processes. Students also grow produce on site and participate in their community farmers' market each week. These educational strategies help students learn through experience the complex interrelationships among humans, their built environment, and ecological systems. Their new building engages deep learning for the community as well as for students. It is ecologically, socially, and economically responsible. You can read more about Hood River Middle Music and Science Building in Brown and Frichtl's (2013) article and these videos:

https://www.youtube.com/watch?v=UxzduaSmVzY

https://www.youtube.com/watch?v=be3_uvcR_kI

https://www.youtube.com/watch?v=7AinARlpbhA

Although not all communities have the knowledge, political support, and financial resources to immediately go out and build new living buildings, every community can begin asking questions about their current practices and imagining possibilities that lead to less industrialized models of schooling. Visions, as images of the future we wish to create together, act as powerful influences. Conceptualizing our future requires imagination and conversations about what might be possible. If all we know and discuss is rooted in the industrial model then how do we break free of these models? The Green School in Bali, Indonesia, and the Hood River Middle School's Music and Science Building are just two examples of school communities with buildings that leave much of the industrial model behind. What about examples of educators transforming their practice with sustainability in mind, but without cutting edge new buildings? Is that possible? Yes, it is and early research suggests that students do not necessarily need to learn in a green building to learn transferable lessons about sustainability (Cole, 2013). We will share just two examples of impressive sustainability-related education taking place in traditional school buildings, one from Boston Public Schools and one from New York City.

Mission Hill of Boston, Massachusetts

Mission Hill is a K–8 school in Boston Public Schools. Deborah Meier, the author of *The Power of Their Ideas* (1995), was founder of the school in 1997. Today the school serves fewer than 250 students, K–8th grades. The school serves a diverse population, with 77% minority students (Asian, Hispanic, Black, and two or more races) and 45% qualifying for free and reduced lunches. This school is grounded in democratic principles and its mission is explained on their website (http://www.missionhillschool.org/about-2/about/). It begins with their stated purpose of public education, "to help parents raise youngsters who will maintain and nurture the best habits of a democratic society, be smart, caring, strong, resilient, imaginative, and thoughtful." It continues with a detailed description of the democratic community they continuously cultivate. It ends with:

> Our mission is to create a community in which our children and their families can best maintain and nurture such democratic habits. Toward these ends, our community must be prepared to spend time even when it might seem wasteful hearing each other out. We must deal with each other in ways that lead us to feel stronger and more loved, not weaker and less loveable. We must expect the most from everyone, hold all to the highest standards, but also respect our different ways of exhibiting excellence. We must together build a reasonable set of standards for our graduates so that they can demonstrate to us their capacity to meet this mission.

If you watch the internet series *Good Morning Mission Hill* or the documentary with the same name, you will hear Principal Ayla Gavins describe the three themes for their 2013–2014 school year, "Being a steward of the land, having meaningful work, and being kind, just really speaks to the work we are going to engage in this year." When you visit this school, watch the video, and/or read the descriptive articles and books, you see that these educators, families, and students are living the work of democracy in transformative and inspiring ways. Their practice of democracy shows up in every aspect of schooling, among the faculty and staff, within classrooms, and within the parent community. Glickman (1993, 2003) described democracy as a theory of learning, as much as an approach to governance; this is certainly true at Mission Hill. Their conception of democracy is broad and inclusive of the natural world. As engaged democratic citizens, they honor their relationship with nature and cultivate awareness and understanding of nature among their students through the formal curriculum, investigation, and outdoor play. They are growing engaged democratic citizens through the work of student-centered, democratic practice. We will discuss more about their approach to teaching and learning through school wide themes later in Chapter 8 (Meier, Knoester, & D'Andrea, 2015).

Green Bronx Machine of New York, New York

Another urban school educator, Stephen Ritz, is transforming the way school works for students, teachers, and communities. Beginning as an after school, alternative high school program that engaged students in urban farming and growing edible walls ("the new green graffiti!") Ritz's program, Green Bronx

Machine (GBM), is now a non-profit organization and a K-12+ school model located in the South Bronx of New York City. The Bronx is a neighborhood with high rates of obesity and related diseases, unemployment, underemployment, food insecurity, and many food stamp recipients. The GBM programming has been inspiringly successful, as these data from their website indicate, "Along the way some of our critical benchmarks have included moving targeted daily attendance rates from 40% to 93%, 100% passing rates on New York State Examinations, and partnering towards 2,200 youth jobs" (http://greenbronxmachine.org/about-us/). The students and community members affiliated with GBM are "growing [their] way into the new economy" (Ritz, 2012, n.p.). Their mission reads:

> Green Bronx Machine builds healthy, equitable, and resilient communities through inspired education, local food systems, and 21st Century workforce development. Dedicated to cultivating minds and harvesting hope, our school-based model using urban agriculture aligned to key school performance indicators grows healthy students and healthy schools to transform communities that are fragmented and marginalized into neighborhoods that are inclusive and thriving.

And their vision:

> We believe that healthy students help drive healthy schools, and that healthy schools are at the heart of healthy communities. We envision growing healthy communities where those who are "apart from" will become "part of" new solutions that benefit 100% of society; a world where people do not have to leave their community to live, learn and earn in a better one. Together, we can grow something greater! Ready, set, GROW!

The Center for Green Schools listed the GBM as one of the Best of Green Schools for 2014. Ritz's students, all special needs learners, English Language learners, homeless, foster care, or adjudicated youth, have contributed to transforming a multi-block area of the South Bronx from community blight to productive urban garden.

> My kids can get a handgun quicker than they can get an organic tomato. That said, when they get involved with nature and they learn to nurture, they feel good about themselves. And, the remarkable thing about plants is that they grow, and grow quickly. And the kids start to feel responsible for taking care of them. (Fried, 2013, p. 167)

His is an inspiring story that did not begin with a clear and big vision; it began with a bag of daffodils that happened to bloom behind his classroom radiator. He noticed the wonder and energy that the daffodils sparked among his typically disengaged students and he followed the student enthusiasm for growing the daffodils, then a garden, then green walls, then edible walls, and eventually a program that is transforming his Bronx neighborhood (Fried, 2013). His story, in particular, highlights the fact that visions may begin as big, powerful images of the future, or not. Sometimes the most powerful visions emerge from learning together how to make it into the next day.

Cultivating the Power of Vision

Vision Basics

We all know that cultivating a shared vision is a critical element for leading transformative change, but truly doing so is not easy work. "Dealing with vision is a bit like trying to carry fog around in a satchel. No area in the school improvement literature is more in need of intellectual architecture" (Murphy & Torre, 2014, p. 2). In our reading of the vision literature, we recall Wheatley's (1999, pp. 53–56) discussion of vision from a Newtonian or factory model perspective vs. vision from a new science or living systems perspective. The Newtonian, linear view, defines vision as a clear picture of the future. How this picture is generated varies across schools. Typically a school leader would have a vision and would then share it with his/her school community. In other cases, school leadership teams might collaboratively generate a clear vision statement and then share it out to the rest of the school community. Less often, school leaders engage a community-wide school visioning process, with the endless wordsmithing that such processes entail. Regardless of the process, once established, vision statements are hung on walls, posted on websites, and this accreditation requirement is complete. Unfortunately, even the broadest and most inclusive processes for establishing a vision will leave the school essentially visionless unless the linear, Newtonian approach is replaced with a living systems approach.

A living system perspective shifts from vision being a thing to accomplish to a continuous process. In Wheatley's words,

> If vision is a field, think about what we could do differently to use its formative influence. We would start by recognizing that in creating a vision, we are creating a power, not a place, an influence, not the destination. This field metaphor would help us understand that we need congruency in the air, visionary messages matched by visionary

behaviors. We also would know that vision must permeate through the entire organization as a vital influence on the behavior of all employees. (1999, p. 55)

From a living systems perspective, cultivating shared vision is complex, messy, and never ending. It should not be a discrete task on an accreditation to-do list every few years, although many school leaders seem to treat it that way (Gurley et al., 2014; Stemler, Bebell, & Sonnabend, 2011). Rather, it should be a continuous process of inquiry, engagement and modeling. Visioning work is both individual and collective (Senge et al., 2012). It requires imagination, creativity and rational practicality all at the same time (Meadows, 1994). Living a vibrant, shared vision requires conversations, many conversations. Truly shared visions emerge from this continuous, individual and collective work. And yet, we must acknowledge the realities of school life today that continue to transition away from factory model expectations. School leaders today must meet their accreditation expectations through stating and posting their vision statements, *and* they have to do the messy work of truly cultivating inspiring, motivating, shared visions among their school community members. Again, we acknowledge that this is not easy work.

A Model of Shared Vision

Drawing on Murphy and Torre's (2014) review of 35 years of educational leadership literature related to school vision and additional references not cited in their article (Capra & Luigi, 2014; Gurley et al., 2014; Kose, 2011; Kurland et al., 2010; Mulford, 2010; Starratt, 2003; Wheatley, 1999; Wiek & Iwaniec, 2014; Ylimaki, 2006), we present a summary model for cultivating shared vision in green schools in Figure 4.1. Table 4.1 provides definitions for the terms used in Figure 4.1.

Our model includes the familiar, rational elements that accreditation bodies want to see. At the same time, it incorporates some fundamental assumptions that may not be explicit in other models. First, the school (or district) is an open system, thus the dashed-line border in Figure 4.1. Although ideas will also flow out beyond the school's borders, in this discussion, we are focused on outside information permeating the school and influencing its visioning processes. Certainly most schools receive guidance on their learning standards from the outside. Depending on state policy and context, the degree to which student learning standards and other outside programming materials inform a school's vision may vary. Second, cultivating a shared vision is a continuous, co-creative process that must be deeply embedded in the local context. Third, when shared, evidence of values, mission, and vision permeate artifacts throughout the school, wise school leaders recognize the

Figure 4.1 Shared Vision Process That Includes Addressing Local and Global Needs in Addition to Meeting Student Learning Standards. The Continuous Co-creative Process Is Context Embedded

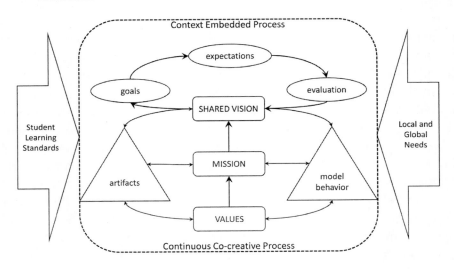

Table 4.1 Basic Definitions

Values	Core beliefs that inform behavior or the way work gets done (Gurley et al., 2014).
Mission	"a statement of why an organization exists, a statement of its fundamental purpose." (Gurley et al., 2014, p. 222)
Vision	"an articulation not of purpose, but of a preferred future for the organization." (Gurley et al., 2014, pp. 222–223) and "organizational clarity about organizational purpose and direction . . . a power, not a place, an influence, not a destination . . . a vital influence on the behavior of all employees." (Wheatley, 1999, pp. 55–56)
Goals	"precisely what level of performance is to be achieved . . . and what steps are to be taken, by whom, in order to achieve the goal." (Gurley et al., 2014, p. 224)
Expectations	"This practice includes leaders demonstrating through their behaviors that they expect a high level of professionalism from staff, hold high expectations for students, and expect staff to be effective innovators." (Sun & Leithwood, 2012, p. 429)
Evaluation	Testing the degree to which behaviors, goals and expectations align with and reflect the school's core values, mission, and vision and then realigning as necessary.
Artifacts	"all the phenomena that you would see, hear, and feel." (Schein, 2010, p. 23)
Model Behavior	individual and collective behavior reflecting the values, mission, and vision.

messaging power inherent in these artifacts, including the grounds, the building itself, the front entrance, posters, student work, etc. These artifacts are present in all schools and they are active contributors to shared vision, or detractors from it. Fourth, individual behavior flows from one's values. While not all individuals may share an exact set of values among each other, cultivating a shared vision benefits greatly from aligning behavior with some shared core values that clearly ground the mission and vision of the school. Finally, green schools also look to local and global needs to inform their vision. In fact, integrating awareness and commitment to address local and global environmental, social, and economic needs may be the very power missing from visions focused solely on improving student learning.

> Teachers and administrators report that students are tired of learn-ing for the sake of learning; however, they are absorbed by learning that addresses their concerns and behaviors to ameliorate the prob-lems of the world. Sustainability as a theme of inquiry addresses the problem of decreasing student engagement and the relevancy of the curriculum. Sustainability as the purpose of education addresses the concerns of the students of today. Beyond purpose, sustainabil-ity gives a common vision to schooling—the vision of a better, more sustainable world and the positive social transformation that accom-panies that vision. (McKeown & Nolet, 2013, p. 15)

Green schools are places where sustainability ethics, a concern for contem-poraries, future generations, and nature (Becker, 2011) inform their shared values, mission and vision.

Visionary Leaders

Individual leaders throughout the school community, including students, parents, community partners, staff, teachers, and positional leaders, can be visionary leaders. Two recent qualitative research studies provided in-depth descriptions of visionary leadership (Kose, 2011; Ylimaki, 2006) that seem to break free of mechanistic approaches. Their descriptions seem far more con-sistent with a living systems model of leadership and they provide excel-lent lessons for school leaders like Tom and Angela who wish to deepen and expand their shared visions for a greener school. Both studies' participants were individuals peer nominated for their visionary, transformative leader-ship. What made them visionaries was not simply that they had a clear vision of a desired future state, but that they were authentic, effective communi-cators, who included traditionally marginalized groups or individuals and were able to see in multiple ways, at multiple scales.

Ylimaki (2006) described visionary leaders as those who use their inner resources of insight, intuition, and perception to continuously cultivate shared vision through their daily work and open, honest interactions with others. Ylimaki's study reported on four leaders, curriculum directors, three that expressed visionary leadership and a discrepant case that followed a more mechanistic approach. The three visionaries did not follow a prescriptive recipe. They understood their context, they met people where they were, and they walked alongside others towards improvement. They led with inquiry and encouragement, not directives and demands. Kose's (2011) description of transformative principal leadership also emphasized the importance of understanding one's context. These principals were selected for their social justice leadership. Changing practices in schools to be more socially just requires deep, second-order change. It requires personal and collective learning that is often uncomfortable. The study's principals led broadly inclusive processes for vision statement development and then they operated consistent with their ideals. The principals' understanding of their context and inclination to support change without pushing too hard, minimized resistance.

The leaders featured in Ylimaki's and Kose's articles remind us of another visionary leader who followed less mechanistic approaches to cultivating shared vision and change, David Hagstrom (2004). He described his personal story of turning around an Alaskan school. As a newcomer to the community, he did not begin with his vision of what should be. Rather, he began with a simple and powerful question, "What do you want for your children, here at Denali School?" From this question emerged a community-wide effort that transformed the school from a low performing school into a vibrant learning community.

Conclusion

Tom and Angela have much to consider as they work to both meet their accreditation body's expectations for written mission and vision statements *and* to continuously cultivate a shared vision within their school communities. Twenty-first century school leaders must master a form of both—and leadership. They have to meet rational, linear expectations grounded in a mechanical age *and* they have to partner with the more irrational realities of organizational life. Sharp (2002) described this dual approach to leading change for sustainability at Harvard:

> It is no accident that the most successful green campus initiatives are the ones that have been able to adapt to the low levels of rationality that exist within the university organization. Instead of operating only to a

strategic plan these initiatives stand ever ready to embrace emerging opportunities, constantly shifting priorities and resources. Instead of depending only on business models and structured growth, these initiatives are highly organic in their growth patterns, with growth rates reflecting opportunities of the day. Instead of relying upon operational structures and fixed staffing levels, these initiatives remain adaptive in their structure and staffing. Rather than relying upon formal links to decision makers and formal decision-making forums these initiatives are extremely adept at building networks of trusting and diverse relationships with a wide range of individuals. In essence, the most successful green campus initiatives are able to thrive in the dynamic complexity of the university because they strike a pragmatic balance between appearing rational (strategic plans, business models, operational structures, and formal decision making forums) and operating irrationally (organic, adaptive, chaotic growth, networks of trust). (pp. 136–137)

As you lead during this time of transition between factory model expectations and living system model possibilities, have the courage to artfully engage both rational and irrational approaches to leading change.

Questions for Discussion

1. Watch the TED Talk, My Green School Dream, by John Hardy (http://www.ted.com/talks/john_hardy_my_green_school_dream?language=en). What possibilities does this story inspire you to see in your own community?

2. Watch Donella Meadows' talk about vision (see four part playlist here: https://www.youtube.com/playlist?list=PLZuD9ySFrYUhzAMaTbE1tesM6079tngW8). How does the vision process she describes relate to your personal vision and collective vision processes in your school?

3. Consider your school's vision and answer the following questions:

   ◆ How was it created?
   ◆ How is it continuously cultivated?
   ◆ In what ways do you see the factory model at work?
   ◆ In what ways do you see a living systems model at work?
   ◆ To what degree is your school's vision shared, powerful, motivating, and inspiring? What would make it more so? To what degree does your vision speak to meeting the needs of the 21st century?

References

Bebell, D., & Stemler, S. (2012). *The school mission statement: Values, goals, and identities in American education.* New York: Routledge.

Becker, C. (2011). *Sustainability ethics and sustainability research.* New York: Springer Science & Business Media.

Brown, C., & Frichtl, A. (2013). A building that teaches. *High Performing Buildings* (Winter), 34–46.

Capra, F., & Luigi, L. P. (2014). *The systems view of life: A unifying vision.* Cambridge: Cambridge University Press.

Cole, L. B. (2013). *The teaching green school building: Exploring the contributions of school design to informal environmental education.* Ann Arbor, MI: The University of Michigan.

Edmonds, R. (1979). Effective schools for the urban poor. *Educational Leadership, 37*(1), 15–24.

Fried, K. (2013). *American teacher: Heroes in the classroom.* New York: Welcome Books.

Gallup. (2014). *Gallup report: State of America's schools.* Retrieved from Washington, DC: http://www.gallup.com/services/178709/state-america-schools-report.aspx

Glickman, C. D. (1993). *Renewing America's schools.* San Francisco, CA: Jossey-Bass.

Glickman, C. D. (2003). *Holding sacred ground: Essays on leadership, courage, and endurance in our schools.* San Francisco, CA: Jossey-Bass.

Gurley, D. K., Peters, G. B., Collins, L., & Fifolt, M. (2014). Mission, vision, values, and goals: An exploration of key organizational statements and daily practice in schools. *Journal of Educational Change, 16*(2), 217–242. doi:10.1007/s10833-014-9229-x

Hagstrom, D. (2004). *From outrageous to inspired: How to build a community of leaders in our schools.* San Francisco: Jossey-Bass.

Hazzard, M., Hazzard, E., & Erickson, S. (2011). *The green school effect: An exploration of the influence of place, space and environment on teaching and learning at green school, Bali, Indonesia.* Retrieved from: http://www.powersofplace.com/pdfs/greenSchoolReport.pdf

Kong, S. Y., Rao, S. P., Abdul-Rahman, H., & Wang, C. (2014). School as 3-D textbook for environmental education: Design model transforming physical environment to knowledge transmission instrument. *Asia-Pacific Journal of Teacher Education, 23*(1), 1–15. doi:10.1007/s40299-013-0064-2

Kose, B. W. (2011). Developing a transformative school vision: Lessons from peer-nominated principals. *Education and Urban Society, 43*(2), 119–136. doi:10.1177/0013124510380231

Kurland, H., Peretz, H., & Hertz-Lazarowitz, R. (2010). Leadership style and organizational learning: The mediate effect of school vision. *Journal of Educational Administration, 48*(1), 7–30. doi:10.1108/09578231011015395

Leithwood, K., Harris, A., & Hopkins, D. (2008). Seven strong claims about successful school leadership. *School Leadership and Management, 28*(1), 27–42. doi:10.1080/13632430701800060

Leithwood, K., & Seashore-Louis, K. (2011). *Linking leadership to student learning*. San Francisco: John Wiley & Sons.

Leithwood, K., & Sun, J. (2012). The nature and effects of transformational school leadership: A meta-analytic review of unpublished research. *Educational Administration Quarterly, 48*(3), 387–423. doi:10.1177/0013161x11436268

Living building challenge 3.0: A visionary path to a regenerative future. (2014). Retrieved from Seattle, WA: https://living-future.org/sites/default/files/reports/FINAL%20 LBC%203_0_WebOptimized_low.pdf

McKeown, R., & Nolet, V. (Eds.). (2013). *Schooling for sustainable development in Canada and the United States* (Vol. 4). New York: Springer.

Meadows, D. (1994, October 24–28). Down to Earth. Paper presented at the International Society of Ecological Economics Conference, Costa Rica. YouTube Playlist retrieved from: https://www.youtube.com/playlist?list=PLZuD9y SFrYUhzAMaTbE1tesM6079tngW8

Meier, D. (1995). *The power of their ideas: Lessons for America from a small school in Harlem*. Boston: Beacon Press.

Meier, D., Knoester, M., & D'Andrea, K. C. (Eds.). (2015). *Teaching in themes: An approach to schoolwide learning, creating community, & differentiating instruction*. New York: Teachers College Press

Mulford, B. (2010). Recent developments in the field of educational leadership: The challenge of complexity. In A. Hargreaves, A. Lieberman, & M. Fullan (Eds.), *Second international handbook of educational change* (pp. 187–208). New York: Springer Science & Business Media.

Murphy, J., & Torre, D. (2014). Vision: Essential scaffolding. *Educational Management Administration & Leadership, 43*(2), 177–197. doi:10.1177/1741143214523017

NBEA. (2015). *Professional standards for educational leaders 2015*. Retrieved from Reston, VA.: http://www.ccsso.org/Documents/2015/ProfessionalStandardsforEducational Leaders2015forNPBEAFINAL.pdf

Palmer, P. J. (1998). *The courage to teach*. San Francisco: Jossey-Bass.

Ritz, S. (2012). A teacher growing green in the South Bronx. Retrieved from https:// www.ted.com/talks/stephen_ritz_a_teacher_growing_green_in_the_south_ bronx?language=en

Schein, E. H. (2010). *Organizational culture and leadership* (4th ed.). San Francisco, CA: Jossey-Bass.

Senge, P. M., Cambron-McCabe, N., Lucas, T., Smith, B., & Dutton, J. (2012). *Schools that learn (updated and revised): A fifth discipline fieldbook for educators, parents, and everyone who cares about education*. New York: Crown Business.

Sharp, L. (2002). Green campuses: The road from little victories to systemic transformation. *International Journal of Sustainability in Higher Education, 3*(2), 128–145. doi:10.1108/14676370210422357

Starratt, R. J. (2003). *Centering educational administration: Cultivating meaning, community, responsibility*. Mahwah, NJ: Lawrence Earlbaum Associates.

Stemler, S. E., Bebell, D., & Sonnabend, L. A. (2011). Using school mission statements for reflection and research. *Educational Administration Quarterly, 47*(2), 383–420. doi:10.1177/0013161X10387590

Strike, K. A. (2004). Community, the missing element of school reform: Why schools should be more like congregations than banks. *American Journal of Education, 110*, 215–232.

Sun, J., & Leithwood, K. (2012). Transformational school leadership effects on student achievement. *Leadership and Policy in Schools, 11*(4), 418–451. doi:10.1080/15700763.2012.681001

Thoonen, E. E. J., Sleegers, P. J. C., Oort, F. J., Peetsma, T. T. D., & Geijsel, F. P. (2011). How to improve teaching practices: The role of teacher motivation, organizational factors, and leadership practices. *Educational Administration Quarterly, 47*(3), 496–536. doi:10.1177/0013161x11400185

Waugh, B., & Forrest, M. S. (2001). *Soul in the computer.* Maui, HI: Inner Ocean Publishing, Inc.

Wheatley, M. J. (1999). *Leadership and the new science: Discovering order in a chaotic world* (3rd ed.). San Francisco: Berrett-Koehler.

Wiek, A., & Iwaniec, D. (2014). Quality criteria for visions and visioning in sustainability science. *Sustainability Science, 9*, 497–512. doi:10.1007/s11625-013-0208-6

Ylimaki, R. M. (2006). Toward a new conceptualization of vision in the work of educational leaders: Cases of the visionary archetype. *Educational Administration Quarterly, 42*(4), 620–651. doi:10.1177/0013161x06290642

Part II

Healthy Ecosystems for Learning

5

Place, Community, and Partnerships

[Our goal is to] enlist upcoming generations in the creation and preservation of con-
vivial places—places where human diversity and species diversity can coexist, where
future generations of children can find good reason to feel attached.

(Chawla, 1992, p. 84)

In their own particular place on the globe, Tom and Angela are holding themselves to account as their schools' lead learners. Together, they are taking time
to clarify their own sense of purpose as educators and challenging themselves to investigate the implications of current societal and environmental
challenges for their work as 21st-century school leaders. This project prompts
them to consider their role as civic leaders across the ecological, social, and
economic systems within which their schools are nested. The potential scope
of their responsibilities can seem overwhelming, and so they craft a laser-
focused vision for their work, a vision grounded in intimate knowledge
of, and care for, the place their students call home. This "think globally, act
locally" stance allows Angela and Tom to grasp the import of their home-
grown efforts on regional, national, and global fronts.

Tom and Angela have long since learned about the importance of extending their reach out into their neighboring community. They have come to
know the needs of their families, and this knowledge informs their work day-
to-day. More recently, a growing confidence in themselves as green school

leaders has them stretching beyond more traditional community engagement strategies to explore how they might position their schools as active agents in the development of healthy communities. According to Angela,

> Some of our families wrestle with the effects of poverty and joblessness. They struggle to provide their kids opportunities to live healthy lives. For a variety of reasons, their homes may not be the healthiest places, and the food they're eating may not necessarily be healthy either. The community garden and healthy food programs we are instituting have potential to improve the quality of everyone's life in the community. As students learn how to grow healthier food and develop and maintain a healthier physical environment, they embrace their healthy selves and seek to share these new life habits with each other and with their families.

Tom is quick to point out that his students' sense of self and place draws on the strengths of culture and heritage inherent within their evermore-diverse community.

> So, within our school's learning garden, we had several of our families adopt beds. Whatever they cultivated, it was theirs to keep. When students were out working in the garden after school, the families were there working alongside them. One Hmong family began showing the students traditional garden practices, like the use of a shorter, wider hoe. It was all hands in!

The places children call home are characterized, not only by their particular landscape and ecology, but also by the socioeconomic and cultural features contained within a given landscape (Smith & Gruenwald, 2008). The interconnectedness of these various aspects of place and community inform our actions as green school leaders, moving from inside the school, to points out in the community, beyond to the school's larger extra-community and natural environment, and back inside again.

This chapter begins with discussion of the primary role place plays in children's identity development, as well as the strong attachments children cultivate with these important places they inhabit. The chapter considers how place-based learning provides important opportunities for students to understand the complex interdependencies at play between human and natural systems, motivating them to appreciate and care for these abundant places they call home, and, by extension, to preserve the homes of other human and nonhuman inhabitants across the planet. The chapter then considers the challenges associated with harnessing this sophisticated and mature knowledge of place in order to shape a sense of 21st-century, global community. We explore the role of green school principals in this community building process, applying the principles and methods of democratic community to engender a sense of collective responsibility and optimism in the face of this wildly challenging 21st-century context. Finally, the chapter explores the benefits of green school leadership and whole-school sustainability as a means to build the sort of authentic community partnerships school leaders have long desired and pursued to revitalize and preserve communities and provide the supportive, connected, and resource-rich learning environments and experiences we know are in the best interest of our children.

The Places We Inhabit

"Place is defined by its human scale: household, neighborhood, community, forty acres, one thousand acres" (Orr, 2005a, p. 88). Researchers across disciplines appear to share the common assumption that through attachment to places, "a person acquires a sense of belonging and purpose which gives meaning to his or her life" (Proshansky, Fabian, & Kaminoff, 1983/1995, p. 90). To the degree that certain places are familiar, useful, and malleable, these places help children maintain a sense of self, including the definition of that self (Proshansky & Fabian, 1987).

Key concepts in the literature on people–place relationships include a *sense of place*, defined as the experiential process created by the setting itself in combination with what a person brings to it (Buttimer, 1980; Hart, 1979; Jorgensen & Stedman, 2001; Tuan, 1980); *place attachment*, defined as people's bonds to particular places (Altman & Low, 1992; Hidalgo & Hernandez, 2001); and *place identity*, defined as the dimensions of self that develop in relation to the physical environment (Proshansky, 1978). Our particular interest in school communities as primary places of meaning for children (as well as for other stakeholders) begs some attention to these concepts. People–place relationships are also foundational to the *place-based learning* that happens within green schools. These place-based learning experiences, allow students to "understand complex phenomena and subject matter mediated through connection to their local communities and natural world of which they are a part" (Williams & Brown, 2012, p. 66). Children's personal relationships with, and emotional attachment to, place are further developed through these experiences (Williams & Brown, 2012).

Place Identity and Attachment

Place identity connotes those dimensions of self that develop in relation to the physical environment (Proshansky, 1978). "Knowedge of a place—where you are and where you come from—is intertwined with knowledge of who you are" (Orr, 2005a, p. 93). As educators, we tend to emphasize the role social environment plays in human development. And yet, "the places a child grows up in, comes to know, prefer, seek out or avoid also contribute significantly to self-identity" (Proshansky et al., 1983/1995, p. 104).

Studies of place preferences in children and adolescents provide similar evidence, with youth also favoring places that bolster self-esteem and nurture self-concept (Newell, 1997), including private, personalized, and natural settings (Owen, 1988; Rivlin, 1990; Sobel, 1990) that are relaxed, calm, and comfortable (Korpela, 2002, p. 366). According to Chawla (1992), enduring memories of favorite childhood places inform more immediate experiences. As these places have provided a sense of security, opportunities for social affiliation, and a context for creative expression and exploration, youth continue to seek similar places to foster their ongoing self-development. In studies of the physical features contained within favorite places, researchers found a significant convergence of characteristics across diverse samples by age, profession, and nationality. Participants frequently, and with attendant intensity, named access to outdoors, to nature, and to freedom of movement in the environment as primary traits of their favorite places (Chawla, 1992, p. 76). In behavior mapping studies, children and adolescents are rarely observed to spend even as much a 15% of their time in neighborhood woods, fields, waterways, and yet, in favorite place analyses, these are most frequently named as their most favorite places (Chawla, 1992, p. 81).

In terms of human development, there is no physical environment that is not also a social environment, and vice versa (Ittleson, Proshansky, Rivlen, & Winkel, 1974). Attachment to significant places and people is often a balance of many social roles children and youth adopt (e.g., Carter, 2006; Violand-Sanchez & Hainer-Violand, 2006). When we become attached to a place we "show happiness at being in it and regret or distress at leaving it . . . [We come to] value it not only for the satisfaction of physical needs but for its own intrinsic qualities" (Chawla, 1992, p. 64). The more, and more varied, children's experiences are within the community and the natural world they inhabit, the stronger is their sense of self as citizens of, and agents for, the significant places in their lives. "Developing a 'sense of place' tends to support an associated responsibility of stewardship of endemic resources, be they ecological, economic, or social" (Williams & Brown, 2012, p. 61).

Engaging Our Children as Champions and Protectors of Place

Later, in Chapter 8, we will explore the tenets of place-based teaching and learning in greater detail. For now, let's consider, more generally, how place itself can become an active "agent in the curriculum," and how students and their communities benefit from such pedagogical choices (Orr, 2005b, p. 103).

For Angela, it means her students take on more responsibility and assume more ownership of their learning *and* their community. She explains:

> For one of our integrated projects, we all go to the river for a clean-up, and it's not just cigarette butts and bottle caps. It is sides of boats and huge pieces of Styrofoam. We put it in the art teacher's truck and lug it all back to the school. We don't throw it away. Instead, we turn it into art. Kids make sculptures. Our tagline is, "How will you engage the world?" As a sustainable community, we see an issue or problem, and we go find a way to contribute to solving it.

The Center for Ecoliteracy (www.ecoliteracy.org), whose mission it is to promote ecological education and encourage schools to teach and model sustainable practices, proceeds with the work according to four core principles: (1) nature is our teacher; (2) sustainability is a community practice; (3) the real world is the optimal learning environment; and (4) sustainability is rooted in a deep knowledge of place (Stone, 2010, p. 36). As discussed in Chapter 3 of this book, we understand that sustainability as a human endeavor addresses the interface between human civilization and the ecological world. The ability of human beings to live within the ecological carrying capacity of planet Earth presently and into the future presupposes deep knowledge of the interrelatedness of social, economic, and ecological systems. Discipline-based approaches to learning and problem solving will not take us where we need to go. If we are to develop new solutions to increasingly complex challenges, we must dramatically improve our capacity to understand interdependencies and learn across traditional disciplines. To do so, we need only look to the familiar places we inhabit, the places right beneath our noses, within earshot, and before our very eyes.

> Places are laboratories of diversity and complexity, mixed in social function and natural processes. A place has a human history and a geological past; it is part of an ecosystem with a variety of microsystems. It is landscape with a particular flora and fauna. Its inhabitants are part of a social, economic, and political order: they import or export energy materials, water and waste, they are linked by innumerable bonds of places … The study of place enables us to widen the focus to examine the interrelationships between disciplines and to lengthen our perception of time. (Orr, 2005a, p. 91)

Call it the three dimensional textbook writ large, "content animated by local interest or tangibility" (Williams & Brown, 2012, p. 74). Chawla calls out the salience of nature within these tangible, "full-bodied" (Chawla, 2007, p. 153) learning experiences, wherein "children … explore and manipulate the natural environment in a liberty denied them amid constructed places and possessions" (Chawla, 1992, p. 76).

Some argue that place-based education is "inherently parochial and narrowing," and yet, to the degree studies of place are imbedded in a wider curriculum that acknowledges "context and the relationship between places" (Orr, 2005a, p. 94), learners are challenged to face "broader consideration of, and collaboration with, those communities 'upstream and downstream'" (Williams & Brown, 2012, p. 61), so to speak. Noddings (2012) reminds us:

> If the well-being of my place depends on the well-being of Earth, I have good reason for supporting the well-being of your loved place. I have selfish, as well as cosmopolitan, reasons for preserving the home-places of all human beings. (Noddings, 2012, p. 66)

At Tom's high school, students took on a project they called "Timber Tags," working in collaboration with the Park Board.

> We went out in the dead of winter. There was not a leaf on a tree. The students got to walk around with arborists and identify trees on our school grounds and then expanded the effort to a dozen other schools. They identified trees, mapped them out, and labeled them, with common and Latin names.

Teachers coupled the mapping effort with research on different species, both locally and in other parts of the world. Students went on to investigate the effects of deforestation on biodiversity across the globe.

> They [the students] are now in the process of developing a public service announcement to be aired across high schools in the district, educating their peers on the power of their purchasing decisions in discouraging companies from perpetuating bad environmental practices.

As Tom's teachers "focus attention on the local particularities of global phenomena" (Williams & Brown, 2012, p. 58), they develop "ecological cosmopolitanism" in their students (Noddings, 2013).

Developing a 21st-Century Sense of Community

Community recognizes and fosters notions of neighborliness, cooperation, and mutual support. We can imagine a closely-knit group of individuals dedicated to a common purpose and, as such, also dedicated to one another. And yet, circumstances have changed since the days of over-the-fence and front-stoop intimacy. We are different, and the world is different. As a citizenry, we speak different languages, inhabit different cultures, and value different traditions. Understanding one another takes time, effort, and empathy.

Within this 21st-century context, community can no longer afford to limit itself to parochial mechanisms and insular concerns. Familiar notions of democracy, liberty, and individuality must grow broad enough to support our nation's differences and strong enough to nurture and protect an ever more complex global community. To succeed in our efforts, we must become students of community, as the creation of a global community requires new forms of local ones (Noddings, 2013). Reaching a 21st-century sense of community requires we balance the familiar and the intimate with the worldly-minded, acknowledging that local actions have "more than local import" (Dewey, 1939/1989, p. 41). The elements of community (i.e., voluntary association, mutual adjustment, the building of common interest) instruct us in the ways to engage divergent points of view toward common ends.

Twenty-first-century citizenship necessitates what Noddings calls "critical open-mindedness" (2013, p. 2), cultivated through engagement in democratic methods themselves. By welcoming diverse opinions, free debate, and the public examination of alternatives, democratic communities (like their scientific counterparts) teach members how to redirect solitary action toward cooperative inquiry. According to Goleman, Bennett, and Barlow (2012), no one person has "the capacity to understand all the ways in which human systems interact with natural systems," and so, ecological intelligence is "inherently *collective*" (p. 7, emphasis in original). Vigorous collective inquiry can begin to unmask the complexities of contemporary social and ecological interdependence and reveal its consequences. Global community is born of these understandings, and "school communities—which like ecosystems—come to life through networks of relationships, are ideal places to nurture this new and essential ecological sensibility" (Goleman et al., p. 7). As discussed in Chapter 3 of this book, designing and leading green, more sustainable school communities requires understanding both the practice of ecological principles and the practice of democratic ones. Vital and dynamic democratic methods reach inside human experiences to enlarge and enrich them.

Leveraging the Role of 21st-Century Civic Leader

Green school leaders are wise to communicate the value-added their community will derive from creating greener, more sustainable schools, welcoming interested members into a two-way dialogue about the opportunities inherent in such an educational program—for students, teachers, parents, and the community at large. As participants debate what is most important and necessary, the experience may tap the talents and skills of citizens. And yet, to do so, participation must move beyond perfunctory advisement. The people who will live within a school must be the ones to undertake the work of determining goals and crafting the structural and organizational means to reach them, and the process must be ongoing. Green school leaders occupy a critical position in this democratic process, with opportunity to facilitate the creation of green, more sustainable schools as central to their comprehensive educational plan.

In designing and building schools, and in the financing of their construction, the community is already part of the process. Taxpayers foot the bill, and, for some, the bottom line may hold more weight than the public ends of schooling. We have a chance to weld commitment when we extend the community's involvement to include deliberations about how we best realize the full potential of these facilities. There will no doubt be differences of opinion. Still, as a green school leader, you are positioned within a new matrix, brokering the complexities of the community and a vision for education. As vocabularies are enriched and knowledge is openly shared, new connections, relationships, and levels of meaning are established. Absent this collective process whereby we discover, absent specific and particular community dialogue, we, as educator, lack understanding of how our communities define purpose and intent, how they see the past and what they expect for the future.

And, our children will be watching us and learning according to our example. Ecoliterate democratic school communities are communities that actively practice both democratic and ecological principles (Henderson & Tilbury, 2004; Higgs & McMillan, 2006; Schelly, Cross, Franzen, Hall, & Reeve, 2010). These effective schools operate as "apprentice communities" (Caine & Caine, 2000, p. 53), providing students ample opportunities to engage with public issues at the local level and, thus, develop their identities as builders and keepers of community (Niemi & Junn, 1998).

Trusting Our Children as Community Builders

To the extent that adults trust children to actively wrestle with the critical concerns that challenge our world, these public issues gain personal meaning within their lives (Chawla & Cushing, 2007, p. 444). As students engage over extended periods of time, they not only learn necessary knowledge and skills, but also achieve valued goals (p. 441).

When the community association in Angela's attendance area expressed interest in launching a community garden, Angela extended the what/why/how discussion to include students, teachers, parents, community association leaders, and members of the business community. In order to justify her time and attention, she knew the project would need to meet important learning objectives for her students, fill tangible resource needs for her school, provide expansive engagement opportunities for her community, and demonstrate legitimate ecological benefits.

> We began with discussions regarding the vision and goals for the garden: from the alignment with particular learning standards all the way to the designation of a specific garden tract for planting vegetables in high demand at the local food bank. This last goal was the students' nonnegotiable. We hashed out the details and worked through disagreements. We have strong community ties. It was Stone-Bridgeport Properties (pseudonym), the big quarry construction company in this area, who initially partnered with us to get the site for the garden up and going.

Angela's students put on a big fundraiser with the district's Urban Ag program and a local grocer. Stone-Bridgeport actually donated what used to be a quarry adjacent to the school. This became the natural area where the community garden sits.

> Through their earth science and botany units, our students now go to other school campuses across the district, helping them get their gardens up and going. We (the students, teachers, and parents) have begun to meet regularly with the community association and other principals in the area. The project has become well integrated into the community in a host of ways, so it will be sustainable. The community association reached their goal, and the students will continue to realize theirs.

According to Chawla (2007), these sorts of primary, "full-bodied" experiences result in personal relationships and place attachments. Through such experiences, children "[draw] motivation to protect the places they love and [build] alliances and competencies to do so" (p. 153). Angela's community garden project illustrates how whole-school sustainability is not one more add on, but instead, "represents a fundamentally different way for schools to function . . . provid[ing] strategies to help young people and their communities deal optimistically and resiliently with a world in change" (Davis & Cooke, 2007, p. 351).

Forging Interdependent Partnerships for Sustainability

The call to forge school–community partnerships is certainly not new to the field of educational leadership. Related knowledge and skills factor prominently within the national standards for school leadership practice. Standard

8 of the new Professional Standards of Educational Leaders addresses the key responsibilities associated with the meaningful engagement of families and communities in the life of schools. According to the standard, "effective educational leaders engage families and the community in meaningful, reciprocal, and mutually beneficial ways to promote *each* student's academic success and well-being" (National Policy Board for Educational Administration, 2015, p. 16, emphasis in original).

From the 1930s on, scholars have argued that, to be successful, school reform efforts necessitate close consideration of the school's community, taking account of context by way of school–community collaborations (Counts, 1932 and Kilpatrick, 1932, as cited in Langhout, Rappaport, & Simmons, 2002, p. 325). And yet, schools have traditionally operated as some combination of open and closed systems, building bridges and responding to the local community while at the same time buffering teachers and the classroom from external threats and disruptions (Crowson & Boyd, 2001). As a school leader, you no doubt feel the tug of your competing responsibilities to reach out and involve others and, at the same time, focus inward and protect the technical core of your organization.

At the cusp of the 21st century, researchers observed an emerging community-based, "back-to-the-neighborhoods" movement in school reform (Crowson & Boyd, 2001, p. 16). Especially in large urban school districts, reformers were directing their attention "toward a revitalizing set of linkages between schools and neighborhoods" (Crowson & Boyd, 2001, p. 17), acknowledging the necessity of parents as partners in improving student learning and achievement (Epstein, 1996); the importance of school-linked social services to support families (Smrekar & Mawhinney, 1999); and even the possibility that local schools might play a central role in the revitalizing the community itself (Schorr, 1997). Driscoll and Kerchner (1999) labeled this rejuvenation of school–community connections as "restoring a sense of place" (p. 394) to public schooling. As described by scholars at the time, these community connections "moved beyond notions of partnering or collaborating, [advancing] a new mental model of schooling" (Golding & Hausman, 2001, p. 199).

> A sense of place in school administration is to be found in efforts toward integrating and exercising agency rather than buffering, in community investment rather than limiting the liability of the school, and in effective partnering with other educative and developmental institutions in the community. (Crowson & Boyd, 2001, p. 24)

These same scholars observed the need for an "ecological sense of 'coproduction' between school and community, a shared revitalization of both the neighborhood and school" (Crowson & Boyd, 2001, p. 17). As observed in Chapter 3, ecological metaphors for organizations (Morgan, 1998), schools (Sirotnik, 2005), and communities (Crowson & Boyd, 2001) have primarily bounded the ecosystems under study to the human systems or cultural ecologies, rarely directing attention to the ways school leaders and schooling impact local and global nonhuman ecological systems. This more narrow focus only encourages an anthropocentric blind spot relative to school leaders' possible opportunities and responsibilities for reducing the environmental impact of school buildings and processes. In contrast, green school leadership widens our point of view, directing our attention to community restoration and revitalization in an economic, social, *and* nonhuman ecological sense. In fact, this expanded leadership focus may just be the catalyst that instigates authentic, productive, sustainable school–community partnerships.

Evidence suggests that ongoing, school–community collaborations are extraordinarily difficult to accomplish and maintain (Smreker & McWhinney, 1994). Warren (2005) observes:

> A strong tradition dating back at least to John Dewey understands schools as foundational institutions for American community and democracy, and sees schools as fundamental to progressive social change. But, even when school reformers appreciate these broad arguments, reform efforts concentrate again and again within the four walls of the school. (pp. 165–166)

Studies of school–community partnership efforts reveal long-held organizational habits and structures that impede the development of necessary inter-organizational relationships (Crowson & Boyd, 2001). Further, teachers, parents, and community members can grow cynical about the many contrived forms of participation they have experienced over time (Anderson, 1998, p. 573). Still, when the stakes are genuine, both in terms of the negative consequences that result from ignoring our interdependence *and* in terms of the potential benefits for our children if we join forces to educate them and protect their future, our motivation may just grow strong enough to realize the partnerships we seek. As a green school leader, your civic capacity in building these alliances will make all the difference (Smreker & Mawhinney, 1994).

"The process of 'greening' a school offers an excellent opportunity to practice working in community" (Stone, 2010, p. 37). Aspiring green school leaders will be relieved and excited to discover substantial pockets of existing expertise, related to sustainability and green school programs, already embedded within their school communities. These pockets include knowledgeable teachers, enthusiastic parents, governmental agencies, and local, regional, and national groups and institutions committed to environmental concerns. As you work to pinpoint and link these centers of activity, you will leverage existing networks and build new ones, making your own expertise visible and available to the larger cause of education for sustainability (EfS). You will discover key champions who operate at various levels of the system, from the classroom, to the school, to the district, to city government, and out into the community at large. Consider creating a school-level Green Team, comprised of students, teachers, custodians, parents, and vested community partners. Your role will be to support and direct these champions and, through their leadership, to help individuals understand how their various role(s) connect, or could connect, within and across initiatives. These person-to-person connections make individuals feel valued and empowered to act. Through these connections, participants learn they are contributing to something larger than themselves, something that has the potential to improve the lives of students and the community.

Your knowledge of the social/cultural dynamics of your community and school system will provide the foundation for establishing new sustainability-focused values, norms, and symbols within your school's learning culture. Keep your sustainability-related goals visible, model commitment to these goals, and persist. The readiness of personnel and community members to attend to sustainability-related learning and changes will no doubt vary. Where responsibility and support for green initiatives is located further down the chain of command, support and direction will be more diffuse. Where there is commitment at the highest levels of the organization, you will receive focused and strategic direction and support. Even within the best of circumstances, you are bound to struggle with competing demands.

Your capacity to solidify and extend emerging green transformations will rest in your development of dense and nimble networks of relationships across the district and out into the community. You will serve as the architect of these connections, acting as facilitator, broker, and champion of all things green. Continuously scan your environment for related activities and critical events, connecting various involved stakeholders with other isolated pockets of innovative work. Celebrate and support already existing efforts and forge the necessary relationships for initiating new work. These ongoing actions will realize value-added and cost saving outcomes for your school, your students, and your community, and the discovered benefits will provide impetus to keep partners energized and engaged.

Empowering Our Children as Partners and Change Agents

"School-in-community" learning experiences reaffirm that human life, culture, and society are firmly embedded within the natural world (Selby, 2000, p. 90). These pro-social, pro-environmental experiences of relatedness constitute the means by which students develop a civic identity (Yates & Youniss, 1999 as cited in Chawla & Cushing, 2007, p. 444). Venturing forth from school to engage in real-world, problem-based learning, children build a sense of individual and collective agency as they undertake meaningful endeavors and succeed (Chawla, 2009, p. 16). Through these experiences, students discover they are wholly capable agents, prepared to make important things happen in the world.

Angela's Green Team wrote a grant to install an energy dashboard so her students could track the school's energy use. "They know how much electricity we are using per week, and they look for ways to reduce. They get excited about it. The children are really the sustainability champions in the school. They put a lot of pressure on the adults to do the right things."

Included in the plans for recent renovations to Tom's school, a rainwater harvesting system was proposed for flushing toilets in the building. Students conducted an energy audit and determined the water savings would be significant. They were excited about the prospects. "Come to find out, the system violated city code, but our students were prepared. They did their homework and lobbied City Council to get that code changed. We now have a fully functioning rain water system."

As we can see, the very goals of sustainability can "redefine the role of schools and their relationship with the community ... [rendering] schools as a focal point where children, adults, and the community interact and learn together" (Henderson & Tillbury, 2004, n.p.) Whole-school approaches to sustainability focus on complex social issues, "such as the links between environmental quality, human rights, and peace and their underpinning politics" (Henderson & Tillbury, 2004, n.p.). These green schools provide ample opportunities for learners to develop the skills and competencies necessary for partnership, participation, and action (Henderson & Tillbury, 2004, n.p.). Within these reimagined, interdependent places of learning, children build a strong foundation for their current and future work as stewards and change agents, engaging in environmentally focused endeavors and sharing their experiences with interested adults (Malone, 2013).

Conclusion

We have long debated what constitutes legitimate activity for a school to undertake. Some believe that education is the instrument whereby larger institutions are gradually changed. If we agree that schools are appropriate places for children and adults to develop 21st-century socio-ecological sensibilities, green school leaders must begin by preparing themselves to speak on behalf of these matters with authority and enthusiasm for the full range of possibilities. As educational professionals and community members discover each other across roles and disciplines, school administrators will find themselves at either a flash point or a point of departure, the latter preferable to the former. School leaders will inevitably be the ones to negotiate the changes warranted by these new ideas, assuring reconciliation, continuity, and a smooth transition from past to present to future.

Green school leaders will need to convince community members, both inside and outside schools, that this is not another fad or fancy, accepted in name alone or once accepted, reduced to so many superficial activities and ceremonies. With all the change, nothing really changes. DiMaggio and Powell (1991) call this "incomplete institutionalization," this tendency for new practices to "take a firm hold for a short period, only to quickly wane [if] their source of normative support erodes" (p. 199).

Similarly, organizational norms and beliefs do not change without attention to actual conditions and specific structures. In a seminal article about reforming schools, Tyack and Tobin (1994) call the "remarkably durable" features of American schools, the "grammar of schooling" (p. 455). They liken the grammatical rules of schooling to those of speech. Like talking, schooling goes on smoothly without conscious knowledge of the rules. These scholars of school history and change maintain "much of the grammar of schooling has become so well established that it is taken for granted as just the way schools are," and they suggest, "it is the *departure* from customary practice in schooling, [like in] speaking, that attracts attention"(p. 454, italics in original).

In an earlier article, Tyack (1991) contended that, even given this compelling grammar, schools do change. "Contrary to the view that schools have been impervious to innovations, schools have changed markedly over time in some respects." However, rather than reforms being truly character changing, they more often result in "growth by accretion," that is, the adding on of new functions and activities (Tyack, 1991, p. 14). As much as reforms change schools, schools change reforms and, in doing so, the whole enterprise tends to grow bigger and more diffuse (Tyack & Tobin, 1994).

Adding a couple of green activities here and a few sustainable practices there only creates another distracting layer of grammatical rules and does little to change the essential character of schools. Think of these as veneers, more coats of paint whatever the color.

> In schools aspiring to be a darker shade of green ... woven into the school ethos ... [is] the development of whole-school policies and practices to foster environmental concern and responsiveness, but also to promote social justice, multiculturalism, holistic health, safe schools, citizenship, and democracy across the school community. (Selby, 2000, p. 91)

Green school leaders work to ensure these practices remain vital and animated. Living them, not merely going through the motions, is what makes sustainable practices in these schools a normal part of things. Whole-school sustainability policies are announced publicly and introduced openly, at the same times green practices find their way more subtlety into daily routines. The direction of effort is horizontal as well as vertical. It moves from the top down and from the bottom up. The work is on a grand scale, while at the same time it is circumscribed and local. It must happen in big and small ways, simultaneously.

Ecological and democratic habits of mind and practice must not only penetrate the classroom walls. We must also find the means to project them out into the attendant community. Stone (2010) reminds us that "a community worth sustaining [is] alive—fresh, vital, evolving, diverse, dynamic" (p. 34). Healthy communities of living organisms provide apt models, as they survive according to strong and diverse networks of relationships that foster resilience (Goleman et al., 2012, p. 13). For a school to provide its children this sort of healthy context for learning, it must be a community in its own right, a place "where learning is the accompaniment of continuous activities . . . which have a social aim. [U]nder such conditions, the school becomes itself a form of social life, a miniature community and one in close association with . . . experience beyond school walls" (Dewey, 1916, p. 418). Such schooling helps develop "interest in the community welfare, an interest which is intellectual and practical, as well as emotional" (1916, p. 418).

On a warm day in April, Angela stopped to comment on the manner in which garden boxes at the school's front entrance were so beautifully weeded and cared for. "This," she said, "is under students' hands. Is that not amazing? They are creating beauty in their community and for the world."

Questions for Discussion

1. Think of your most productive school–community partnership. Describe who is involved, how long they have been involved, and its purposes. How does, or might, this partnership help you realize your vision for a green, more sustainable school community? As a green school leader, what do you do to ensure this partnership is authentic, productive, and sustainable?

2. Prepare a five-minute elevator speech on the value-added your community will derive from creating greener, more sustainable schools. Touch on the inherent opportunities for students, teachers, parents, and the community

at large. Convince your audience that whole-school sustainability will not be just another passing fad.

3. Describe a time when students at your school served as environmental stewards and change agents. How was your community influenced by their actions?

References

Altman, I., & Low, S. M. (1992). Place attachment: A conceptual inquiry. In I. Altman & S. M. Low (Eds.), *Human behavior and environments: Advances in theory and research. Volume 12: Place attachment* (pp. 1–12). New York: Plenum Press.

Anderson, G. L. (1998). Toward authentic participation: Deconstructing the discourses of participating reforms in education. *American Education Research Journal, 35,* 571–603.

Buttimer, A. (1980). Home, reach and sense of place. In A. Buttimer & D. Seamon (Eds.), *The human experience of space and place* (pp. 73–85). London: Croom Helm.

Caine, G., & Caine, R. N. (2000). How the brain learns. In Z. Barlow & M. Crabtree (Eds.), *Ecoliteracy: Mapping the terrain* (pp. 51–57). Berkeley, CA: Center for Ecoliteracy / Learning in the Real World.

Carter, P. (2006). Straddling boundaries: Identity, culture, and school. *Sociology of Education, 79,* 304–328.

Chawla, L. (1992). Childhood place attachments. In I. Altman & S. M. Low (Eds.), *Human behavior and environments: Advances in theory and research. Volume 12: Place attachment* (pp. 63–86). New York: Plenum Press.

Chawla, L. (2007). Childhood experiences associated with care for the natural world: A theoretical framework for empirical results. *Children, Youth, and Environments, 17,* 144–170.

Chawla, L. (2009). Growing up green: Becoming an agent of care for the natural world. *Journal of Developmental Processes, 4*(1), 6–23.

Chawla, L., & Cushing, D. F. (2007). Education for strategic environmental behavior. *Environmental Education Research, 13,* 437–452.

Counts, G. S. (1932). *Dare the school build a new social order?* New York: John Day.

Crowson, R. L., & Boyd, W. L. (2001). The new role of community development in educational reform. *Peabody Journal of Education, 76,* 9–29, doi:10.1207/ S15327930pje7602_2

Davis , J. M., & Cooke, S. M. (2007). Educating for a healthy sustainable world: An argument for integrating health promoting and sustainable schools, 22, 346–353

Dewey, J. (1916). *Democracy and education.* New York: Macmillan Company.

Dewey, J. (1939/1989). *Freedom and culture.* Buffalo, New York: Prometheus Books.

DiMaggio, P. J., & Powell, W. W. (Eds.). (1991). *The new institutionalism in organizational analysis.* Chicago: University of Chicago Press.

Driscoll, M. E., & Kerchner, C. T. (1999). The implications of social capital for schools, communities, and cities. In J. Murphy & K. S. Louis (Eds.), *Handbook of research on educational administration* (2nd ed., pp. 385–404). San Francisco: Jossey-Bass.

Epstein, J. (1996). School and family connections: Theory, research, and implications for integrating sociologies of education and family. *Marriage and Family, 15,* 99–126.

Goldring, E. B., & Hausman, C. (2001). Civic capacity and school principals: The missing links for community development. In R. Crowson (Ed.), *Community development and school reform* (pp. 193–209). London: Elsevier.

Goleman, D., Bennett, L., & Barlow, Z. (2012). *Ecolierate: How educators are cultivating emotional, social, and ecological intelligence.* San Francisco, CA: Joseey Bass.

Hart, R. (1979). *Children's experience of place.* New York: Irvington.

Henderson, K., & Tilbury, D. (2004). *Whole-school approaches to sustainability: An international review of whole-school sustainability programs.* Canberra, Australia: Austrailian Research Institute in Education for Sustainability.

Hidalgo, M., & Hernandez, B. (2001). Place attachment: Conceptual and empirical questions. *Journal of Environmental Psychology, 21,* 273–281.

Higgs, A., & McMillan, V. (2006). Teaching through modeling: Four schools' experiences in sustainability education. *The Journal of Environmental Education, 38*(1), 39–53.

Ittleson, W. H., Proshansky, H. M., Rivlen, L. G., & Winkel, G. H. (1974). *An introduction to environmental psychology.* New York: Holt, Rinehart, and Winston.

Jorgensen, B., & Stedman, R. (2001). Sense of place as an attachment, Lakeshore owners attitudes toward their properties. *Journal of Environmental Psychology, 21,* 233–248.

Kilpatrick, W. H. (1932). *Education and the social crisis: A proposed program.* New York: Liveright.

Korpela, K.M. (2002). Children's environments. In R. Bechtel & A. Churchman (Eds.), *Handbook of environmental psychology* (pp. 363–373). New York: John Wiley & Sons.

Langhout, R. D., Rappaport, J., & Simmons, D. (2002). Integrating community into the classroom: Community gardening, community involvement, and project-based learning. *Urban Education, 37,* 323–349.

Malone, K. (2013). The future lies in our hands: Children as researchers and environmental change agents in designing a child-friendly neighborhood. *Local Environment, 18,* 372–395.

Morgan, G. (1998). *Images of organizations.* San Francisco, CA: Berrett Koehler.

National Policy Board for Educational Administration. (2015). *Professional standards for educational leaders.* Retrieved from Reston, VA: http://www.ccsso.org/Documents/2015/ProfessionalStandardsforEducationalLeaders2015forNPBEAFINAL.pdf

Newell, P. B. (1997). A cross-cultural examination of favorite places. *Environment and Behavior, 29,* 495–514.

Niemi, R. G., & Junn, J. (1998). *Civic education: What makes students learn.* New Haven, CT: Yale University Press.

Noddings, N. (2012). *Peace education: How we come to love and hate war.* Cambridge: Cambridge University Press.

Noddings, N. (2013). *Education and democracy in the 21st century*. New York: Teachers College Press.

Orr, D. W. (2005a). *Place and pedagogy*. In M. K. Stone & Z. Barlow (Eds.), *Ecological literacy: Our educating children for a sustainable world* (pp. 85–95). San Francisco: Sierra Club Books.

Orr, D. W. (2005b). Recollection. In Stone, M. K. & Z. Barlow (Eds.), *Ecological literacy: Educating our children for a sustainable world* (pp. 96–106). San Francisco: Sierra Club Books.

Owen, P. E. (1988). Natural landscapes, gathering places, and prospect refuges: Characteristics of outdoor places valued by teens. *Children's Environmental Quarterly, 5*, 17–24.

Proshansky, H. M. (1978). The city and self-identity. *Environment and Behavior, 10*, 147–169.

Proshansky, H. M., & Fabian, A. K. (1987). The development of place identity in the child. In C. S. Weinstein & T. G. David (Eds.), *Spaces for children, the built environment and child development* (pp. 21–24). New York: Putman.

Proshansky, H. M., Fabian, A. K., & Kaminoff, R. (1983/1995). Place identity: Physical world socialization of self. In L. Groat (Ed.), *Readings in environmental psychology: Giving places meaning* (pp. 87–114). London: Academic Press. [Originally published in *Journal of Environmental Psychology*.]

Rivlin, L. G. (1990). Home and homelessness in the lives of children. *Children and Youth Services, 14*, 5–17.

Schelly, C., Cross, J., Franzen, W., Hall, P., & Reeve, S. (2010). Reducing energy consumption and creating a conservation culture in organizations: A case study of one public school district. *Environment and Behavior, 43*(3), 316–343.

Schorr, L. B. (1997). *Common purposes: Strengthening families and neighborhoods to rebuild America*. New York: Anchor.

Selby, D. (2000). A darker shade of green: The importance of ecological thinking in global education and school reform. *Theory into Practice, 39*, 88–96.

Sirotnik, K. A. (2005). Ecological images of change: Limits and possibilities. In A. Lieberman (Ed.), *The roots of educational change* (pp. 169–185). The Netherlands: Springer.

Smith, G., & Gruenewald, D. (Eds.). (2008). *Place-based education in the global age: Local diversity*. New York: Lawrence Erlbaum Associates.

Smrekar, C. E., & Mawhinney, H. B. (1999). Integrated services: Challenges in linking schools, families, and communities. In J. Murphy & K. S. Louis (Eds.), *Handbook of research on educational administration* (2nd ed., pp. 443–461). San Francisco: Jossey-Bass.

Sobel, D. (1990). A place in the world: Adults' memories of childhood special places. *Children's Environments Quarterly, 7*, pp. 5–12.

Stone, M. (2010). A schooling for sustainability framework. *Teacher Education Quarterly, 37*, 33–46.

Tuan, Y. F. (1980). Rootedness versus sense of place. *Landscape, 24*, 3–8.

Tyack, D. (1991). Public school reform: Policy talk and institutional practice. *American Journal of Education, 100*(1), 1–19.

Tyack, D., & Tobin, W. (1994). The "grammar" of schooling: Why has it been so hard to change. *American Education Research Journal, 31*(3), 453–479.

Violand-Sanchez, E., & Hainer-Violand, J. (2006). The power of positive identity. *Educational Leadership, 64*(1), 36–40.

Warren, M. R. (2005). Communities and schools: A new view of urban education reform, *Harvard Review, 75*, 133–173.

Williams, D. R., & Brown, J. D. (2012). *Learning gardens and sustainability education: Bringing life to schools and schools to life*. New York: Routledge.

Yates, M., & Youniss, J. (Eds.). (1999). *Roots of civic identity*. Chicago: University of Chicago Press.

6

Green School Buildings as Dynamic Learning Environments

Architects must integrate many aspects of design to create a whole and wholesome learning environment … responding to the needs of the user, the community, and the Earth. Educators, in turn, must identify the current needs of active, whole learners while expanding their own understanding of built, natural, and cultural environments as teaching and learning tools.

(Taylor, 2009, p. xvii)

As we have discussed in Chapter 5, place plays an important role in our development as people and as leaners. Our emotional and cognitive conceptions of physical environments inform our understandings of ourselves, both as individuals and members of social groups (Knez, 2005). Outside the home, students spend the greatest portion of their time in school (Gump, 1978; Rivlin & Weinstein, 1995). Here they continue to develop a sense of self and build their capacity to relate to peers and adults. Given its primacy in children's cognitive, social, and emotional development, "school as *place* [warrants close] attention as a physical entity and continuing experience in [students'] lives" (Rivlin & Weinstein, 1995, p. 256, emphasis in original).

In the early decades of the 20th century, American philosopher and educator John Dewey wrote an essay which appeared in the *New York Times* on April 23, 1933, within which he described his conception of the ideal, "utopian" school. His discussion began not with curriculum, instructional method, or administration, but with physical space. Dewey wrote about "large grounds," "gardens," and "greenhouses." He described interiors as "open-air." His school replaced "mechanical rows of screwed-down desks" with effects more resembling those found in "a well-furnished home." He added to these a "variety of equipment," "workshops," "laboratories," and "books everywhere" (Dewey 1989a, p. 136). Place figured high on Dewey's list of ideals and he was not shy about emphasizing beauty, comfort, excitement, *and* connection to the environment.

Now, within the early decades of the 21st century, as we consider "global and ecological patterns—networks, cycles, flow, and sustainability—we begin to see implications for a new dynamic, a 'living' and ecologically responsive approach to the design of school and the educational systems they house" (Taylor, 2009, p. 47). The children who attend these ecologically responsive schools have the opportunity to develop a 21st-century *sense of place*, created as they learn, play, and discover within these green schools, bringing their own sense of self and the world to bear on these experiences (Buttimer, 1980; Hart, 1979; Jorgensen & Stedman, 2001; Tuan, 1980).

This chapter begins with a discussion of the primary role schools play in children's development as learners and, in particular, the role the building plays in supporting students' learning and well-being. The chapter then considers the uphill climb many school leaders face as they attempt to ensure their students and communities have access to high-quality, dynamic learning environments. Finally, the chapter builds a compelling case for why the provision of such high-quality, sustainable school facilities is in the best interest of the children who attend, both for realizing their current learning potential and for protecting their future quality of life. We end with a tour of a healthy, high-performing school, a school built and managed for socio-ecological sustainability, imagining the possibilities for leveraging green school leadership.

Experiencing School Buildings as Primary Places for Development and Learning

As young children transition from the familiarity of home and neighborhood to school, the physical structure of the school building introduces them to forms and ideas outside the range of their earliest experiences (Uline, 2000). To the degree educators, planners, and designers are willing "to make judgments based on the overall quality of a facility rather than [mere] adherence to myriad individual standards" (Genevro, 1992, p. 10), school buildings, as structures, begin to provoke thought and encourage learning just as powerfully as they protect occupants from the elements.

In the case of green schools, children have the opportunity to interact in, and with, ecologically responsive learning environments that reveal connections to the larger society and natural world. Through active, problem- and project-based learning experiences, students begin to build a sense of responsibility for, and commitment to, their community, their planet, and each other. In green schools, the building design and systems, themselves, demonstrate environmental stewardship, here in the place "where children first learn what it is to be in the world in the society of other people" (Gelfand, 2010, p. 3). In fact, recent research suggests sustainable school design is the best predictor of children's environmental attitudes, facilitating their connectedness with nature and increasing their awareness of the impact of the built environment on the natural environment (Izadpanahi, Elkadi, & Tucker, 2015).

Given the myriad variables influencing students' academic performance, including age difference of students, socio-economic status (SES), available district and school resources, the quality of teaching, the quality of buildings themselves (in terms of age, design, building systems, characteristics, operation and maintenance practices), and the difficulty in isolating and controlling for these confounding factors, researchers acknowledge "the effect of the built environment will necessarily appear small" (National Research Council, 2007, p. 38). Still, a growing body of research connects the quality of school facilities to student outcomes, including achievement and attitude, as well as teacher attitude and behavior (see Earthman, 2004; Earthman & Lemasters, 1996, 1998; Higgins, Hall, Wall, Woolner, & McCaughey, 2005; Lemasters, 1997; Schneider, 2002, 2003).

Specific building features and conditions have been shown to influence student achievement, including climate control and indoor air quality (Cash, 1993; Earthman, 2004; Hines, 1996; Lanham, 1999); lighting (Barrett, Zhang, Moffat, & Zobbacy, 2013; Heschong Mahone Group, 1999; Kuller & Lindsten, 1992; Mayron, Ott, Nations, & Mayron, 1974; Wurtman, 1975); views to the outside (Heschong & Mahone, 2003); acoustical control (Evans & Maxwell, 1997; Haines, Stansfeld, Job, Berglund, & Head, 2001; Hygge, Evans, & Bullinger, 2002; Maxwell & Evans, 2000); building age (Bowers & Burkett, 1988; Chan, 1979; Earthman & Lemasters, 1996; McGuffey & Brown, 1978; O'Neill, 2000; Phillips, 1997; Plumley 1978); and non-modernized versus modernized and refurbished buildings (Maxwell, 1999; McGuffey & Brown, 1978; Plumley, 1978). In addition, design classifications have been found to influence student outcomes, including flexible classroom arrangements, movement and circulation, and positive outdoor spaces (Tanner, 2008, 2009; Tanner & Lackney, 2006). The places where students learn make a difference in their performance, their sense of themselves as learners, and their overall well-being.

Acknowledging the Uphill Climb to Dynamic Learning Environments

And yet, even as evidence mounts, school leaders, particularly those in poorly resourced districts, struggle to convince policy makers and taxpayers of the need to invest resources in replacing or renovating inadequate school facilities. A 2006 national report conducted by Building Education Success Together (BEST) describes public school construction over a ten-year period in the United States (2006). The report described the scale, scope, and distribution of school facility investments nationwide. Public school districts in the United States built more than 12,000 new schools during the prior decade, and more than 130,000 renovations and other improvement projects were completed. More than $304 billion were spent on such capital expenditures as new construction, renovation, and modernization. Data revealed that students in poorly resourced districts received much smaller shares of the overall expenditure on adequate facilities.

Findings in a contemporary study that calculated capital stock and unmet capital investment requirements of districts in Michigan indicate that under-resourced districts continue to have the greatest need (Arsen & Davis, 2006). Their findings confirmed those of BEST (2006). Together these studies help to refine and focus earlier estimates of need,[1] confirming that many of the most challenged school districts continue getting by with poor quality buildings (Mead, 2005, p. 1). Community and school district leaders, particularly those in poorly resourced urban and rural districts, struggle to convince policy makers and taxpayers of the need to expand the available building stock, replacing inadequate school facilities with 21st-century learning spaces (Uline, Wolsey, Tschannen-Moran, & Lin, 2010). It appears many remain unimpressed with the seriousness of the problem, challenging the relative impact of capital investments on student achievement when compared with other factors that demand the attention of policy makers, administrators, teachers, and members of the community. In fact, empirical evidence suggests that such either/or decisions about where best to invest our resources may be shortsighted (Crampton, 2009).

A recent study, entitled *State of Our Schools: America's K–12 Facilities 2016*, examined 20 years of publicly available national and state data to estimate the cost of operating, maintaining, modernizing, and meeting the enrollment growth of the K–12 public schools in the United States, from 1994 through 2013 (Filardo, 2016). Nationally, states and districts spent a total of $925 billion (in 2014 dollars) on maintenance and operations, an annual average of nearly $46 billion per year. In addition to maintenance and operations spending, states and districts invested $973 billion, an average of $49 billion per year, for new school construction and improvements to existing schools. Over the past three years (2011–2013), the combined spending totaled nearly $99 billion per year. This sounds like a tremendous investment in educational infrastructure, and yet, according to industry standards, states and districts should be spending approximately $145 billion per year to maintain, operate, and renew facilities "so that they provide healthy and safe 21st century learning environments for all children" (Filardo, 2016, p. 4):

> Comparing historic spending against building industry and best-practice standards for responsible facilities stewardship, we estimate that national spending falls short by about $8 billion for M&O [maintenance and operations] and $38 billion for capital construction. In total, the nation is under spending on school facilities by $46 billion—an annual shortfall of 32 percent. Gaps vary by state and local district, depending on investments by local communities and the structure of school facilities funding at the state level. Nevertheless, investment levels in all states but three will not meet the standards.

And students are not the only ones affected by poor quality buildings. The nature and quality of the built learning environment also has been shown to affect the community's ongoing engagement with a school (Berner, 1993), as well as teacher attitudes, behaviors, performance (Buckley, Schneider, & Shang, 2004; Earthman & Lemaster, 2009; Lowe, 1990; Schneider, 2003), and their choices about where to work (Fuller et al., 2009; Horng, 2009). Research by Fuller and colleagues (2009) suggests that new elementary schools in Los Angeles attract younger, more recently trained members of the teaching ranks. Horng (2009) surveyed 531 California elementary teachers, asking them to choose between various workplace characteristics, "trading off" student demographics, salaries, and working conditions, including school facilities, administrative support, class sizes, and salaries. In response to earlier studies that suggested teachers avoid schools with significant populations of low-income, minority, and low-performing students, Horng sought to "disentangle student characteristics from other characteristics of teaching jobs" and better understand if student characteristics served as proxies for the working conditions common in schools attended by low-income, minority, and low-performing students (p. 690). Data from this study suggest that when teachers choose among schools, on average, the condition of the school facility is more than twice as important as student demographic variables and 30% more important than salary.

The places where teachers teach make a difference to their performance, their sense of themselves as professionals, and their overall well-being. In fact, the enhanced image of a school designed to environmental principles may help to recruit and retain high-quality, 21st-century-trained teachers.

Research suggests these professionals are drawn to work places that deliver a clear message about the value of learning and teaching (Edwards, 2006). To the degree green schools signal an investment in occupant health and well-being, the buildings themselves contribute to students' learning, teachers' satisfaction, and, possibly, the welfare of the wider community (Edwards, 2006).

What Makes a Green School Building Green?

In 2010, the American Institute of Architects (AIA), ICLEI-USA Local Governments for Sustainability, the Redford Center, and the U.S. Green Building Council (USGBC) brought together national experts and local leaders, including mayor and superintendent teams from ten cities, to develop a plan for achieving the vision that every child in America will attend a green school within this generation. The resulting *National Action Plan for Greening America's Schools* underscored the billions of dollars spent each year on building and operating U.S. schools (representing the largest construction sector in the United States, $80 billion from 2006 to 2008). According to the plan, too many schools are designed to minimum standards, waste millions of dollars in energy consumption, and fail to meet the learning needs of the students who attend them. The plan also highlighted green schools from across the country, built at or below the cost of these more conventionally designed buildings and constructed and operated with a focus on occupant health and energy efficiency (Rainwater & Hartke, 2011, p. 5).

Widely accepted definitions describe such green schools as healthy and high performing (Collaborative for High Performance Schools (CHPS), n.d.). A green school creates a healthy environment that is conducive to learning while saving energy, resources, and money (USGBC, n.d.). Commonly referred to as high performance buildings, these schools apply sustainable, energy conservation techniques across all building systems. They are designed with particular attention to ambient features such as acoustic, thermal, and visual comfort. Green school buildings also utilize energy analysis tools along with lifecycle cost analyses, to ensure ongoing cost effectiveness. As stated in Chapter 1 of this book, 1,732 public school projects in the United States have obtained some level of LEED certification, a number representing just over 1% of all public schools in the United States. Although these data are heartening, school districts and communities face significant challenges in realizing the *National Action Plan for Greening America's Schools* vision, that every child in America will attend a green school within a generation.

How Do Green School Leaders Make the Case?

As a 21st-century school leader, you no doubt acknowledge the uphill battle and ask yourself, where do I possibly begin to make the case for this ecologically responsive approach to school design? Further, given the nature and the weight of my current responsibilities, how do I justify the time and effort necessary for the task? Understandably, planning a sustainable school "raises the stakes," with design, construction, and management practices that are new to school districts (Gelfand, 2010, p. 19). And yet, consider a recent study of primary schools in Great Britain wherein Edwards (2006) compared 42 pairs of schools, green versus conventional with similar characteristics in terms of geography, size, grade level, SES and numbers of students with special needs and for whom English is a second language. The study considered five sets of performance factors, including performance on standardized tests, absenteeism, bullying, teacher turnover and teaching days lost due to illness, and qualitative interview data from teachers and department heads regarding their work experiences.

Schools designated as green were designed based on ecological principles, demonstrating evidence of energy efficiency, health (both physically and psychologically), comfort, responsiveness, and flexibility. Research findings demonstrated a 3–5% improvement in test scores consistently displayed in all but one green school, with more significant improvements for younger students who stay in one classroom longer. Data also revealed lower teacher absenteeism and turnover rates, reduced rates of student absenteeism and bullying in green schools, as well as an enhanced image on the part of the community for their school. Holistic green design strategies, where design, construction, and curriculum practices were integrated, appeared to offer greater advantages over concentration on a single aspect of green design. In addition, schools that prioritized daylight and natural ventilation generally out performed other schools, both in urban and rural contexts (Edwards, 2006).

Intentionally designed, high performance schools appear to provide school leaders a singular opportunity to influence the ways in which occupants and the community at large construct meaning from a school's physical features, conditions, and local context. These understandings likely influence the community's commitment to their school, shape the nature of the school's learning climate in significant ways, and ultimately, impact the learning and performance of students and teachers. Given the nature and weight of your current responsibilities, it seems you can't afford not to consider the benefits of green, ecologically responsive school facilities.

Choosing Sustainable Design Elements in the Best Interest of Children

According to the National Research Council (2007), green schools have two complementary goals and resulting outcomes (p. 2):

◆ First, green schools aim to "support the health and development (physical, social, intellectual) of students, teachers and staff by providing a healthy, safe, comfortable, and functional physical environment," and

◆ Second, green schools seek to have "positive environmental and community attributes."

When approached in an integrated fashion, the location and design of a green school, including the nature of school site; the building orientation; the envelope; the heating, ventilation, and air conditioning systems; the acoustics; and the lighting systems, result in a physical learning environment with appropriate levels of moisture, ventilation, air quality, noise, and lighting (LPA, Inc., 2009; National Research Council, 2007). Such well-conceived buildings function as dynamic learning environments. They are healthier and more environmentally responsible. Green schools are also less expensive to operate and, in the best cases, the buildings themselves function as interactive tools for learning.

For Sake of Our Children's Present

In Chapter 2 we took a critical look at educators' inclination to advance best-interests-of-children arguments when considering the decisions before them—big or small, immediate or long-range. We observed that contemporary understandings of best-interest concepts limit themselves to anthropocentric, localized, and present-day frames of reference, with little or no attention paid to the impact day-to-day decisions may have on children beyond the school walls or in future generations. Here we consider how well-conceived, sustainable school building designs serve the best interest of our children, now and in the future, at the same time they address local and global ecological, social, and economic needs.

It Is in the Best Interest of Children to Provide an Abundance of Clean Indoor Air

Indoor air quality, which results from the presence/absence of outdoor and indoor air pollutants, thermal comfort, and sensory loads (odors, freshness), can affect the heath of children and adults and may affect student learning and teacher productivity (National Research Council, 2007, p. 54). Pollutants and allergens in indoor air, including mold, dust, bacterial and fungal products, volatile organic compounds (VOCs), and particulate matter have been associated with asthma and other respiratory symptoms, as well as eye, nose, and throat irritations, headaches, and fatigue (National Research Council, 2007). Elevated CO_2 levels have also been associated with student absenteeism (Shendell et al., 2004) and reduced rates of attention in primary school students (Coley & Greeves, 2004).

To assess the connection between indoor environmental quality in Finnish elementary school buildings and the health of sixth grade students, researchers surveyed 297 schools, with 4,248 participants completing heath questionnaires (estimated response rate 62.6%). Indoor environmental conditions were also assessed via ventilation rate and thermal condition measurements of classrooms in a subsample of 56 schools. Students reported stuffy nose, fatigue, and headache as their most common symptoms, with noise and stuffy air/poor indoor air quality (IAQ) identified most frequently as factors causing inconvenience and discomfort within classrooms (Turunen et. al., 2014).

Design decisions that allow for natural ventilation in classrooms, combining operable windows with well-designed mechanical systems that can operate in tandem, ensure an abundance of fresh air (National Research Council, 2007). For example, displacement ventilation systems introduce clean, fresh, tempered air at the floor level closer to the occupants, accomplishing greater comfort with less airflow. In this case, the lower 4 to 6 feet of space is made comfortable with less air movement, making acoustics and energy use easier to control. Less air mixture also minimizes the distribution of dust and microbes (Gelfand, 2010).

A multiple building study of 39 schools in Sweden identified a 69% reduction in two-year incidence of asthma among students in schools that received a new displacement ventilation system with increased fresh air supply rates and reduced humidity, as compared to students in schools that did not receive a new ventilation system (Smedje & Norback, 2000). Wargocki and Wyon's (2005) longitudinal studies of ventilation and temperature (holding other conditions constant) demonstrated increased task completion and modest improvements in student performance on weekly tests of verbal and math skills. When reduced temperature was combined with increased ventilation rates, task completion increased in a test of logical thinking. In a recent study conducted across 70 elementary schools in southwestern United States, researchers surveyed students and monitored multiple indoor environmental quality (IEQ) parameters in a subset of classrooms during the academic year of 2008–2009. A multi-level analysis, based on measurement data from 140 fifth grade classrooms and student level data ($N = 3,109$) on socioeconomic variables and standardized test scores, revealed a statistically significant association between ventilation rates and mathematics scores. Students' mean mathematics scores (average 2,286 points) were increased by up to 11 points (0.5%) per each liter per second per person increase in ventilation rate. Effects of similar magnitude, but with higher variability were observed for reading and science scores (Haverinen-Shaughnessy & Shaughnessy, 2015). In another widely cited study, students in classrooms where windows could be opened were found to progress 7 to 8% faster than those with fixed windows (Heschong Mahone Group, 1999).

It Is in the Best Interest of Children to Ensure Ample Access to Daylight, as Well as High-quality Artificial Lighting Systems

Throughout a school day, students engage in a wide variety of learning experiences and tasks, most of which include some visual dimension. In fact, "[t]he visual qualities of a learning environment are some of the most crucial building aspects to design properly since children depend heavily on sight in the learning process" (Baker & Bernstein, 2012, p. 10). Both the quantity and quality of light are important factors in design decisions, with wide agreement on appropriate quantity firmly established and additional research required on issues regarding quality (Baker & Bernstein, 2012).

High-quality natural light helps to create a sense of physical and mental comfort with benefits beyond aiding sight (Barrett & Zhang, 2009). Building orientation constitutes a fundamental design choice for the control of light, given the variations in available daylight at east, west, north and south facing facades. Additional daylight design strategies, including the size and placement of windows in combination with clerestories, skylights, solar tubes, and light shelves, optimize daylight distribution and bring light deeper into a given space. Frosted glass and easily operable shades help to eliminate glare and provide teachers necessary control of lighting across the day and for different learning activities.

Windows and views, as well as various forms of light, have been linked to student health, learning and behavior, with daylight offering a more positive effect on student outcomes, potentially due to its biological effects on the human body. For example, a study by Kuller and Lindsten (1992) determined that students who lacked access to natural light experienced delayed seasonal cortisol production, a hormone positively associated with concentration. The Heschong Mahone Group (1999) analyzed data from 2,000 classrooms across school districts in Orange County, California, Seattle, Washington, and Fort Collins, Colorado. Test results of 21,000 students, demographic data, architectural plans, aerial photographs, the presence of skylights, maintenance records, and daylighting conditions were among the factors considered. Findings revealed students in daylit classrooms showed greater improvements across one school year in math and reading than did students in windowless classrooms.

Hathaway (1995) conducted a two-year study of the effects of various lighting systems (full spectrum florescent, full spectrum florescent in combination with ultraviolet light supplements, cool white florescent, and high-pressure sodium vapor) on elementary students' dental health, attendance, growth and development, vision, and academic achievement. Results demonstrated that students who received ultraviolet light supplements had fewer dental cavities, better attendance, greater gains in height and weight, and better academic performance than students who didn't receive the supplements. Students under the high-pressure sodium vapor lighting had the slowest rates of growth in height and academic performance, as well as lower rates of attendance.

Schools typically rely upon lighting systems that combine artificial and natural sources, taking account of different room configurations, layouts, and surfaces. Ideal school daylighting solutions admit diffuse or reflected sunlight but not summer heat, admit solar heat in the winter where needed, allow views but prevent glare, and include electric lighting controls that adjust artificial sources in response to available daylight and user need (Gelfand, 2010). The control of light in accordance with various learning activities and the role it plays in the occupants' mood, school security, and time on task constitute important factors (Uline, Tschannen-Moran, & Wolsey, 2009).

It Is in the Best Interest of Children to Plan for Effective Classroom Acoustics

Acoustic performance involves the control of ambient and external noise within an enclosed space in order to provide high-quality conditions for producing and receiving desired sounds. The control of noise and the quality of auditory perception primarily determine the nature and quality of the acoustic environment (Barrett & Zhang, 2009). A substantial body of research underscores the importance of minimizing background noise and maximizing speech intelligibility in order to ensure students have optimal opportunities to learn (Berg, Blair, & Benson, 1996; Knecht, Nelson, Whitelaw, & Feth, 2002). School design decisions that take account of location to avoid excessive external noise consider layout of academic spaces to minimize intrusive internal noise, and plan for room features that incorporate sound absorbent materials to reduce sound reverberations, ensure high-quality acoustic performance. And yet, too often, students and teachers struggle within poor, acoustically performing classrooms (Feth & Whitelaw, 1999; Sato & Bradley, 2008).

Excessive noise and reverberation in classrooms is a problem for all children, but especially students who are hearing impaired (Finitzo-Hieber & Tillman, 1978; Nábělek & Pickett, 1974), students with learning difficulties (Bradlow, Krauss, & Hayes, 2003; Elliot et al., 1979), and students for whom English is a second language (Nábělek & Donahue, 1984). Results from a recent study of elementary students in Germany indicate significant effects of reverberation on speech perception and short-term memory of spoken items (Klatte, Hellbrück, Seidel, & Leistner, 2010). Children from classrooms with increased reverberation time also judged their relationships with peers and teachers as less positive than children who enjoyed higher quality acoustic environments.

Ecologically sound design decisions can alleviate problems through high-quality heating, ventilation, air conditioning, and plumbing systems. Control of outdoor noise and noise from adjacent spaces also results from careful siting and space configuration plans, as well as careful consideration of the acoustical quality of windows, walls, and doors. In sum, effective classroom acoustics result from thoughtful planning that takes account of external and internal sources of noise, sets criteria for ambient noise levels, and verifies outcomes through a commissioning process (National Research Council, 2007) We describe the commissioning process in greater detail in Chapters 7 and 9.

It Is in the Best Interest of Children to Maintain Thermal Comfort within the Classroom

Thermal comfort within the built environment is maintained through control of temperature, humidity, and airflow. A well-designed building envelope (exterior building shell) helps to mediate external conditions when combined with high-efficiency and double-paned windows, siting for solar access and ventilation, and high R-value (thermal resistance) insulation (Taylor, 2009). High performance heating, ventilation, and air conditioning (HVAC) systems help to minimize distractions and allow for focused learning. When a classroom is too hot, cold, or damp, students and teachers have difficulty settling in. Understandably, they'd rather be somewhere else, and so, instead of fully engaging in the work at hand, their thoughts stray to some more inviting and comfortable place.

A robust literature documents the effects of temperature and humidity on occupants' comfort and productivity in office buildings (Wang, Federspiel, & Arens, 2005; Wyon, 2004). Similarly, a well-respected and often cited review of research regarding the effects of school facilities on student outcomes recommends that humidity levels rest between 40% and 70% and temperatures range between 68 and 74 degrees for maximum student comfort and performance (Schneider, 2002). Research by Wyon and Wargocki (2007) connects reduced room temperatures with increases in students' speed of test completion and levels of test performance. Results from a field intervention in two classrooms of 10-year-old students conducted by Wargocki et al. (2005) also revealed a significant relationship between reduced temperature and increased task completion in subtraction and reading.

A desire for individual control over physical comfort features prominently across studies. Teachers appear to greatly value their ability to open windows and adjust room temperatures in accordance with changes in environmental conditions and classroom activity levels (Heschong & Mahone, 2003; Uline et al., 2009; Worgocki et al., 2005). For energy conscious school leaders, "[q]uestions remain . . . regarding how to provide individual thermal control while keeping energy use in check" (Baker & Bernstein, 2012, p. 13).

It Is in the Best Interest of Children to Provide Ample Access to Nature and the Outdoors

A carefully conceived school site reinforces a sense of place, honors pre-existing landforms, supports circulation, mitigates heat islands, and provides opportunity for resource conservation and habitat protection. Ecologically sensitive site designs create learning landscapes (Taylor, 2009) with a myriad of interconnected features including *natural* (climate, plants, animals, soil and rocks, wetlands), *built* (play structures, bermed earth, pathways, sports venues, seating), *multisensory* (texture, patterns, colors, patterns, sounds, smells), *cultural* (gathering spaces, local materials, student and public art, indigenous design), *agricultural* (gardens, land management areas, orchards), and *outdoor classroom* (weather stations, solar and wind energy stations, trails, greenhouses, water harvesting systems) elements (Taylor, 2009). In combination, these features of a sustainable school site provide diverse settings for a multitude of learning activities (Gelfand, 2010). When designing a schoolyard, or any aspect of a school campus, the choice of features that serve multiple educational functions may constitute the wisest investment, with "[o]ne design choice . . . hav[ing] cascading positive benefits" (Cole, 2013, p. 222).

> For example, native plantings . . . can [include] static signage that educates the passerby about the environmental benefits [and] can also be integrated into the biology curriculum for student observation. The view of such greenery through the classroom window additionally offers restorative benefits for mentally fatigued students and teachers. (Cole, 2013, p. 220)

A significant body of research demonstrates a positive relationship between access to nature and the well-being of children and adults (Kuo & Faber Taylor, 2004; Louv, 2005; Noddings, 2006, 2013); the healing effects of views of nature (Ulrich, 1984); and nature's positive influence on mental health (Zarghami & Fatourechi, 2015). Further, outdoor activities have been shown to encourage more creativity than those in classrooms (Lindholm, 1995), demonstrating possible effects on learning (Fjortoft, 2004).

Barrett, Davies, Zhang, and Barrett (2015) studied the impact of physical classroom features on the academic progress (as measured by students' performance on standardized achievement tests) of 3,766 students in 153 classrooms across 27 primary schools in the UK. Barrett et al. were interested to explore the "holistic impacts of space on users ... experienced via multiple sensory inputs in particular spaces" (Barrett et al., p. 119). Such an approach foregrounds "inside-out and sensory sensitive" designs that keep the learner at the center of all decisions (Barrett et al. 2015, p. 131). The researchers considered three design principles, including *Individualization* (ownership, flexibility, and connection); *Stimulation* (complexity and color); and *Naturalness* (light, sound, temperature, air quality, *and* links to nature). The combined impact of the built environment factors on learning scales explained 16% of the variance in learning progress, with the *naturalness factors* accounting for approximately 50% of the facility design's impact on learning (Barrett et al., 2015).

Well-designed schoolyards create transitions from indoors to outdoors (Taylor, 2009), allowing learning to sprawl beyond classroom walls, thus challenging the architecture of self-contained classroom instruction (Uline et al., 2009). When learning landscapes are designed in a way that allows children to sense an internal logic to spaces and the paths of movement, they feel safe and at ease in these natural surroundings. And, when children are allowed to experience nature, with all its variety, color, shape, texture, sound, and smell, they are apt to respond with excitement, curiosity, and determination. These are beautiful experiences, and "[t]he hope is that students who understand, use, and feel connected to the natural environment will grow into adults who appreciate and protect its healthy, functional, and aesthetic properties" (Taylor, 2009, p. 327). We return to discussions of all these benefits in Chapter 8.

For Sake of Our Children's Future

According to Gelfand (2010), "people experience a building ... through movement and memory, not awareness of the mechanical and structural systems at work" (p. 53). And yet, mechanical and structural systems, and the ongoing maintenance and operation of these systems, play a central role in minimizing negative environmental effects. Further, green school design practices have potential to transform the way we experience the built environment. As transparent green design solutions render building systems visible, children and adults have the opportunity to experience and interact with them, learning how efficient and renewable energy systems, resource conservation systems, waste management systems, and ecologically sensitive building sites work together in integrated fashion to "amplify the effectiveness of the constituent parts" (p. 54). It is in the best interest of children to implement integrated design solutions that utilize ecologically sound mechanical and structural systems in our schools, not only because these actions influence the quality of our children's learning environments today, but also because they have potential to profoundly affect the quality of life our children will inherit. We will examine these systems in greater detail in Chapter 7 when we explore how sustainable operation and maintenance practice save money and reduce a school's carbon footprint. For now, consider these examples.

We Protect Our Children's Future When We Design Systems for Increasing Energy Efficiency and Generating Power on Site

Along with energy efficient lighting, heating and cooling, and ventilation systems, green school leaders are utilizing wind power, biomass, geo-thermal and small hydroelectric plants to power their schools. Green roofs also provide insulation, reduce heat loss, and reduce or eliminate rooftop heat island effects.

We Protect Our Children's Future When We Design Systems for Conserving Resources

Along with water-conserving plumbing fixtures in kitchen facilities, restrooms, and gymnasium locker rooms, green school leaders are incorporating bioswales that help to purify water runoff into their school landscapes. They are also implementing purchasing practices that take account of construction material production and transport, utilizing locally produced, rapidly renewable materials and materials with high recycled content.

We Protect Our Children's Future When We Design Systems for Managing Waste

Along with construction waste reduction systems that maximize the recycling, composting, and/or salvaging of construction, demolition, and land-cleaning waste, green school leaders are developing school-wide norms and routines, expecting and celebrating responsible, waste-conscience habits.

We Protect Our Children's Future When We Design Systems for Promoting Habitat Protection

The reuse of existing school sites, in combination with compact school designs, help to preserve undeveloped, open spaces. In addition, green school leaders are taking account of their school sites as natural systems, respecting and preserving wetlands and other existing habitats as laboratories for learning.

In these ways, green school buildings become vehicles for visualizing sustainability in action (Seibold-Bultman, 2007), and through integrated application of these ecologically sound systems and practices, our school campuses begin to play a significant role in ensuring the sustainable future our planet and our children deserve. And yet, skeptics continue to maintain that green systems and technologies are too complicated for school maintenance staff; green materials aren't durable; and, most frequently, that the cost of going green is too high. In fact, good daylighting, ventilation, site design, and effective integration of building systems should not cost more (LPA, Inc., 2009). Where certain materials, controls, and sensors are expensive by themselves, these components should be carefully considered within the context of the entire system (Gelfand, 2010).

A national report, authored by Gregory Kats in 2006, documented the financial costs and benefits of green schools compared to conventional schools. Data gathered between 2001 and 2006 from 30 green schools built in ten states revealed the cost per square foot for green design was $4 more than conventional design, while the operating benefits of green design realized approximately $68 per square foot in savings. Thus, green schools cost less than 2% more than conventional schools but provide financial benefits that are 20 times as large. And yet, like Tom and Angela, principals who are experimenting with green school leadership practices too often struggle with the limitations of their current school facilities and situations. Imagine if they enjoyed all that is possible in green design and sustainable district management practices. Let's consider the prospects.

When Green School Leadership Takes Hold in Our Schools

You leave your car or the bus, park your bike, or just walk down the sidewalk. The building stands before you, big as life. You pass under a canopy of photovoltaic panels that shade you and produce energy for the school you are about to enter. A marquee out front celebrates student achievements and announces upcoming events. You know things about this place without being told. Whether you are in a city, the suburbs, or a rural area, you know students come to this place each morning, Monday through Friday. Once inside, they find their way to certain classrooms, to their assigned chairs and, when there, to the matters at hand. Each day, students join the hidden rhythms of their school building, the hubbub of energy, and the spirit of school as place.

You may be a teacher yourself or a principal of your own school. You may sit on your community's school board or be the superintendent of a district with numbers of schools to manage. Even if you've never worked inside a school, there is much you remember from your own days as a student. And yet, this school is different; it is a green school.

You notice a plaque at the side of the front door that indicates this building is LEED certified, indicating that it met the USGBC's high standards for green building design. As you enter, you find a lobby with comfortable and inviting benches, live plants, and an abundance of natural light from skylights overhead. The lobby serves as the hub of classrooms, the library, and even an auditorium. It feels welcoming and fresh, hinting at new possibilities for learning. The principal's office sits across the lobby behind a glass wall. This is your first stop on the way inside, your point of entry. One wall holds a rack of mail slots, each with a different person's name beneath it. Below is a conveniently located recycling bin to catch the unwanted paper. There is a counter to speak over, and behind it are desks where a secretary or secretaries answer phones and greet people as they arrive. Behind them is a door with the principal's name on a small plaque.

The activity around you holds your attention. Children and adults come and go in a fairly steady stream. After several moments, you sign in on a visitors' roster. A secretary gives you a clip-on visitor's badge and points you in the right direction. The hallway is wider than one might expect. Here and there classroom doors stand open, and students spill out to work in small groups on comfortable benches that line the hallway walls. The doors and spaces around the doors appear to be used as extensions of the learning space. Content-area posters and student-created artwork related to topics studied in various classrooms are prominently displayed. You take note of the distance from one door to the next and notice that the wall is different in this section of the hallway. The wall is clear, Plexiglas maybe, and you can see the pipes and wires that are typically hidden. A sign explains the flow of water and energy through the building. Right now you can hear the sound of your shoes on the tile floor. You stop at one of the open doors and poke your head inside. A student comes to welcome you in.

The room is large, rectangular in shape, and has eye-level windows along one wall. You see shelves and a number of tables, but no individual desks. There are multiple groups of students talking with each other, but the room is not loud; the room's acoustical design supports engaged learning by absorbing rather than magnifying the noise. The room is also rich with technology. Groups of students sit at the tables with laptop computers. An electronic white board is mounted on the front wall. The board is surrounded by another group of students, with the teacher leading exploration of their local watershed. The students will engage in studying their watershed across the content areas, with opportunities to learn about present and historic land use and water quality through research, field trips, and data collection. They are developing a state of the watershed report for their local watershed board. At the time you enter, all the people in the room are busy.

You choose a suitable time to move on. As you walk along, you notice that the building is well maintained. The floors and windows shine. Beside you, a student stoops to pick up stray papers from the hallway floor, depositing them in a recycle bin before moving on. You stop in the restroom and notice this space is also very clean; it smells fresh without a hint of air freshener or strong chemicals. There are educational signs explaining water saving strategies by the toilets and sink. Users have the option of an energy efficient hand dryer or paper towels made of recycled paper; the paper towels will be composted as explained by the sign. The extra trashcan collects non-compostable trash.

Back in the hallway, the air in the building is also fresh and devoid of noxious odors. You notice that, in many classrooms, windows stand open. You imagine teachers, like most of us, value their ability to open windows to allow the circulation of fresh air. In crowded classrooms with poor air circulation, it does not take long for carbon dioxide levels to increase and students' attention to wander. An abundance of natural light also streams in through these windows. In addition, three large skylights open the hallway ceiling at intersections where grade-level wings diverge from the central hallway.

For some students it's lunchtime. They move toward the cafeteria and you follow. The dining area features a long wall of glass that provides a full view of green open space including athletic fields, play areas, and gardens. The cafeteria is thoughtfully designed to promote healthy food choices. The salad bar features vegetables grown locally and even in the school's garden. Students are quick to choose these delicious vegetables before they're gone. They have participated in their planting and care; they know where this food came from. The main dishes for the day are not the hot dogs and tater tots you might remember; this food is minimally processed and attractively presented. Healthy school lunches are a key ingredient to student success.

The building is flanked by parking lots and playgrounds, and, if it happens to be a secondary school, by athletic fields and bleachers. The degree to which schoolyards offer opportunities for students to learn and play within natural surroundings depends in part on geography. This school's property is a vital feature of their learning community. The space invites learning and benefits from the learning. For example, a few years ago the students noticed that a play area would flood and stay wet long after the rains had left, restricting their play. As part of their learning about watersheds, they discovered strategies for better managing the water flow that was impeding their play and providing a haven for mosquito larvae. They designed and built a beautiful rain garden featuring native plants, with guidance from a community partner. Community members now come to workshops on the school property to learn how to do the same in their yards.

It is coming time for you to leave. Your own concerns take you out and away. Your time here was well spent. When you arrived you carried with you certain ideas about what you thought you would find or should find. While here, you've learned some things and now leave, changed by the experience. As you move back through the town or the city that is home to this school, retracing your earlier course, you are reminded that schools are continuous with their larger communities. From the individual school building, up through the various levels of school district structure, out into the local community and beyond to the state and the nation, schools and their constituents expect from and depend upon each other. Communities entrust the schools with their future. School entrusts communities with theirs. Their lives and their livelihoods are interdependent now and as they move into the future unknown.

Conclusion

We build to accommodate ourselves, but we also build beyond ourselves, casting backward and reaching forward in time. Dewey wrote that "architecture ... expresses ... enduring values of collective human life" (Dewey, 1989b, p. 225). And yet, in discussions of capital outlay and school facility planning, too many communities lack the resources, or the will, to move beyond the tough-minded concerns of budgets and bottom lines. Ideas of comfort, beauty, and imagination are often regarded as esoteric and expensive. Still, if we wish our schools to be centers of excellence and to support community values, locally and globally, perhaps it is time to seek a more future-focused balance. Perhaps school leaders should engage in a dialogue about quality that reaches beyond the parameters of isolated local communities, teaching each other about the challenges and benefits of going green on behalf of the students, families, and communities they serve.

According to Taylor (2009), "the ideal educational environment is a carefully designed physical location composed of natural, built, and cultural parts that work together to accommodate active learning across body, mind, and spirit" (Taylor, 2009, p. 31). When schools, as significant places in students' lives, reflect sustainable design principles, they become rich, varied, and dynamic learning environments within which students gain a sense of agency as local and global citizens who can make a difference for their own and each other's futures. Further, these green schools are "ideal place[s] to plant an idea that is meant to propagate throughout a community" (Gelfand, 2010, p. 7). And so, students, through their physical engagement with the environmental features of their school—vegetable gardens, demonstration kitchens, compost piles, energy system monitors, ponds—model responsibility, stewardship, and active engagement in learning.

They derive meaning and purpose from these carefully conceived spaces and gain confidence in teaching others about the important discoveries they make.

Questions for Discussion

1. Reflect on the following questions regarding your school building:

   ◆ What spaces/places on my school campus make my students feel like they belong?
   ◆ Where do my students go when they need to concentrate?
   ◆ Which space(s) are their favorite places to learn with classmates?

Ask a sample of students at your school to answer these questions for themselves. How do your answers compare?

2. Ask your teachers to describe the learning activities they have planned for an upcoming day in terms of the physical features of the learning environment they will utilize. Record the conversations. What do you learn from these conversations?

3. Make a list of ten ways your school building serves the best interest of the students who attend. List ten ways it fails to do so. Over which aspects of these conditions/features do you have control? Develop and implement a plan for improving at least one, if not all, of these conditions/features for which you have control.

Note

1 According to national estimates, 21% of U.S. schools are more than 50 years old and another 50% are at least 30 years old, requiring a total of $127 billion dollars in new construction and retro-fitting (Office of Education Research and Improvement, 2000). A National Education Association (NEA) study placed the need at more than double these estimates, bringing the cost of modernizing America's schools to $268 billion. Add to this $52 billion for technology needs and the total surges to $322 billion (National Education Association, 2000).

References

Arsen, D., & Davis, T. (2006). Taj Mahals or decaying shacks: Patterns in local school capital stock and unmet capital need. *Peabody Journal of Education, 81*(4), 1–22.

Baker, L., & Bernstein, H. (2012). *The impact of school buildings on student health and performance*. Washington, DC: McGraw-Hill Research Foundation and The Center for Green Schools.

Barrett, P., Davies, F., Zhang, Y., & Barrett, L. (2015). The impact of classroom design on pupils' learning: Final results of a holistic, multi-level analysis. *Building and Environment, 89*, 118–133.

Barrett, P., & Zhang, Y. (2009). *Optimal learning spaces: Design implications for primary schools* (SCRI Report No. 2). Salford: SCRI.

Barrett, P., Zhang, Y., Moffat, J., & Kobbacy, K. (2013). A holistic, multi-level analysis identifying the impact of classroom design on pupil learning. *Building and Environment, 59*, 678–689.

Berg, F. S., Blair, J. C., & Benson, P. V. (1996). Classroom acoustics: The problem, impact, and solution. *Language, Speech, and Hearing Services in Schools, 27,*16–20. doi:10.1044/0161-1461.2701.16

Berner, M. M. (1993). Building conditions, parental involvement, and student achievement in the District of Columbia Public School System. *Urban Education,* 28 (1), 6–29.

Bowers, J. H., & Burkett, C. W. (1988). Physical environment influences related to student achievement, health, attendance and behavior. *Council of Educational Facility Planners Journal, 26,* 33–34.

Bradlow, A. R., Krauss, N., & Hayes, E. (2003). Speaking clearly for students with learning disabilities: Sentence perception in noise. *Journal of Speech, Language, and Hearing Research, 46,* 80–97.

Buckley, J., Schneider, M., & Shang, Y. (2004). *The effects of school facility quality on teacher retention in urban school districts.* Washington, DC: National Clearinghouse for Educational Facilities. Retrieved from: http://www.edfacilities.org/pubs/teacherretention.htm

Building Education Success Together. (2006). *Growth and disparity: A decade of US public school construction.* Washington, DC: Building Education Success Together (BEST).

Buttimer, A. (1980). Home, reach and sense of place. In A. Buttimer & D. Seamon (Eds.), *The human experience of space and place* (pp. 73–85). London: Croom Helm.

Cash, C. S. (1993). *Building condition and student achievement and behavior.* Unpublished dissertation, Virginia Polytechnic Institute and State University, Blacksburg, VA.

Chan, T. C. (1979). *The impact of school building age on the achievement of eighth-grade pupils from the public schools in the State of Georgia.* Unpublished dissertation, University of Georgia, Athens, GA.

Cole, L. B. (2013). *The teaching green school building: Exploring the contributions of school design to informal environmental education.* Unpublished dissertation, University of Michigan, Ann Arbor, MI.

Coley, P. A., & Greeves, R. (2004). *The effects of low ventilation rates on the cognitive function of a primary school class* (Report R102 for DfES). Exeter, UK: Exeter University.

Collaborative for High Performance Schools (CHPS). (n.d.). Website. Retrieved from: http://www.chps.net/dev/Drupal/node

Crampton, F. (2009). Spending on school infrastructure: Does money matter? *Journal of Educational Administration, 47*(3), 305–322. doi: 10.1108/09578230910955755

Dewey, J. (1989a). Dewey outlines utopian schools. In J. Boyston (Ed.), *Volume IX: The Later Works 1925–1952* (pp. 136–140). Carbondale & Edwardsville: Southern Illinois University Press (First Published 1935).

Dewey, J. (1989b). Art as experience. In J. Boyston (Ed.), *Volume X: The Later Works 1925–1952* (p. 225). Carbondale & Edwardsville: Southern Illinois University Press.

Earthman, G. I. (2004). *Prioritization of 31 criteria for school building adequacy.* Baltimore, MD: American Civil Liberties Union Foundation of Maryland.

Earthman, G. I., & Lemasters, L. (1996, October). *Review of the research on the relationship between school buildings, student achievement, and student behavior.* Paper presented at the annual conference of the Council of Educational Facility Planners International, Tarpon, FL.

Earthman, G. I., & Lemasters, L. (1998, February). *Where children learn: A discussion of how a facility affects learning*. Paper presented at the annual meeting of Virginia Educational Facility Planners, Blacksburg, VA.

Earthman, G. I., & Lemasters, L. (2009). Teacher attitudes about classroom conditions. *Journal of Educational Administration, 47*(3), 323–335.

Edwards, B. W. (2006). Environmental design and educational performance. *Research in Education, 76*, 14–32.

Elliot, L., Conners, S., Kille, E., Levin, S., Ball, K., & Katz, D. (1979). Children's understanding of monosyllabic nouns in quiet and in noise. *Journal of the Acoustical Society of America, 66*, 12–21.

Evans, G. W., & Maxwell, L. (1997). Chronic noise exposure and reading deficits: The mediating effects of language acquisition. *Environment and Behavior, 29*(5), 638–656.

Feth, L., & Whitelaw, G. (1999). *Many classrooms have bad acoustics that inhibit learning*. Columbus, OH: Ohio State.

Filardo, M. (2016). *State of our schools: America's K–12 facilities 2016*. Washington, DC: 21st Century School Fund, U.S. Green Building Council, Inc., & the National Council on School Facilities.

Finitzo-Hieber, T., & Tillman, T. W. (1978). Room acoustics effects on monosyllabic word discrimination ability for normal and hearing-impaired children. *Journal of Speech and Hearing Research, 21*, 440–458.

Fjortoft, I. (2004). Landscape as playscape: The effects of natural environments on children's play and motor development. *Children, Youth and Environments, 14*(2), 21–44.

Fuller, B., Dauter, L., Hosek, A., Kirschenbaum, G., McKoy, G., Rigby, J., & Vincent, J. M. (2009). Building schools, rethinking quality? Early lessons from Los Angeles. *Journal of Educational Administration, 47*(3), 336–349

Gelfand, L. (2010). *Sustainable school architecture*. Hoboken, NJ: John Wiley & Sons, Inc.

Genevro, R. (1992). Introduction. In The Architectural League of New York (Ed.), *New schools for New York: Plans and precedents for small schools* (p. 10). New York: Princeton University Press.

Gump, P. V. (1978). School environments. In I. Altman & J. F. Wohlwill (Eds.), *Children and the environment* (pp. 131–174). New York: Plenum Press.

Haines, M. M., Stansfeld, S. A., Job, R. F. S., Berglund, B., & Head, J. (2001). Chronic aircraft noise exposure, stress responses, mental health and cognitive performance in school children. *Psychological Medicine, 31*, 265–277.

Hart, R. (1979). *Children's experience of place*. New York: Irvington.

Hathaway W. E. (1995). Effects of school lighting on physical development and school performance. *The Journal of Educational Research, 88*, 228–242.

Haverinen-Shaughnessy, U., & Shaughnessy, R. J. (2015). Effects of classroom ventilation rate and temperature on students' test scores. *PLoS ONE, 10*(8): e0136165. doi:10.1371/journal.pone.0136165

Heschong Mahone Group. (1999). *Daylighting in schools: An investigation into the relationship between daylighting and human performance.* Fair Oaks, CA: Heschong Mahone Group.

Heschong, L., & Mahone, D. (2003). *Daylighting in schools: Reanalysis report.* Sacramento, CA: California Energy Commission.

Higgins, S., Hall, E., Wall, K., Woolner, P., & McCaughey, C. (2005). *The impact of school environments: A literature review.* London: Design Council.

Hines, E. W. (1996). *Building condition and student achievement and behavior.* Unpublished dissertation, Virginia Polytechnic Institute and State University, Blacksburg, VA.

Horng, E. L. (2009). Teacher tradeoffs: Disentangling teachers' preferences for working conditions and student demographics. *American Educational Research Journal, 46*(3), 690–717.

Hygge, S., Evans, G. W., & Bullinger ,M. (2002). A prospective study of some effects of aircraft noise on cognitive performance in school children. *Psychological Science, 13,* 469–474.

Izadpanahi, P., Elkadi, H., & Tucker, R. (2015). Greenhouse effect: The relationship between the sustainable design of schools and children's environmental attitudes. *Environmental Education Research.* Retrieved from: http://dx.doi.org/10.1080/13504622.2015.1072137

Jorgensen, B., & Stedman, R. (2001). Sense of place as an attachment, Lakeshore owners attitudes toward their properties. *Journal of Environmental Psychology, 21,* 233–248.

Kats, G. (2006). *Greening America's schools: Costs and benefits.* Retrieved from: www.usgbc.org/showfile.aspx?Document ID—2908

Klatte, M., Hellbrück, J., Seidel, J., & Leistner P.(2010). Effects of classroom acoustics on performance and well-being in elementary school children: A field study. *Environment and Behavior, 42,* 659–692, doi:10.1177/0013916509336813

Knecht, H. A., Nelson, P. B., Whitelaw, G. M., & Feth, L. L. (2002). Background noise levels and reverberation times in unoccupied classrooms predictions and measurements. *American Journal of Audiology, 11,* 65–71.

Knez, I. (2005). Attachment and identity as related to a place and its perceived climate. *Journal of Environmental Psychology, 25,* 207–218.

Kuller, R., & Lindsten, C. (1992). Health and behavior of children in classrooms with and without windows. *Journal of Environmental Psychology, 12,* 305–317.

Kuo, F. E., & Faber Taylor, A. (2004). A potential natural treatment for Attention-Deficit/Hyperactivity Disorder: Evidence from a national study. *American Journal of Public Health, 94*(9), 1580–1586.

Lanham, J. W. (1999). *Relating building and classroom conditions to student achievement in Virginia's elementary schools.* Unpublished PhD thesis, Virginia Polytechnic Institute and State University, Blacksburg, VA.

Lemasters, L. K. (1997). *A synthesis of studies pertaining to facilities, student achievement, and student behavior.* Unpublished dissertation, Virginia Polytechnic Institute and State University, Blacksburg, VA.

Lindholm, G (1995). Schoolyards: The significance of place properties to outdoor activities in schools. *Environment and Behaviour, 27,* 259–293.

Louv, R. (2005). *Last child in the woods: Saving our children form nature deficit disorder.* New York: Workman Publishing Company, Inc.

Lowe, J. (1990). *The interface between educational facilities and learning climate in three elementary schools.* Unpublished dissertation. Texas A & M University, College Station, TX.

LPA, Inc. (2009). *Green school primer.* Victoria, Australia: The Images Publishing Group.

Maxwell, L. (1999). *School renovation and student performance: One district's experience.* Scottsdale, AZ: Council for Educational Facility Planners International.

Maxwell, L. E., & Evans, G. W. (2000). The effects of noise on pre-school children's pre-reading skills. *Journal of Environmental Psychology, 20,* 91–97.

Mayron, L. W., Ott, J., Nations, R., & Mayron, E. L. (1974). Light, radiation and academic behavior. *Academic Therapy, 10*(1), 33–47.

McGuffey, C. W., & Brown, C. L. (1978). The impact of school building age on school achievement in Georgia. *Council of Educational Facility Planners Journal, 16,* 6–9.

Mead, S. (2005). Schooling's crumbling infrastructure: Addressing a serious and underappreciated problem. *Education Week.* Retrieved from: http://www.edweek.org/ew/articles/2005/06/15/40mead.h24.html

Nábělek, A., & Donahue, A. (1984). Perception of consonants in reverberation by native and non-native listeners. *Journal of Acoustical Society of America, 75,* 632–634.

Nábělek, A. K., & Pickett J. M. (1974). Reception of consonants in a classroom as affected by monaural and binaural listening, noise, reverberation, and hearing aids. *Journal of Acoustical Society of America, 56,* 628–639.

National Education Association. (2000). *Modernizing our schools: What will it cost?* Washington, DC: National Education Association.

National Research Council. (2007). *Green schools: Attributes for health and learning.* Washington, DC: The National Academies Press.

Noddings, N. (2006). *Critical lessons: What our schools should teach.* New York: Cambridge University Press.

Noddings, N. (2013). *Education and democracy in the 21st century.* New York: Teachers College Press.

Office of Education Research and Improvement. (2000, June). *Condition of America's public school facilities: 1999.* Washington, DC: U.S. Department of Education.

O'Neill, D. (2000). *The impact of school facilities on student achievement, behavior, attendance, and teacher turnover rate at selected Texas middle schools in Region XIII ESC.* Unpublished dissertation, Texas A & M University, College Station, TX.

Phillips, R. W. (1997). *Educational facility age and the academic achievement and attendance of upper elementary school students.* Unpublished dissertation, University of Georgia, Athens, GA.

Plumley, J. P. (1978). *The impact of school building age on the academic achievement of pupils from selected schools in the State of Georgia.* Unpublished dissertation, University of Georgia, Athens, GA.

Rainwater, B., & Hartke, J. (2011). *Local Leaders in Sustainability—special report for Sundance, a national action plan for greening America's schools.* Washington, DC: U.S. Green Building Council, Inc. and The American Institute of Architects.

Rivlin, L. G., & Weinstein, C. S. (1995). Educational issues, school settings, and environmental psychology. In D. Canter (Ed.), *Readings in environmental psychology: The children's environment* (pp. 243–260). London: Academic Press.

Sato, H., & Bradley, J. S. (2008). Evaluation of acoustical conditions for speech communication in working elementary school classrooms. *The Journal of the Acoustical Society of America, 123*(4), 2064.

Schneider, M. (2002). *Do school facilities affect academic outcomes?* National Clearinghouse for Educational Facilities. Retrieved from: http://www.edfacilities.org/pubs/outcomes.pdf

Schneider, M. (2003). *Linking school facility conditions to teacher satisfaction and success.* National Clearinghouse for Educational Facilities. Retreived from: http://www.edfacilities.org/pubs/teachersurvey.pdf

Seibold-Bultman, U. (2007). What sustainability looks like: Green architecture as an aesthetic proposition. *Interdisciplinary Science Review, 32,* 3–6.

Shendell, D. G., Prill, R., Fisk, W. J., Apte, M. G., Blake, O., & Faulkner, D. (2004). Associations between classrooms' CO_2 concentrations and student attendance in Washington and Idaho. *Indoor Air, 14,* 333–431.

Smedje, G., & Norback, D. (2000). New ventilation systems at select schools in Sweden: Effects on asthma and exposure. *Architecture Environmental Health, 1,* 18–25.

Tanner, C. K. (2008). Explaining relationships of student outcomes and the school's physical environment. *Journal of Advanced Academics, 19*(3), 444–471.

Tanner, C. K. (2009). Effects of school design on student outcomes. *Journal of Educational Administration, 47*(3), 381–400. doi:10.1108/09578230910955809

Tanner, C. K., & Lackney, J. A. (2006). The physical environment and student achievement in elementary schools. In C. K. Tanner & J. A. Lackney, *Educational facilities planning: Leadership, architecture, and management* (pp. 266–294). Boston, MA: Pearson Education, Inc.

Taylor, A. (2009). *Linking architecture and education: Sustainable design of learning environments.* Albuquerque: University of New Mexico Press.

Tuan, Y. F. (1980). Rootedness versus sense of place. *Landscape, 24,* 3–8.

Turunen, M., Toyinbo, O., Putus, T., Nevalainen, A., Shaughnessy, R., & Haverinen-Shaughnessy, U. (2014). Indoor environmental quality in school buildings, and the health and wellbeing of students. *International Journal of Hygiene and Environmental Health, 217,* 733–739.

Uline, C. L. (2000). Decent facilities and learning: Thirman L. Milner Elementary School and beyond. *Teacher College Record, 102,* 444–462.

Uline, C. L., Tschannen-Moran, M., & Wolsey, T. D. (2009). The walls still speak: The stories occupants tell. *Journal of Educational Administration, 47*(3), 400–426. doi:10.1108/09578230910955818

Uline, C. L., Wolsey, T. D., Tschannen-Moran, M., & Lin, C. (2010). Improving the physical and social environment of school: A question of equity. *The Journal of School Leadership, 20,* 597–632.

Ulrich, R. S. (1984). View through a window may influence recovery from cancer. *Science, 224,* 420–423.

USGBC. (n.d.). Website. Retrieved from: http://www.usgbc.org/

Wang, D., Federspiel, C. C., & Arens, E. (2005). Correlation between temperature satisfaction and unsolicited complaint rates in commercial buildings. *Indoor Air, 15,* 13–18.

Wargocki, P., & Wyon, D. (2007). The effects of moderately raised classroom temperatures and classroom ventilation rate on the performance of schoolwork by children. *HVAC&R Research, 13,* 193–220.

Woolner, P., Hall, E., Higgins, S., McCaughey, C., & Wall, K. (2007). A sound foundation? What we know about the impact of environments on learning and the implications for Building Schools for the Future. *Oxford Review of Education, 33*(1), 47–70.

Wurtman, R. J. (1975). The effects of light on the human body. *Scientific American, 233*(1), 68–77.

Wyon, D. P. (2004). The effects of indoor air quality on performance and productivity. *Indoor Air, 14,* 92–101.

Wyon, D. P., & Wargocki, P. (2007). *Indoor environmental effects on the performance of school work by children* (1257-TRP). ASHRAE.

Zarghami, E., & Fatourechi, D. (2015). Impact of sustainable school design on primary school children's mental health and well-being. *International Journal of Advances in Agricultural and Environmental Engineering, 2,* 31–38.

7

Operations and Maintenance for Whole School Sustainability

It makes good business sense for school divisions to take a holistic approach to sustainability initiatives. If a school division can significantly reduce its operation and maintenance budget, improve student and staff health, and improve test scores while preparing students to face the complexities of the 21st century, we should be promoting that news at every opportunity. All it takes is a willingness to think big, start small, and act now.

(Tim Cole, Sustainability Officer,
Virginia Beach City Public Schools, 2015, p. 34)

We build schools to human dimensions: a body's length, width, and mass, with considerations for perceiving space and moving through it, for how we reach, sit, walk and interact. For example, the average person takes up 1 foot, 8 inches of space when standing and 2 feet, 5½ inches when sitting. On average, three people standing together occupy 5 feet, 7 inches of space, while one person in a wheelchair may require up to 6½ feet. Add to these dimensions the distance covered by an outstretched arm, the length of a stride, the momentum accomplished with each turn of a wheelchair's wheels. How we engineer the shape of a room, the width of a hallway, the rise of a ramp, are determined by human dimensions. These understandings of the body's structures and functions direct our plans for enclosing the spaces we inhabit. This is to say, we build our schools around ourselves. We would not think to build to dimensions outside our physical nature. For reasons of safety and efficiency, ease of motion and accessibility, we require a fit (Uline, 2000).

Increasingly, we are coming to understand that buildings must also be constructed in ways that accommodate and sustain the structures and functions of the natural world. Just as we would not think to build to dimensions outside our own physical nature as human beings, we are beginning to grasp the foolhardiness of building without consideration for an environmental fit. Concerns for the long-term environmental impact of traditional construction have building owners looking to more sustainable options. In a recent study of the economic contributions of green and Leadership in Energy and Environmental Design (LEED) building construction to the U.S. gross domestic product (GDP), jobs, labor earnings, individual states' tax contributions, and environmental indicators at the national and state levels, the U.S. Green Building Council (USGBC) discovered that green building construction growth currently outpaces general construction. Data sources from the 2015 Dodge Construction Outlook report, which provides the forecast of U.S. construction starts, further demonstrated that green building construction growth will continue to do so through 2018, with annual green construction spending expected to grow 15.1% year over year (YoY) for 2015–2018, increasing from $150.6 billion in 2015 to $224.4 billion in 2018 (Hamilton, 2015).

Likewise, McGraw-Hill Construction's 2013 Education Green Building Smart Market Report estimated that 45% of the 2012 total construction starts in the education sector were green. Over 80% of the K–12 schools surveyed had conducted at least some green retrofits and operational improvements, and the percentage of those doing over 90% of these green improvements was expected to grow to just under one-third by 2015 (McGraw-Hill Construction, 2013).

Just as schools are built to human dimensions, and, in the case of green schools, in accordance with the dimensions and dynamics of the surrounding ecosystem, they are also built to particular structural, mechanical, and technical specifications. Building codes are the rules that regulate capacity and specify materials. Codes establish requirements for building structure, fenestration size/locations, egress, heating, ventilation, plumbing, sewage, lights, alarms, site drainage, and storage. These rules exist for reasons of health, safety, and general welfare. They are the application of knowledge born of observation, experience, testing, and consensus. Yet, in their recent State of Our Schools report, the Center for Green Schools estimates it will take approximately $271 billion to bring school buildings in the United States up to working order and into compliance with current building codes (Center for Green Schools, 2013). In failing to keep the best interest of our children at the center of our public consciousness, we dismiss these rules as overly burdensome, continuing a cycle of minimum commitment.

According to the U.S. General Accounting Office, upwards to 14 million students attend schools considered to be substandard or even dangerous, with close to two-thirds of school building features deemed in need of extensive repair or replacement (U.S. General Accounting Office, 1995). As a nation, we have allowed too many of our schools to fall into a state of disrepair we would not accept in the places where we work, eat, recreate, or shop. We justify the violation of basic health and safety codes, because the doors must be ready to open on Monday morning.

In 2007, the National Center for Educational Statistics reported nearly 44% of principals were displeased with their school facility's condition and perceived that deficiencies were interfering with instruction (Chaney & Lewis, 2007). Too often, chronic funding shortages place building maintenance and repairs low on the list of school district priorities, resulting in the degradation of basic heating, ventilation, lighting systems (Kats, 2006), particularly in schools serving high concentrations of low-income students (National Center for Education Statistics, 1995). A recent study by UC Berkeley's Center for Cities and Schools found that between 2008 and 2012, more than half of California districts failed to meet industry benchmarks for spending on capital renewals and more than 60% failed to meet the benchmark for basic operations and maintenance (Vincent & Jain, 2015a). Districts serving low-income students disproportionately drew more from general operating funds for operations and maintenance than districts serving higher income students, leaving fewer dollars for education programs. "Overall, these findings suggest that many districts—particularly those serving high-need students—risk grossly underfunded facilities budgets, deteriorating schools, and declining educational outcomes" (Vincent & Jain, 2015b, p. 2). Recent data reveal similarly disturbing inequities in facility funding across districts nationally (Filardo, 2016).

As demonstrated in Chapter 6, poor indoor environmental conditions, including inadequate and poor-quality lighting, excessive noise, poor indoor air quality, dampness, surface contamination, and inadequate ventilation impact the health of teachers and students, adversely affecting classroom instruction and hindering learning (National Research Council, 2007). Further, research suggests that physical disorder and neglect is significantly related to a climate of social disorder within schools, as these conditions can invoke fear among students and erode a school's sense of collective efficacy (Plank, Bradshaw, & Young, 2009). On the other hand, data also suggest that as school buildings move from poor to fair, average achievement scores can be expected to increase by 5.455 points, while improvement from poor to excellent results in a 10.9 point increase (Berner, 1993). Even in the face of this compelling evidence, too often we choose shortsighted and miserly habits of mind, policy, and practice, undermining our efforts to close achievement gaps and improve the life chances of our nation's children.

As we seek to address the needs of students and communities in the 21st century, we have the opportunity to reverse this trend, sharpening our focus on the human dimensions of school life and increasing our understanding of interdependencies between human and natural/nonhuman dimensions. As we learn to articulate the benefits, indeed the necessity, of such an enlarged perspective, we may just muster the public will to meet existing codes and even exceed these minimum requirements, providing high-quality, sustainable learning environments for all our children, regardless of their socio-economic status. Such schools not only improve the life chances of our children, but also of our planet.

In this chapter we explore how the practical functions of operating and managing school facilities take on new meaning as we acknowledge their importance in ensuring the well-being of children and the well-being of the planet. First, we underscore the needs of the whole child, reminding ourselves of the role the physical learning environment plays in students' physical, social, emotional, and cognitive well-being. We then examine how sustainability-focused principals, in concert with their facilities colleagues, manage healthy, safe, and sustainable learning environments in ways that reduce energy, conserve natural resources, and minimize waste. We consider how these green operations and maintenance routines provide opportunities for leveraging the three-dimensional textbook (Taylor, 2009) we inhabit day-to-day. Finally, we remind ourselves of the case we must build together as green leaders, convincing our publics of the benefits inherent within green schools, benefits for our children, our planet, *and* our bottom line.

Whole Child-Focused Building Management

In recent years, educators and health professionals have acknowledged the need for a unified approach to school health and child well-being, one that promotes greater alignment between health and educational outcomes (Lewallen, Hunt, Potts-Datema, Zaza, & Giles, 2015). For the past decades, these professionals have worked somewhat in isolation from one another. In 1987, the U.S. Centers for Disease Control and Prevention (CDC) implemented a systems approach to health promotion and disease prevention in schools through the Comprehensive School Health Program, a Coordinated School Health (CSH) approach widely accepted by the health community but not necessarily known or embraced by educators at the school level. Twenty years later, the Association for Supervision and Curriculum Development (ASCD) launched the Commission on the Whole Child, challenging educators to look beyond narrow definitions of school success in order to ensure that all students enjoy good health and feel supported, challenged, engaged, and safe at school (ASCD, 2007).

During spring 2013, the ASCD and the CDC convened a panel of experts from the fields of education and health to explore lessons learned from implementation of CSH and Whole Child approaches and to consider joint development of a new model that would incorporate the knowledge gained from these efforts (Lewallen et. al., 2015). The Whole School, Whole Community, Whole Child (WSCC) approach resulted from this collaboration, combining and extending the elements of the Whole Child model and the CSH approach to create a unified model that supports a systematic, integrated, collaborative approach to student health and learning. According to the authors, "[t]he WSCC model is an ecological approach that is directed at the whole school, with the school in turn drawing its resources and influences from the whole community and serving to address the needs of the whole child" (ASCD & CDC, 2014, p. 6).

Healthy, safe, engaged, supported, challenged students sit at the center of the WSCC model. Surrounding the whole child is the socioecological system of school and community, although natural ecosystems do not explicitly appear in the model or the model description. The model includes ten school health components: physical education and physical activity; nutrition environment and services; health services; counseling, psychological, and social services; social and emotional climate; physical environment; employee wellness; family engagement; community involvement; and health education (ASCD & CDC, 2014). Unlike the earlier Whole Child model and CSH approach, the WSCC includes a separate component dedicated to the physical environment, thus encouraging greater attention to the concerns discussed within this chapter. According to the WSCC model:

> The physical school environment encompasses the school building and its contents, the land on which the school is located, and the area surrounding it. A healthy school environment will address a school's physical condition during normal operation as well as during renovation (including ventilation, moisture, temperature, noise, or natural and artificial lighting), and protect occupants from physical threats (such as crime, violence, traffic, or injuries) and biological and chemical agents in the air, water, or soil as well as those purposefully brought into the school (including pollution, mold, hazardous materials, pesticides, or cleaning agents). (Lewallen et al., 2015, p. 733)

This deliberate attention to the management of physical learning environments is too often missing from discussions about learning and teaching. By underscoring the importance of the physical school environment in meeting the needs of the whole child, the WSCC model elevates the role of green school leaders (be they principals, custodians, plant managers, or district shop foremen), emphasizing the necessary functions and responsibilities associated with providing a healthy and safe learning environment.

In their efforts to grow as green school leaders, Angela and Tom sought counsel with key members of their school district's operations and maintenance department. They were interested to investigate ways they might increase the health of their school buildings, and, at the same time, decrease their schools' carbon footprints. They wanted to learn more about the district's efforts toward these ends. This knowledge would serve as foundation for the establishment of school-level Green Teams, with teachers, students, and parents assuming leadership roles in implementing changes to organizational habits. They knew of teachers already motivated to take the reins, yet they also knew the operations and maintenance department would need to embrace any efforts they might pursue. Inviting these experts to the table would build capacity for informed decisions, as well as organizational support for future actions. Tom shared his impressions of their first meeting with district shop foremen.

> The operations and maintenance folks were so excited to be a part of the process. Some of these gentlemen have been here for 40 years and their dads had worked here before them. They went to these schools, and so they're truly invested in the community. They're craftsmen. We have nine different shops led by nine different foremen who possess actual specialty trades. This represents an enormous store of knowledge to bring to the table, and nobody had ever asked.

In order to manage the school facility in ways that meet the needs of the whole child, we must draw upon resources and influences from the whole school and the whole community (ASDC & CDC, 2014). We are wise to extend a heart-felt invitation, never underestimating the capacity, or the desire, of colleagues on the operations side of the house. Curriculum and instruction and operations and maintenance need not exist in separate silos. In fact, green schools provide a case in point for what happens when we link arms.

Maintaining Healthy, Safe, Sustainable Physical Learning Environments

In Chapter 4 you were introduced to a number of green schools around the globe where facilities professionals work in concert with their curriculum colleagues. In these schools, green school leaders build bridges between the historically divided curriculum and facilities sides of the academic house, leveraging the resulting combined expertise to manage physical learning environments in ways that enhance teachers' instructional effectiveness and improve students' well-being and academic outcomes. In addition, these schools become vital teaching tools, utilized to develop the necessary values, knowledge, dispositions, and agency that comprise a sustainability worldview (Nolet, 2016). Orr (1993) reminds us "the design, construction, and operation of buildings is a curriculum in applied ecology" (p. 27). He elaborates:

> Buildings can be designed to recycle organic waste through minia-ture ecosystems, which can be studied and maintained by the users. Buildings can be designed to heat and cool themselves using solar energy and natural air flows. They can be designed to inform the occu-pants of energy and resource use. They can be landscaped to provide shade, break winter winds, propagate rare plants, provide habitat for animals, and restore bits of vanishing ecosystems. Buildings and land-scapes, in other words, can extend our ecological imagination. (p. 227)

In igniting our collective imagination, we transform our thinking as it relates to school building operations and maintenance, replacing a laundry list of mundane tasks with an integrated plan for leveraging the three-dimensional textbook we inhabit day-to-day. Standard 9 of the new Professional Standards of Educational Leaders addresses the key responsibilities associated with the operations and management of schools. According to the standard, "effective educational leaders mange school operations and resources to promote each student's academic success and well-being." The elements of the standard most closely associated with school facilities management are as follows:

◆ Seek, acquire, and manage their fiscal, *physical*, and other resources to support curriculum, instruction, and assessment; student learning community; professional capacity and community; and family and community engagement;
◆ [Function as] responsible, ethical, and accountable stewards of the school's monetary and *non-monetary* resources;
◆ Employ technology to improve the quality and efficiency of operations and management; and
◆ Develop and maintain data and communication systems to deliver actionable information for classroom and school improvement.
(National Policy Board for Educational Administration, 2015, emphasis added)

Effective green school leaders understand the shared nature of this work. They know that they fulfill the elements of Standard 9 to the degree they collaborate with their facilities colleagues, extending the reach of these functions in ways that "help learners clarify their own roles and responsibilities with respect to sustainability-related issues and develop efficacy and agency to act on these responsibilities" (Nolet, 2016, p. 74). Student involvement in operations, "act as a catalyst for . . . discussions about sustainability and give students opportunities to try new, sustainable behaviors" (Higgs & McMillan, 2006, p. 45). In green schools, building operations and maintenance becomes a community affair.

Ensuring High Quality Indoor Air

In the recent McGraw-Hill Construction (2013) report mentioned above, 88% of K–12 respondents considered enhanced occupant health and well-being to be a primary catalyst for their greening efforts, roughly equivalent to energy use reductions and operating cost savings. Further, products and practices that improve indoor environmental quality (IEQ) were deemed essential to achieving this goal, with 87% of respondents ranking indoor air quality IAQ practices as highly important, the largest percentage for any green practice.

As noted in Chapter 6, integrated design decisions, combining operable windows with well-designed mechanical systems, ensure an abundance of fresh air within classrooms (National Research Council, 2007). Designers, well versed in sustainable practices, urge school leaders to "think simplicity, not high tech, . . . starting with windows that open and close" (LPA, Inc., 2009, p. 28). In earlier research, we learned that teachers highly valued influence and control over their physical settings, especially the ability to open windows and allow the circulation of fresh air (Uline, Tschannen-Moran, & Wolsey, 2009).

Careful placement of fresh air intakes also limits the intrusion of exhaust and other pollutants generated by motor vehicles and equipment that frequent school sites. Careful maintenance of ventilation pathways controls pollutants and moisture from incoming air. Angela and Tom's school district went a step further to control outdoor pollutants, replacing 14 buses past their 25–30 year lifecycle with compressed natural gas vehicles. They also adopted 5% biofuel for use in the fleet's older buses. The district transportation director acknowledged the necessity for educating the workforce:

> I remember, when compressed natural gas buses first came out, no one wanted to drive them. They thought they were a gas bomb going down the road. But with a few years of education, it's now it just part of life. Our fuel changeover to 5% biofuel is also going pretty well.

One of the obstacles we anticipate involves biofuel's cleaning capacity. It acts as a detergent for the engine and the pump. However, if you go higher than B5, it can really mess up the engine. It cleans too well! These are just things to keep an eye out for. I remember the days when I would come to work early in the morning and see this big blue cloud of smoke hanging over the transportation yard. You don't see that anymore. It's rather pleasant.

Green school guidelines call for the elimination of gas-fired pilot lights and discourage the use of fossil fuel burning equipment indoors. These practices reduce the potential accumulation of exhaust fumes and the development of combustion products and particulate matter (National Research Council, 2007). Guidelines also call for dedicated exhaust systems for spaces that might house chemicals, including cleaning equipment and supply storage areas, photography labs, copy/print rooms, and vocational spaces (National Research Council, 2007).

Even before school construction is completed and the building is occupied, dust and outgassing contaminants, introduced by conventional construction materials, influence IAQ in negative ways. Sustainably sourcing naturally made building materials, including flooring, acoustic ceiling tiles, insulation, signage, and wall paneling eliminates these contaminants. As construction progresses, daily high-efficiency particulate arrestance (HEPA) vacuuming of all soft surfaces, replacement of all filters at the completion of construction, and 28 days of continuous flushing of the building with outside air prior to occupancy are all proactive steps to maintaining clean indoor air (National Research Council, 2007).

To avoid long-term indoor air problems, green school leaders are establishing indoor health and safety programs (National Research Council, 2007). The U.S. Environmental Protection Agency (EPA) provides extensive resources to assist educational leaders in developing a plan for resolving current IAQ problems, preventing future IAQ problems, and maintaining good indoor air quality (http://www.epa.gov/iaq-schools). The IAQ Tools for Schools Action Kit outlines practical strategies for addressing indoor air problems at little or no cost. The kit includes best practices, industry guidelines, model policies, and a sample IAQ management plan. A complementary document, the *IAQ Reference Guide*, helps schools understand how IAQ problems develop, the importance of good IAQ, and its impact on building occupants. The guide's appendices offer detailed information on IAQ-related topics including: mold, radon, secondhand smoke, asthma, portable classrooms, basic measurement equipment, hiring professional assistance, codes and regulations, and integrated pest management. In addition, EPA's

IAQ Design Tools for Schools provides guidance for all phases of facilities planning and management, from preliminary design to ongoing operations and maintenance. The guide includes practical strategies for controlling pollutants; ensuring healthy and efficient heating, ventilating, and air conditioning (HVAC) systems; controlling moisture; commissioning building; renovating and repairing existing schools; and addressing the particular challenges associated with portable classrooms.

The Tools for Schools Action Kit includes a "Teacher's Classroom Checklist" that provides opportunity for engaging students in promotion of high-quality indoor air. Students might assist in completing the checklist, brainstorming strategies, and assuming appropriate levels of responsibility for maintaining general classroom cleanliness, managing animals in the classroom, reducing moisture sources, and taking other preventative actions to ensure healthy indoor air. Students might also examine construction materials within the classroom and sort by type: renewable, nonrenewable, recyclable, natural, man-made to learn more about their potential benefits and/or harm as it relates to IAQ (Taylor, 2009, p. 196).

Controlling Moisture

The building envelope physically separates the interior and exterior of a building and includes the foundation, walls, floors, roofs, fenestrations, and doors. Any building assembly exists in dynamic relation to its external environment (National Research Council, 2007). Thus, integrated decisions related to building siting, building design, and building materials increase our ability to control moisture. Building scientists conduct "source-path-driving force" analyses to determine the source of the moisture, the path it follows, and the force that drives the moisture along the pathway. "If a building designer is able to control at least one of the three elements in this chain, moisture can be effectively controlled. Controlling more than one element provides for valuable redundancy" (National Research Council, 2007, p. 46).

Certain construction materials, such as masonry walls, have the capacity to store moisture and then dry without harmful effects (National Research Council, 2007). Well-designed drainage systems and HVAC condensation drainage systems also prevent water accumulation. On the exterior of the building, eaves and roof overhangs direct rainwater away from building walls, while surrounding ground, sloped away from the building, carries runoff out from the walls and foundation (Freed, 2010).

Building operations and maintenance strategies also play a key role in avoiding moisture and diagnosing moisture sources when they occur. Keeping site irrigation to a minimum, using walk-off grills and mats to prevent rain and snow from entering the building, inspecting regularly for building leaks, and storing construction materials in dry and well-ventilated areas, all constitute sound moisture control strategies.

Keeping Things Clean in Safe and Healthy Ways

Traditional cleaning supplies adversely affect the environment, the occupants of schools, and, in particular, the people employed to clean them (Gelfand, 2010). To avoid these hazards, green school leadership teams increasingly choose environmentally responsible cleaning supplies and procedures. "Many states, school districts, and individual schools have voluntarily implemented green cleaning through mechanisms ranging from ad-hoc changes initiated at the school level, to school district policies, to state procurement approaches or technical assistance programs" (Arnold & Beardsley, 2015, p. 2). Since 2005, ten states, including Connecticut, Hawaii, Illinois, Iowa, Maine, Maryland, Missouri, Nevada, New York, Vermont, and the District of Columbia have enacted laws addressing green cleaning in schools. Recent findings suggest these laws have potential to raise awareness and encourage use of green cleaning products and practices in schools (Arnold & Beasley, 2015).

The Healthy Schools Network (www.healthyschools.org) offers guidance for these choices. Recommendations include the use of products that contain no probable or possible carcinogens; are nonirritating to skin and eyes; are nonreactive in combination; are not packaged in aerosol cans; are biodegradable; are suitable for multiple tasks to reduce container waste; are made with ingredients from renewable resources; are packaged in reusable and recyclable containers, to name a few.

Tom's school provides an apt example of green practice, implemented through collaboration between the district facilities department and Tom's school-level leadership team, including operations and maintenance professionals. During recent renovations to his school, the team decided to experiment with concrete polishing "as a green way of going." The school's existing hallway floor was concrete.

> It was poured many moons ago with the colors added. The floor was in pretty rough shape, but, when we polished it, the colors came up. The effect is pretty nice. We put a seal coating on it and now maintain it only with water. You don't use any detergents. You don't have to strip it. If you have to repair the floor, you rescrub, refinish, and move on.

As we learned in Chapter 6, a growing body of evidence demonstrates we act in the best interest of the whole child when we implement integrated design solutions that utilize ecologically sound mechanical and structural systems in our schools. We also know these mechanical and structural systems are influenced by occupant use over time *and* by operations, maintenance, repair, and cleaning practices (National Research Council, 2007, p. 3). We are wise to keep green design strategies simple and understandable (Edwards, 2006; Gelfand, 2010; LPA, Inc., 2009). In this way, facilities professionals can better teach principals, teachers, and students sustainable operations and maintenance practices and procedures that will save money and reduce a school's carbon footprint.

Operating Energy Efficient Schools

Along with energy efficient lighting, heating and cooling, and ventilation systems, green-minded siting and building orientation allow green school leaders to "[take] advantage of the site's free gifts" (LPA, Inc., 2009, p. 24). Such mindful building orientation practices allow for maximum use of natural daylighting and increased opportunities for natural ventilation via prevailing breezes (LPA, Inc., 2009). Green school leaders are also utilizing renewable energy technologies to power their schools. Geothermal systems draw heat from the Earth and expel heat back into the Earth to heat and cool the building. Biomass systems utilize biological waste materials to generate electricity, while photovoltaic systems utilize solar panels on roofs, shade surfaces, and facades (LPA, Inc., 2009). A 2014 study by the Solar Foundation and the Solar Energy Industries Association revealed that America's K–12 schools are among the fastest adopters of solar power in the United States, adding 3,000 new solar installations between 2008 and 2012, a fivefold increase. Initially, school districts appeared to adopt solar for the educational or symbolic value of small systems, but today schools are tapping solar on a much larger scale. According to the authors of the report, 3,752 solar-equipped schools now yield 490 megawatts, "enough to power tens of thousands of classrooms while offsetting nearly 443,000 metric tons of carbon dioxide emissions annually" (Cusick, 2014).

School districts can also enter into solar power purchasing agreements (PPA) to receive energy from an outside vendor or sell energy back to the grid. In addition, the purchase of Renewable Energy Credits assures schools are powered by alternative energy sources. Finally, Energy Service Companies (ESCos) have been working with schools for decades to provide performance contracts wherein the ESCo makes efficiency improvements and is later paid via a percentage of utility bill savings. This procurement tool allows school districts to use future energy savings to fund the upfront costs of energy upgrades. In green schools, students can learn about energy stewardship by collecting and comparing electricity use data from schools across their district. They can trace the path of their school power, from "source to outlet," experiencing alternative energy and energy conservation in a hands-on manner (Taylor, 2009, p. 202).

Insulating Well

Insulation is "a simple and vital means of conserving energy," as it "keeps hot air out and cool air in during summer and warm air in and cold air out during winter" (LPA, Inc., 2009, p. 37). Insulation begins with the building frame. "A 2 x 4-framed wall, for example, will have an insulating value of R13 using conventional fiberglass batt insulation. A 2 x 6-framed wall, however, accommodates R19 insulation, which provides 50 percent more insulation" (p. 37). As you increase the R-value of insulation you increase its effectiveness. It should be noted that soy-bean-based or cotton insulation avoids toxins (LPA, Inc., 2009).

Thermally broken windows, with separator material between inner and outer window frame, prevent temperature transfer. High thermal-mass materials, such as concrete and stone, can also help maintain a consistent internal temperature. Outside the building, earth berms and green screens, placed along exterior walls, provide further insulation from heat gain, reducing HVAC use and energy consumption. These landscape design elements also provide green transitions.

Utilizing the Light That Comes Naturally

Daylighting can cut a school building's lifetime energy costs by 30–70%, with diffuse light provided by means of baffles, roof monitors, skylights, and clerestories (Olson & Kellum, 2003). Operable windows with low-E laminated glazing minimize the ultraviolet and infrared light that can pass through glass without compromising the amount of visible light that is transmitted, stopping the direct transfer of heat but not sunlight. Abundant natural light reduces the need for artificial light sources, which are responsible for up to 60% of a school building's energy consumption (Gelfand, 2010). A coordinated system that utilizes daylighting in combination with indirect and energy efficient artificial lighting options, such as advanced florescent lamps and ballasts, light emitting diodes (LEDs), and/or high intensity discharge (HID) bulbs go a long way to providing high-quality lighting and reducing overall costs.

Classroom dimming systems automatically dim or shut down indirect and direct artificial lighting when sufficient daylighting is present. Occupancy sensors shut off lighting when no one is present. And, "[i]f nothing else is done, replacing bulbs or lamps in existing florescent fixtures can provide instant energy savings" (Gelfand, 2010, p. 102). Gelfand further emphasizes that "[a]lthough light sources and controls have been developed rapidly, the most energy savings solution of all is the use of daylighting," along with its benefits for children's health and well-being as discussed in Chapter 6 (Gelfand, 2010, pp. 102–103).

Angela's school relies upon a number of portable classrooms as less than ideal physical learning environments. Although the classrooms offer freedom from interruptions, they tend to be dark and must be regularly inspected for mold. The district's recent efforts to refurbish and upgrade these structures included installation of 21-inch solar tubes as a daylighting experiment in select classrooms. Angela, along with her teachers and students, learned the mechanics of these daylighting devices.

> The prismatic lenses you see on the top will transmit and diffuse any light from sunrise to sunset. Whatever angle the sun is coming in, the tubes suck it in. You have the lens on the top and a highly reflective tube in the middle. The light bounces around and then another lens on the bottom spreads the light out into the classroom. With skylights, you get whatever sun is available at that angle, whereas the tubes harvest it a lot better. There are also louvers that allow you to shut the sun off!

Informed students become green school leaders' best monitors of daytime use, reminding teachers and peers to turn off unnecessary lights when not in use and turn down lighting levels when possible. They can go a step further to chart the savings that result from responsible artificial and natural light usage. Students might also describe all the artificial light sources throughout their school, exploring the differences between high-pressure sodium, fluorescent, full spectrum (Taylor, 2009, p. 191).

Heating and Cooling Efficiently

As discussed in Chapter 6, low-energy heating and cooling methods, such as underfloor displacement air distribution, reduce energy costs and maintain comfortable, consistent temperatures for building occupants. High-performance heating, ventilation, and cooling systems share common characteristics such as (Gelfand, 2010, p. 145):

- ◆ over-size condenser coils that lead to higher equipment efficiencies;
- ◆ water-cooled as opposed to air-cooled condensers;
- ◆ mechanical systems that recover unwanted heat or water in one part of the building and transfer it to another part that requires heat;
- ◆ extended periods of economizer cycle operation.

Efficiency is increased and indoor pollutants minimized through regular maintenance of HVAC systems, utilizing high-efficiency filters and ducted returns. Students might conduct a walking tour of their school, measuring building temperature in different locations. They could diagram the human circulatory system and compare it to their school's building systems (Taylor, 2009, p. 199).

Monitoring Building Performance

In order to realize and maintain a green school's potential health and productivity benefits, green school leaders are wise to utilize monitoring and diagnostic feedback regarding building performance (National Research Council, 2007). The ability to effectively track the long-term savings realized through sustainable practices supports the case for future investments in green building and retrofits (McGraw-Hill Construction, 2013). Monitoring systems, combined with interactive energy dashboards, also provide opportunities for learning as students observe, analyze, and report results. "Transparency in the school's efforts and operations is essential to making facilities effective teaching tools . . . ensuring that the ecological, social, and economic impacts . . . (both positive and negative) are obvious to students and others" (Higgs and McMillan, 2006, p. 45).

EPA's ENERGY STAR Portfolio Manager is a web-based utility tracking tool that allows eligible facilities (including K–12 schools) to record, track, and benchmark their energy and/or water performance against that of similar facilities across the country. EPA's ENERGY STAR energy performance scale indicates how efficiently buildings use energy on a 1–100 scale. An ENERGY STAR energy performance score of 50 indicates average energy performance while an ENERGY STAR Score of 75 or better indicates top performance. Energy dashboards provide students the opportunity to monitor building performance and report results, functioning as the energy conscience of their school community.

Faced with a funding shortfall during the Great Recession, Pennsylvania's North Penn School District (NPSD) set SMART (specific, measurable, attainable, relevant, and time-bound) goals and tracked their energy usage in near real time. A newly hired Manager of Energy and Operational Facilities (Energy Manager) took responsibility for tracking data, developing reports, and responding quickly to aberrations in energy use. As schools met their initial goal of 75 on the ENERGY STAR scale, recognition and celebrations followed, and the goal advanced to 90. North Penn School District was a 2013 ENERGY STAR Partner of the Year, realizing a 30% reduction in energy use across their facilities and saving more than $1.1 million in utility costs. These savings allowed them to meet the educational needs of children across the district, as they retained teachers and educational programming during severe economic turbulence (Kensler & Uline, 2015).

Conserving Resources

Green schools are designed to consume fewer natural resources and create a harmonious relationship between the building and it's natural surroundings (LPA, Inc., 2009). By seeing schools as built from the interior out, that is, as learner-centered (National Center for the 21st Century Schoolhouse, n.d.), at the same time we acknowledge their impact on the natural world, we enhance our point of view. As green school leaders, we meet the needs of whole child to the degree we also address the essential requirements for healthy natural ecosystems.

Reducing Water Use

School campuses are often large enough to influence water quality and quantity beyond their boundaries (Harrington, 2010). Along with water-conserving plumbing fixtures in kitchen facilities, restrooms, and gymnasium locker rooms (including low-flow toilets and aerators on the sinks), green roofs also reduce water runoff, becoming a piece of local habitat (Freed, 2010). Angela and Tom's school district experimented with a green roof on one of their largest high schools. As a river city school district, district officials faced legal action taken by the EPA to reduce the amount of sewer waste washing into the river during strong rains. The district facilities director explained:

> When we had heavy rain events, the sewers overflowed with storm water and sewage mixed together, backing up into homes and flowing out into the river. The EPA sued the metropolitan sewer district just as we started our project. Instead of taking the traditional approach of making bigger underground sewers, we became a laboratory to test different ideas, and the sewer district brought the money. This building now has 33,000 square foot of green roof, which is the largest in this region. The plantings are in replaceable trays for easy maintenance and repair. The roof catches that first inch of rain, which actually is the worst part for these combined sewer overflows. It comes down hard and would sheet off, but the green roof captures every bit of that first inch.

Grass, gravel, and resin paving, unit pavers, and porous asphalt all allow water to percolate and/or plants to grow, while also reducing heat islands (Harrington, 2010, p. 171). At the same school in Tom and Angela's district, the metropolitan sewer district also funded a project to minimize hard sur-face paving. "It is a rain garden with native and adaptive plants. It is also soaking up the water; and that is what matters." This collaboration between the school and the sewer districts represents the sort of ecological approach advocated by the WSCC model, with the school drawing resources and influ-ences from the whole community to address the needs of the whole child. Not only do the roof and the rain garden contribute to a healthy ecosystem for children, they also provide rich additions to the school's three-dimensional textbook.

Green school leaders are incorporating bioswales into school grounds with native species that help to purify water runoff. Drought tolerant grasses require less irrigation, and water recapture systems for irrigation reduce water use, moving in the direction of net zero (Harrington, 2010). Strategies such as avoiding midday watering, zoning irrigation by plant location and type, maintaining heads and filters, utilizing smart controllers, and using low-volume irrigation for gardens, trees, and shrubs together provide an integrated strategy for conserving water (Eley, 2006; Gelfand, 2010). Students can assist by graphing monthly water bills and acknowledging and celebrat-ing the efforts of their school's operations and maintenance team.

Preserving and Protecting Habitats

The reuse of existing school sites, in combination with compact school designs, help to preserve undeveloped, open spaces. In addition, green school leaders are taking account of their school sites as natural systems, respecting and preserving wetlands and other existing habitats as laboratories for learning.

The National Wildlife Federation (NWF) assists schools in developing outdoor classrooms called Schoolyard Habitats®, where educators and stu-dents learn how to attract and support local wildlife. The program sponsors a listserve for organizations working on schoolyard improvement. Web pages for National Wildlife Foundation (www.nwf.org), the Evergreen Foundation (www.evergreen-foundation.com) and Project Wild (www.projectwild.org) provide information and links to other similar projects (Rivkin, 1997).

The NWF Schoolyard Habitat Program has certified schoolyards in every U.S. state and two territories, with international sites in Thailand, Italy, and the United Kingdom. These wildlife habitats become places where students learn about wildlife species and ecosystems, while at the same time honing academic skills and nurturing creativity (https://www.nwf.org/How-to-Help/Garden-for-Wildlife/Schoolyard-Habitats.aspx). Schools engaged in habitat preservation and development usually start small with projects such as butterfly gardens, bird feeders and baths, tree planting, sundials, weather stations, and native plant gardens. Larger projects, often initiated in concert

with new construction, include wetlands, nature trails, meadows, stream restoration, shelters for small animals, and large vegetable gardens (Rivkin, 1997).

> There is a trend to choose ecologically valuable projects over simple
> beautification ones, e.g., turf converted to meadow contributes more
> to the local ecology than azaleas planted around the school's founda-
> tion. Optimally, students are involved in the planning, implementing,
> and maintenance of projects. Important curriculum aims can be
> served as well as a sense of ownership and stewardship encouraged.
> (Rivkin, 1997, p. 64)

In addition to developing and caring for schoolyard habitats, students' sense
of ownership and stewardship might be enriched through a process of identifying, photographing, and archiving the native plants and animals thriving
within their schoolyard habitat.

Managing Waste

Construction waste reduction systems maximize the recycling, composting, and/or salvaging of construction, demolition, and land-cleaning waste.
Informed by the Cradle-to-Cradle Framework (C2C) for making, using, and
recycling things, these systems can encourage active consideration of the life-
cycle of things, with the waste products of one cycle becoming the raw materials of the next (McDonough & Braungart, 2002).

Increasingly, green school leaders are developing district- and school-
wide norms and routines, expecting and celebrating responsible, waste-
conscience habits. The Cincinnati City School District in Cincinnati, Ohio,
recently worked in collaboration with the city's Park Board to implement a
unique recycling effort that has become a point of pride for the community.
The Park Board was forced to take down a significant number of ash trees due
to an emerald ash borer infestation that hit the area hard. Typically, downed
trees from the city's regular preventative maintenance cycle become firewood
and mulch for use in the parks, but, with the infestation, the Park Board had
many more thousands of logs. The school district facilities director shared the
details of their solution:

> Ash is a good hard wood, so we partnered with Park Board to get
> ahold of some and also partnered with a furniture company to create
> classroom furniture, including mobile cubbies (for coats and belong-
> ings) and mobile bookcases.

As these trees come down and the district buys the lumber, some of funds then go to reforesting the urban canopy. We've created bookmarks that tell the story of the urban timber program and the emerald ash borer. We also have wood sample chains so students can compare the different species of wood on the chain with the wood on their cubby, "This is oak; this is ash." They experience the story. They touch it every day.

From replacement of paper with electronic memos and online assignments, to purchasing cafeteria trays that can be composted or recycled, to ensuring that recycling receptacles are regularly used throughout the school, to school-wide sorting of recyclable, compost, and landfill waste, green school leaders encourage a culture of shared responsibility for waste reduction and management, often with students at the helm.

Making the Case

Typically, green schools cost 1–2% more than conventional buildings, with an average cost premium of 1.7% or $4 more per square foot (Kats, 2006). This cost differential is often referred to as the "green premium," resulting from the increased cost of sustainably sourced materials, more efficient mechanical systems, and other high-performance building features (Kats, 2006). Any increase in upfront costs raises concerns for already financially strapped districts, and yet, growing evidence suggests, in the case of green schools, each dollar spent today realizes two dollars in future savings (Gelfand, 2010). Sustainability-focused organizational practices require we adopt the routine of lifecycle costing, factoring in the costs of installation, operation, and disposal over the entire life of a material or system. Rather than relying upon first-cost analyses, this more thorough price accounting reveals the actual cost of green versus convention school buildings (Eley, 2006; Gelfand, 2010), helping green school leaders build the case for future returns on initial investment.

Green schools realize an average of 33% energy reduction over conventionally designed schools as a result of efficient lighting, greater use of daylighting and sensors, more efficient heating and cooling systems, and better insulated walls and roofs (Kats, 2006). They experience a 32% reduction in water use as a result of efficient plumbing fixtures, green roofs, water catchment systems, and the like (Kats, 2006). Durable construction materials and thorough building commissioning processes also reduce operations and maintenance costs. In fact, a study of the costs and benefits of greening California public buildings across 40 state agencies found an $8 per square foot saving in operations and maintenance costs over a 20-year period (Kats et al., 2003). Green school leaders should avail themselves of these compelling data at same time they amass their own evidence of building performance over time.

In a recent article for *School Business Affairs,* Tim Cole, Sustainability Manager for the Virginia Beach City School District (VBCPS), tells the story of how VBCPS "moved toward an educational and operational model that embraces the triple bottom line of social, economic, and environmental effects when measuring profit and loss" (Cole, 2015, p. 32). Cole reports on the resulting savings realized by the school district:

> VBCPS has been moving in a direction that eased the transition to tough economic times . . . By constructing [eight] new buildings according to LEED criteria and focusing on Energy Star and performance contract work for HVAC and lighting in existing buildings, VBCPS has reduced energy costs. Since 2006, the school division has increased in square footage by 9%—to 10.6 million square feet. At the same time, energy use per square foot has decreased by 21%. (Cole, 2015, p. 33)

VBCPS's experiences also challenge the accuracy of the green premium. When compared with construction costs across the states of Delaware, the District of Columbia, Maryland, Virginia, and West Virginia, all eight VBCPS LEED projects were built for less than the regional average. Cole is quick to point out that most of the comparison schools are non-LEED buildings (Cole, 2015).

Green project certification, resulting from a third-party verification process, helps to make a compelling case for going green. Certification systems, such as USGBC's LEED and Collaborative for High Performance Schools (CHPS) provide public confirmation of sustainability efforts, building public trust in the quality of the outcomes. In addition, a comprehensive building commissioning process (a systematic quality assurance procedure that begins with the first stages of planning and extends through design, construction, and post-occupancy) increases the chances that the finished product will successfully meet the needs of students, their teachers, their community, and the natural world. In addition, Educational Commissioning informs teachers, students, even parents and community partners, of the design intentions, helping them to best leverage all aspects of the physical learning environment (Lackney, 2005). We will revisit the commissioning process in greater detail in Chapter 9.

Conclusion

Operating and managing schools with a green frame of mind increases the likelihood that our schools will support the whole child, not only creating the conditions for their academic success, but also addressing their needs in terms of physical, emotional, social, and cognitive well-being. As we sharpen and extend our focus on the human as well as the natural dimensions of school life, the facility-related job functions of principals, custodians, plant managers, and district shop foremen take on new importance and present exciting possibilities for reducing a school's carbon footprint, for saving precious dollars, for enriching students' learning experiences, and for meeting our children's needs, now and into the future.

Questions for Discussion

1. Partner with your facilities team and take you teachers on a field trip of your school building. Pose these and/or similar questions related to the operation and maintenance of the building. How is it that the water comes to bubble from the fountain? Where is the furnace and how efficiently does it do its job? Is the roof leaking? What sorts of light fixture illuminate the classrooms? What do we use to clean our floors?

2. Describe a time when your school facility helped you to marshal community support. How do you continue to engage your community as owners of their building?

3. Devise a specific activity or project that will require interaction between the curriculum and facilities professionals within your school organization. Describe one process you might design for continuing this collaboration. You might generate some ideas during the field trip you take together, as suggested in the first discussion question.

References

Arnold, E., & Beardsley, E.R. (2015). *Perspectives on implementation and effectiveness of school green cleaning laws*. Washington, DC: U.S. Green Building Council.

ASCD. (2007). *The learning compact redefined: A call to action*. Alexandria, VA: ASCD. Retrieved from: http://www.ascd.org/ASCD/pdf/Whole%20Child/WCC%20 Learning%20Compact.pdf

ASCD & CDC. (2014). *Whole school, whole child, whole community: A collaborative approach to learning and health*. Retrieved from: http://www.ascd.org/ASCD/pdf/siteASCD/publications/wholechild/wscc-a-collaborative-approach.pdf

Berner, M. M. (1993). Building conditions, parental involvement, and student achievement in the District of Columbia public school system. *Urban Education, 28*, 6–29. doi:10.1177/0042085993028001002

Center for Green Schools. (2013). *State of our schools report*. Washington, DC: U.S. Green Building Council. Retrieved from: http://www.centerforgreenschools.org/sites/default/files/resource-files/2013%20State%20of%20Our%20Schools%20Report%20FINAL.pdf

Chaney, B., & Lewis, L. (2007). *Public school principals report on their school facilities: Fall 2005* (NCES 2007–007). U.S. Department of Education. Washington, DC: National Center for Education Statistics.

Cole, T. (2015). Why sustainability makes good economic sense. *School Business Affairs*, March, 32–34.

Cusick, D. (2014, September 19). Renewable energy: U.S. schools quickly climbing learning curve in solar power. *Climate Wire*. Retrieved from: http://www.eenews.net/stories/1060006112/print

Edwards, B. W. (2006). Environmental design and educational performance. *Research in Education, 76*, 14–32.

Eley, C. (2006). High performance school buildings. In H. Frumkin, R. J. Geller, & I. L. Rubin (Eds.), *Safe and healthy school environments* (pp. 341–350). New York: Oxford University Press.

Filardo, M. (2016). *State of our schools: America's K–12 facilities 2016*. Washington, DC: 21st Century School Fund, U.S. Green Building Council, Inc., & the National Council on School Facilities.

Freed, E. C. (2010). Building structure and envelope. In L. Gelfand (Ed.), *Sustainable school architecture: Design for primary and secondary schools* (pp. 111–136). Hoboken, NJ: John Wiley & Sons, Inc.

Gelfand, L. (2010). *Sustainable school architecture*. Hoboken, NJ: John Wiley & Sons, Inc.

Hamilton, B. A. (2015). *Green building economic impact study*. Washington, DC: USGBC. Retrieved from: http://go.usgbc.org/2015-Green-Building-Economic-Impact-Study.html

Harrington, S. (2010). Landscape and site design. In L. Gelfand (Ed.), *Sustainable school architecture: Design for primary and secondary schools* (pp. 163–196). Hoboken, NJ: John Wiley & Sons, Inc.

Higgs, A. L., & McMillan, V. M. (2006). Teaching through modeling: Four schools' experiences in sustainability education. *The Journal of Environmental Education, 38*(1), 39–53. doi:10.3200/JOEE.38.1.39-53

Kats, G. (2006). *Greening America's schools: Costs and benefits*. Retrieved from: www.usgbc.org/showfile.aspx?Document ID—2908

Kats, G., Alevantis, L., Berman, A., Mills, E, Berkeley, L., & Perlman, J. (2003). *The costs and financial benefits of green buildings: A report to California's sustainability task force*. October, 2003. Retrieved from: http://www.usgbc.org/Docs/News/News477.pdf

Kensler, L. A. W., & Uline, C. L. (2015). The transformation of a school district from energy hog to energy star. In S. J. Gross & J. P. Shapiro (Eds.), *Democratic ethical educational leadership: Reclaiming school reform* (pp. 54–58). New York: Routledge: Taylor & Francis Group.

Lackney, J. (2005). Educating educators to optimize their school facility for teaching and learning. *Design Share*. Retrieved from: http://www.designshare.com/index.php/articles/educational-commissioning/

Lewallen, T. C., Hunt, H., Potts-Datema, W., Zaza, S., & Giles, W. (2015). The Whole School, Whole Community, Whole Child model: A new approach for improving educational attainment and healthy development for students. *Journal of School Health, 85*, 729–739.

LPA, Inc. (2009). *Green school primer*. Victoria, Australia: The Images Publishing Group.

McDonough, W., & Braungart, M. (2002). *Cradle to cradle: Remaking the way we make things*. New York: North Point Press.

McGraw-Hill Construction. (2013). *New and retrofit green schools: The cost benefits and influence of a green school on its occupants*. Bedford, MA: McGraw-Hill Construction.

National Center for Education Statistics (NCES). (1995). *Disparities in public school district spending 1989–90*. Washington, DC: U.S. Department of Education.

National Center for the 21st Century Schoolhouse. (n.d.) Website. Retrieved from: http://go.sdsu.edu/education/schoolhouse/

National Policy Board for Educational Administration. (2015). *Professional standards for educational leaders 2015*. Reston, VA: National Policy Board for Educational Administration.

National Research Council. (2007). *Green schools: Attributes for health and learning*. Washington, DC: The National Academies Press.

Nolet, V. (2016). *Educating for sustainability*. New York: Routledge.

Olson, S. L., & Kellum, S. (2003). *The impact of sustainable buildings on educational achievement in K–12 schools*. Madison, WI: Leonardo Academy, Inc.

Orr, D. (1993). Architecture as pedagogy. *Conservation Biology, 7* (2), 226–228.

Plank, S. B., Bradshaw, C. P., & Young, H. (2009). An application of "Broken Windows" and related theories to the study of disorder, fear, and collective efficacy in schools. *American Journal of Education, 115*(2), 227–247.

Rivkin, M. (1997). The Schoolyard Habitat Movement: What it is and why children need it. *Childhood Education Journal, 25*(1), 61–66.

Taylor, A. (2009). *Linking architecture and education: Sustainable design of learning environments*. Albuquerque: University of New Mexico Press.

Uline, C. L. (2000). Decent facilities and learning: Thirman L. Milner Elementary School and beyond. *Teacher College Record, 102*, 444–462.

Uline, C. L., Tschannen-Moran, M., & Wolsey, T. D. (2009). The walls still speak: The stories occupants tell. *Journal of Educational Administration, 47*(3), 400–426. doi:10.1108/09578230910955818

U.S. General Accounting Office. (1995). *School facilities: America's schools not designed or equipped for the 21st century* (General Accounting Office Report # HEHS-95-95). Washington, DC: U.S. General Accounting Office.

Vincent, J. M., & Jain, L. S. (2015a). *Going it alone: Can California's K–12 school district adequately and equitably fund school facilities?* Berkeley, CA: Center for Cities and Schools. Retrieved from: http://citiesandschools.berkeley.edu/uploads/Vincent__Jain_2015_Going_it_Alone_final.pdf

Vincent, J. M., & Jain, L. S. (2015b). *Going it alone: Can California's K–12 school district adequately and equitably fund school facilities? Policy brief.* Berkeley, CA: Center for Cities and Schools. Retrieved from: http://citiesandschools.berkeley.edu/uploads/GiA_2015_2_page_brief.pdf

Part III

Meaningful, Purposeful, Engaged Learning

8

For the Love of Learning

Schooling for students is profoundly voluntary. Children have to "go to school." The decision to "do schooling" is substantially their own. This means, of course, that they are key decision makers in the learning production.

(Murphy, 2015, p. 725)

Tom and Angela just finished a walkthrough and post walkthrough conversation with a team of teachers from their district. Walkthroughs provide the opportunity for teachers and administrators to learn together about current instructional practices and how to improve student learning (Kachur, Stout, & Edwards, 2013). On this day, Tom invited a team of elementary school teachers into his high school to observe student engagement. The elementary teachers provided honest and frank feedback. Consistent with research, they saw a wide range of student engagement in classrooms, from disengaged to deeply engaged and productive (Shernoff, Tonks, & Anderson, 2014). Angela commented to Tom:

> The elementary teachers were really impressed with the interdisciplinary approach to designing the bond funded projects! Those students were fully engaged—they were working together to find solutions to opportunities for building improvements that they identified. It was obvious that these students felt purposeful excitement in their learning.

It was a dramatic difference from some of the other classes where teachers were fighting to keep students' attention.

Tom responded:

> It was really about bringing student voice, conceptualizing and putting students at the center of their schools, giving them an opportunity to assess their individual school sites, to learn about their school sites in terms of how much energy they consumed, how much water they used, the kinds of materials their buildings were made out of, looking at their grounds and how they handled wastes, the kinds of cleaning and chemicals they used, and to come up with a plan of action. This bond funding has really lit a fire in some classes. Everyone participating seems highly motivated to improve this old building!

"All students can learn" is a familiar mantra featured in many school vision and/or mission statements, but is it enough? What if we shift the focus from "can" to "love?" All students love to learn. Humans, as a species, seem to generally love learning; the transition from cave dweller to the high tech 21st century has certainly required extensive learning through the ages. Do we believe all students have an innate love of learning? If so, what might that look like in schools? If not, when and why do children stop loving to learn? We see a vibrant love of learning in our toddlers. If we believed that all students, no matter their age or abilities, have an innate love of learning, what would that mean for our schools and classrooms? When resistance to learning and lack of engagement show up, what would we do? Would we demand that they love it? Would we put them in detention until they loved it? Or would we examine the context and our practice to see what was interfering with their innate love of learning and then remove those barriers, while at the same time facilitating more engaging learning opportunities? The new Professional Standards for Educational Leaders (PSEL) specifically calls for school leaders to promote *each* student's "love of learning" and to attend to student well-being (NBEA, 2015, p. 12), two highly interdependent concepts that facilitate students' academic performance. As Murphy's opening quote for this chapter emphasizes, students choose to "do schooling" or not. Green schools are places where students' love of learning and academic performance are likely to thrive because their school leaders effectively attend to their students' physical, social, emotional, and cognitive well-being.

Where students' well-being is high, they are more likely to love learning, be fully engaged, and achieve at higher levels (Awang-Hashim, Kaur, & Noman, 2015; Shernoff et al., 2014; Sznitman, Reisel, & Romer, 2011). As we have discussed extensively in this book, green schools aim to be healthy places for vibrant, engaged learning; they attend to the best interests of our students, our communities, and our planet. Engaged student learning is the focus of this chapter. We begin with a look at human learning as a vital ecosystem service, building on our understanding of schools as living systems not factories. An overview of mind, brain, and educational (MBE) science follows. We then connect the science of learning to education for sustainability. We demonstrate the potential for green schools to maximize student learning while at the same time cultivating stronger, healthier local communities and reducing the school's ecological footprint. In short, green schools have the capacity to contribute substantially to our world's most pressing challenges by both addressing those challenges through their present day practice and maximizing student learning for a lifetime love of learning.

Learning as an Ecosystem Service

Theoretically, green schools are grounded in a living systems model of organization and schooling. They have the potential to break free from the industrial model and maximize student learning. Academic gains occur within an overall healthy learning ecosystem; they are the result of students' well-being and love of learning. Well-being, "in its broadest sense encompasses all aspects of the human experience as perceived by an individual at any given time" (Gillett-Swan & Sargeant, 2014, p. 136). Gillett-Swan and Sergeant explain that well-being is dependent on context and includes social, economic, environmental, psychological, emotional, and cognitive components. Student perception of their own well-being serves as a source of energy and attention for learning.

Without subjective well-being (individual perception that all is well), an individual lacks the capacity to focus on learning. Scholars identify well-being as a dynamic, interdisciplinary, multifaceted concept that is both a state and a process (Dodge, Daly, Huyton, & Sanders, 2012; Gillett-Swan & Sargeant, 2014). Thus, when it comes to well-being, school leaders have the responsibility to (1) design, lead, and manage for healthy contexts—conditions that support individual perceptions of well-being; and (2) build students' adaptive skills—their capacity to identify and use their resources such that they can care for their own well-being presently and into the future.

Facilitating student well-being is central to green school leadership. Leaders attend to the physical well-being of their students through healthy building conditions; through high-quality, nutritious food; through abundant availability of clean drinking water; through daily outdoor play; and through time in nature. They attend to the social and emotional well-being of their students through cultivating positive, inclusive, and culturally relevant school climates and cultures. And they attend to their students' cognitive well-being through the promotion of student-centered learning grounded in their local socio-ecological community. Leaders in green schools facilitate students' love of learning by addressing the whole ecology of student well-being and engagement in learning.

We might think of the love of learning as an ecosystem service of the human race. Human learning has value, remarkable value, for all of us. Just imagine where the human species would be without the capacity to learn. Human learning has resulted in magnificent leaps in innovation and adaptation. As humans learned into and through the industrial age, we became so enamored with efficient production that we applied factory-model-inspired lessons to many areas of our lives; in particular, schools. We applied these engineering lessons to "improve" the process of learning. What is a natural process and a valuable human-ecosystem service, became a target of engineering throughout the industrial age. The factory model has deeply influenced today's educational theory, policy, and practice (see Senge, Cambron-McCabe, Lucas, Smith, & Dutton, 2012) leaving us with an over-engineered learning ecosystem.

Nature's systems, what we call ecosystems, provide valuable services when allowed to function in their more natural state. These services include provisioning services (e.g., crops, water, wild foods, plant-derived medicines), regulating services (e.g., pollination, wetland water filtration, water cycle, carbon storage, wetland protection from flooding), cultural services (e.g., recreation, spiritual and aesthetic values, education), and supporting services (e.g., soil formation, photosynthesis, nutrient cycling) (Sukhdev et al., 2010, p. 7). Increasingly humans are recognizing that valuable ecosystem services may be lost through attempts to engineer improvements. For example, consider the Florida Everglades. This ecosystem in its natural state covered 3 million acres. Over the past 100 years, engineering restricted and redirected the flow of water for agriculture and development purposes. This left the ecosystem less than half its original size and greatly reduced its capacity to provide valuable ecosystem services such as improving water quality, fishing, hunting, and tourism. A recent report found that investing in restoring the natural function of the Everglades would result in a 4:1 benefit to cost ratio (Houten, Reckhow, Loomis, Cunningham, & Casey, 2012). The natural ecosystem services are worth more economically than the degraded, over-engineered system. They are certainly worth more environmentally as well!

Another impressive example is from New York. Rather than engineering new water treatment plants at a cost of $6–8 billion for New York City's water supply, city officials spent only $1.5 billion for watershed farmers and landowners to reduce run-off and pollution (Sukhdev et al., 2010). Partnering with, and caring for, the natural ecosystem was far more cost effective than not. And doing so was also beneficial for the whole watershed system.

Vibrant learning is humanity's most valuable ecosystem service. Of course, it produces economic benefits. At the same time, learning is the source of innovation and adaptation for living more sustainably on planet earth. Green school leaders have the opportunity to partner with nature in numerous ways to design, lead, and manage vibrant, flourishing learning communities. We propose that the green schools movement is more of a learning-ecosystem restoration movement than a school reform or renewal movement. Nature sits in the center of this effort's learning circle for three reasons. First, earth's natural systems are in peril; humans must learn to live differently on and with our planet (Wijkman & Rockstrom, 2012). Second, humans have a tight evolutionary bond with nature (Wilson, 1984) and time in nature promotes human health and well-being (e.g., see comprehensive reviews Kuo, 2015; Russell et al., 2013). Third, there are lessons we can learn from nature that will help us de-engineer our learning ecosystems. In Wheatley's (1999) words, "We look hopefully to nature to teach us how to do what living systems accomplish with such skill—learn, adapt, change" (p. 158). Looking to nature for design inspiration, the emerging field known as biomimicry is fast becoming common practice across disciplines (Baumeister & Herzlich, 2015; Benyus, 1997, n.d.; Wilson, 1984). Mimicking nature has applications in design of everyday items, buildings, and even organizational processes (Seeley, 2010). In considering schools, we need to understand two primary aspects of natural learning ecosystems: (1) the nature of human learning; and (2) the role of nature itself in facilitating human learning.

Ecosystem restoration projects require a deep understanding of the pristine, natural system. For learning-ecosystem restoration work, we need to better understand the conditions in which our well-being and love of learning thrives, and then we need to design, manage, and lead for those conditions. Humans' innate capacities for learning and affiliation for nature guide this work.

Student Learning

The Nature of Learning

Fifteen years ago, The National Academies Press released the expanded edition of *How People Learn: Brain, Mind, Experience, and School* (Bransford, Brown, & Cocking, 2000). This edited book brought together diverse scientific perspectives on human learning. Ten years later, the Center for Educational Research and Innovation within the Organisation for Economic Co-operation and Development released *The Nature of Learning: Using Research to Inspire Practice* (Dumont, Istance, & Benavides, 2010). Also out that year was Tokuhama-Espinosa's (2010) book, *The New Science of Teaching and Learning: Using the Best of Mind, Brain, and Educational Science in the Classroom.* These works present research on learning from disciplines as diverse as cognitive, social, and educational psychology, human development, anthropology, sociology, computer science, and neuroscience. A robust, evidence-informed and cohesive picture of human learning is now emerging. The guiding principles for educators are consistent and clear, if not complete. Nature is not yet a prominent player in the guiding principles, although we will soon discuss emerging evidence for including nature.

MBE science teaches us, without a doubt, that learning is an ecological phenomenon involving interactions among the whole child, content, and multiple contexts. Figure 8.1 represents our synthesis of MBE recommendations for facilitating student learning. Three primary references informed our synthesis (Bransford et al., 2000; Dumont et al., 2010; Tokuhama-Espinosa, 2010). We note a missing element across the three frameworks—nature. Before we explore the emerging research related to nature, human well-being and learning, let's look a bit more closely at the state of MBE recommendations for educators.

Figure 8.1 Synthesis of MBE Recommendations for Facilitating Student Learning (Bransford et al., 2000; Dumont et al., 2010; Tokuhama-Espinosa, 2010), with Nature Added as a Critical Component of the Learning Context in Green Schools

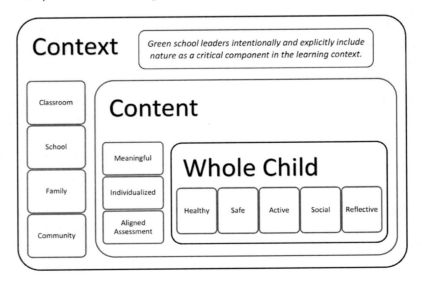

Context for Learning

Learning takes place in context. MBE research tells us that family, community, school, and classroom are all part of a student's learning context, or ecosystem. These contexts define the conditions in which students develop as physically, emotionally, cognitively, and socially healthy individuals. When we look specifically at the school organization,

> Learning scientists know a lot about the nature of learning and instruction but tend to know less about the organisations and cultures in which these routinely play out … In other words, understanding how individuals learn is not a sufficient basis for designing the environments in which they might learn better—this requires attention at the least to the other half of the equation, the environments themselves. (Dumont et al., 2010, p. 28)

Learning contexts are complex, dynamic socio-ecological systems. Learners continuously influence and are influenced by their physical environment and their social environment. We have argued in this book that ecological and democratic principles undergird the design of healthy organizational contexts. Ecological principles apply primarily to the physical context and relate directly to the physical health and well-being of students. Democratic principles apply to the social context and relate directly to the socio-emotional health and well-being of students.

We have described earlier how ecological principles inform partnering with the laws of nature, helping us live more responsibly within them while also benefiting from the healthier conditions they create. What tends to be environmentally responsible, also tends to be healthy for humans. Green school buildings, in addition to treading more lightly ecologically, are characterized by clean air and water, ample daylight, effective acoustics, thermal comfort, and ample access to nature and the outdoors (see Chapter 6). Green school leaders also attend to the food environment by aiming to serve the healthiest of healthy food, sourcing as much local, minimally processed, and organic food as possible. These features of the physical context[1] contribute to school occupants' health and well-being, reduce absenteeism, increase attention, and through these pathways support learning (Chan, Mense, Lane, & Richardson, 2015; Frumkin, Geller, Rubin, & Nodvin, 2006).

The social context or climate of classrooms and schools influence student emotions. The social climate may evoke feelings of belonging or alienation, of trust or fear, of joy or sadness, of delight or boredom, and so on. "Emotions are vital in learning as a whole" (Tokuhama-Espinosa, 2010, p. 105). More democratic classrooms—classrooms characterized by care, respect, openness, responsiveness, and participation—cultivate healthy social systems in which relationships and learning thrive. These classrooms and schools, whether labeled as democratic or not, improve student outcomes by generating belonging, trust, joy, delight, and engagement (Jennings & Greenberg, 2009; Mager & Nowak, 2012; Thapa, Cohen, Guffey, & Higgins-D'Alessandro, 2013; Vieno, Perkins, Smith, & Santinello, 2005). Deborah Meier, a prominent leader in the democratic schools movement, defined democratic schools as, "where you're continuously exploring how everybody's voice can be heard and acted upon, effectively" (as quoted in Knoester, 2012, p. 12). Hearing student voices—truly listening deeply to each individual and meeting their learning needs—is the challenging work of educators. While it may not be easy work, it is the foundation for effectively teaching content.

Content for Learning

MBE research informs curriculum design for teaching content. We've summarized their research-based recommendations for content as meaningful, individualized, and aligned. Once again, the student is the central focus. Students will choose to engage with and learn content that is meaningful to them. This means that teachers have to know their students well and be connection making masters. Connections between new material and each student's prior knowledge, personal interest, and developmental stage need to be visible to students. Given the fact that no two students have had the exact same lived experiences, their embodiment of prior knowledge, interest, and developmental stage is unique. Thus, MBE research consistently calls for some degree of individualization of content for facilitating student learning.

Connection making mastery does not end with individualization for students. Horizontal connections across content areas and contexts must also be made. These horizontal connections help to develop accurate frameworks of knowledge (Dumont et al., 2010). Alignment between learning goals and mode of assessment is also critical. Assessment serves student learning needs when it provides timely and specific feedback that informs continued learning. These general content guidelines apply to every developmental stage and to all disciplines. Whether teaching math or social studies (or better yet, math and social studies in an integrated fashion!), or any other content, the material should feel meaningful to students, meet their individual learning needs, and include appropriate feedback through aligned assessment.

The Whole Child Learns

MBE teaches us that learning is about making new meaning. Learning requires time spent thinking about new ideas. Although much of this thinking may take place in the brain, our cognitive function depends on physical, emotional, and social well-being. The brain is a physical, social, and emotional organ. MBE science tells us unequivocally that learning emerges best when humans are healthy, happy, active, and socially engaged. With this knowledge in mind, the Association for Supervision and Curriculum Development (ASCD) and the Center for Disease Control and Prevention (CDC) recently partnered to develop a new guiding model for educators, health professionals, and policy makers. We introduced the Whole School, Whole Community, Whole Child Model (WSCC) (Lewallen, Hunt, Potts-Datema, Zaza, & Giles, 2015) in Chapter 7. The WSCC model reflects current MBE science. Cognitive growth and development does not happen in isolation, it happens within the whole child. Thus educators must design, manage, and lead contexts and content that engage the whole child. Education in the 21st century is about developing the full capacity of whole children to know themselves, engage with others, and contribute to a sustainable future (Goleman, Bennett, & Barlow, 2012; Goleman & Senge, 2014). Green school leaders, as systems thinkers, strive to lead learning in this more integrative way. Their approach breaks free of the factory model and even extends beyond the WSCC model, by explicitly and intentionally bringing nature into children's learning experiences.

Nature and Learning

Although not a prominent player in mainstream MBE frameworks and guidelines, mounting evidence demonstrates the critical role that contact with nature plays in children's well-being, development, and learning. Nature, as we are using it here, is broadly defined as all the biological and physical elements of the world that are not human or created by humans. Humans experience nature either by spending time out of the built environment or by bringing nature into the built environment. Nature is increasingly incorporated into the built environment through expansive windows that flood the interiors with natural light and views of nature; and through including living plants, fish tanks, water fountains, etc. in working and learning spaces (Gillis & Gatersleben, 2015; Kellert, Heerwagen, & Mador, 2008). Green school leaders are connecting children with nature by getting their students outside and by bringing nature inside.

Numerous recent reviews of research demonstrate that contact with nature is associated with benefits associated with overall health and well-being, including specific aspects of emotional, physical, social, and cognitive well-being (Hartig, Mitchell, de Vries, & Frumkin, 2014; Kuo, 2015; Louv, 2008; Russell et al., 2013). Kuo's 2015 review argued that time in nature benefits human health (reductions in ADD/ADHD, anxiety disorders, depression, migraines, cancer, cardiovascular disease, among many others) by way of enhancing immune system function. She concluded, "The multiplicity of nature–health pathways identified here lends credibility to the hypothesis that nature actually promotes health, as well as a potential explanation for the startling size and scope of nature's apparent impact" (p. 6). Since Louv's (2008) book, *Last Child in the Woods*, reviews have focused specifically on the benefits of contact with nature for children (Chawla, 2015; Gill, 2014; Mustapa, Maliki, & Hamzah, 2015). The evidence is substantial—children benefit from contact with nature. Although fewer studies have yet to investigate the direct connection between contact with nature and specific learning outcomes (Russell et al., 2013), we know that well-being is foundational to engagement in learning. Thus, we argue that including contact with nature as an explicit component of children's school experiences will contribute positively to their well-being and therefore, their academic performance.

Nature and Physical Well-being

Physical activity is critical for children. It is both a health promotion and disease prevention strategy. Over a decade ago, an extensive review of the evidence resulted in an expert panel recommending that "school-age youth should participate every day in 60 minutes or more of moderate to vigorous physical activity that is enjoyable and developmentally appropriate" (Strong et al., 2005, p. 736). Physical activity that takes place in nature adds additional benefits. Mustapa et al. (2015) reviewed studies from the mid-1990s to 2013 that investigated the relationship between children's contact with nature and developmental needs. Outdoor play is associated with healthy physical development and motor fitness for children. Their review highlighted studies that have shown that young children who play in natural areas like a forest develop motor fitness more readily than those who play in traditional playground areas.

Chawla (2015), in her review of the research, reported that children who have access to and spend time in nature benefit from healthier weight, lower blood pressure, more physical activity, and Vitamin D from exposure to sunlight. She also highlighted the importance of maintaining natural play areas without the use of herbicides or pesticides, as these chemicals are associated with "a long list of adverse effects, including miscarriages, low birth weight, birth defects, childhood cancers, respiratory and lung diseases, reduced IQs, attention deficit disorder (ADD) and other learning disabilities, and autism spectrum disorder" (Chawla, 2015, p. 443). Finally, extensive support exists for the use of gardens for promoting children's healthier food choices (Williams & Brown, 2011; Williams & Dixon, 2013).

Nature and Social Well-being

Children who play in more natural settings have been found to engage in more prosocial behaviors with their peers (Chawla, 2015; Gill, 2014; Mustapa et al., 2015). The reviewed studies have investigated preschool through middle school aged children. They have found that children in natural play spaces that include diverse features (e.g., trees, hills, vegetation, moveable branches, logs, and rocks, etc.) engage in more imaginative, collaborative, and diverse forms of play. This play provides a foundation for forming healthy social relationships, friendships, and social skills. Chawla also reported on the importance of the school philosophy in reaping these rewards for children. In schools where natural settings may be available, but there is not a focus on promoting play, children's play is less creative and beneficial. Gardens are another place where children collaborate and work together while developing their social skills (Williams & Brown, 2011; Williams & Dixon, 2013). Friendships and social skills are a key ingredient for sustaining emotional well-being.

Nature and Emotional Well-being

Time in nature has the potential to be restorative, to reduce the effects of stress and nurture emotional well-being. Studies have shown that children, regardless of income, who spend time in nature, feel lower levels of stress, higher levels of self-worth, and lower rates of depression than those who do not (Chawla, 2015; Mustapa et al., 2015). Children of all ages have self-reported feeling free, relaxed, calm, and overall positive moods when in nature. In addition, Chawla (2015) pointed out that young children who have positive experiences in nature are more likely to report that nature buffers their stress in adolescence. Adolescents who do not have a history of positive experiences in nature may feel a sense of fear and anxiety rather than peace when in unfamiliar natural areas. This point suggests that schools have an important role to play in introducing children to nature at an early age, so that they will be more likely to value and benefit from nature as adolescents and adults. Given the cognitive benefits associated with time in nature, schools have good reason to make this effort.

Nature and Cognitive Well-being

Boston Public Schools began renovating their schoolyards in the mid-1990s. Prior to renovation, school properties were unwelcoming and in many cases, unsafe, for children. By the early 2000s nearly 66% of schools had substantially improved their schoolyard. The improvements included restoring the areas with natural features such as small hills, vegetation, boulders, logs, and moveable elements to encourage imaginative play, in addition to some traditional play equipment. A study of fourth grade student performance (aggregated at the school level) found that students in schools with improved schoolyards performed better on standardized testing, even after controlling for demographic characteristics such as income and race (Lopez, Campbell, & Jennings, 2008). Although their study did not explain the positive correlation between the more natural schoolyards and student performance, other studies shed light on this relationship.

Academic performance depends in large part on students remaining focused and engaged in their learning. Emerging research is consistently showing that time in nature improves students' capacity to focus (Chawla, 2015). Multiple studies report that students with attention deficit disorder (ADD) and attention deficit and hyperactivity disorder (ADHD) benefit from reduced symptoms after contact with nature. In a recent study, not cited in the reviews we have been discussing here, Berto, Pasini, and Barbiero (2015) found that 9–11-year-old students' attentional performance was best after time in woods, the area that students also reported as the most restorative, as compared to time in the classroom or playground. Further research is needed to better understand the causal linkages between contact with nature and cognitive well-being. However, the emerging evidence certainly suggests that student academic performance will likely benefit with time in nature. As school leaders consider how to improve student learning, they will be well served to look beyond the classroom walls.

Learning in and for the 21st Century

Here in the 21st century we know more about learning than we have ever known. We also find ourselves needing to maximize our capacity to learn, as never before. The needs of the 21st century demand that we learn how to live differently for a flourishing future. The challenges and opportunities in this age are not simple problems for which tweaking our lifestyles will be enough. Rather we are in an age for which deep, adaptive learning is needed (Barth & Michelsen, 2012; Kagawa & Selby, 2010). This requirement for adaptive learning touches and will continue to touch every aspect of our lives and every field of endeavor. "Society envisions graduates of school systems who can identify and solve problems and make contributions to society throughout their lifetime—who display the qualities of 'adaptive expertise'" (Bransford et al., 2000, p. 133). Bransford and colleagues (2000) further explained,

> Adaptive experts are able to approach new situations flexibly and to learn throughout their lifetimes. They not only use what they have learned, they are metacognitive and continually question their current levels of expertise and attempt to move beyond them. They don't simply attempt to do the same things more efficiently; they attempt to do things better. (p. 48)

If schools are to purposefully serve the needs of the 21st century, they need to engage students in opportunities for developing adaptive expertise. Students in green schools are frequently engaged in this type of learning. They are learning for sustainability through engaging deeply in places, and developing their competency for citizenship.

Engaging Deeply in Places

As we learned in Chapters 5 and 6, the places where we live provide relevant, meaningful, and powerful opportunities for engaged learning. Sobel (2004) described place-based education as:

> The process of using the local community and environment as a starting point to teach concepts in language arts, mathematics, social studies, science, and other subjects across the curriculum. Emphasizing hands-on, real-world learning experiences, this approach to education increases academic achievement, helps students develop stronger ties to their community, enhances students' appreciation for the natural world, and creates a heightened commitment to serving as active, contributing citizens. Community vitality and environmental quality are improved through the active engagement of local citizens, community organizations, and environmental resources in the life of the school. (p. 7)

In the decade since Sobel's landmark review of place-based education, educators and researchers have continued to demonstrate the profound value of using local communities as a central learning resource (Demarest, 2015; Gruenewald & Smith, 2014; Sobel, 2008). The power of place is highlighted in a recent and comprehensive review of student engagement research (Lawson & Lawson, 2013). These authors conceptualized student engagement broadly, "as the conceptual glue that connects student agency (including students' prior knowledge, experience, and interest at school, home, and in the community) and its ecological influences (peers, family, and community) to the organizational structures and cultures of school" (p. 433). Their recommendations for maximizing student engagement in learning include forgoing "one-size-fits-all interventions in favor of those tailored to fit local student, school, and community needs, contexts, and cultures" (p. 457). Place-based education does just this. It deeply engages students in local learning that empowers and enlivens them.

> The creation of curriculum to meet the diverse needs of students and communities becomes a fluid undertaking and brings life to what has become—in many places—a deadened exchange of information. When

the students and community are engaged in generating knowledge, it becomes a more vibrant process. There is a hum, a convergence of purpose, self-direction, knowledge, and future possibilities. (Demarest, 2015, p. 166)

Place-based education brings democratic principles to life in the classroom and community. Students "do democracy" rather than simply learn about democracy. "Democracy has always been a struggle for meaning and for change, and place-based education must demonstrate to students the challenges and potentialities of collective effort" (Gruenewald & Smith, 2014, p. xx). These place-based learning opportunities might start small within a particular classroom, as teachers learn their way into this fundamentally different way of teaching and learning. Or, they may go school wide, with place-based and/or thematic learning as the way learning happens for everyone (Meier, Knoester, & D'Andrea, 2015). Deborah Meier's work leading schools in New York City (Meier, 1995) and Boston (Knoester, 2012; Meier et al., 2015) provide inspiring examples of engaged student learning in democratic schools.

Place-based learning has long been a part of environmental education that deepens children's connection to nature, with investigations of natural ecosystems such as local creeks, ponds, forests, meadows, and coastal areas that are within a short walk from classrooms (Krapfel, 1999). As described early in this chapter, Tom's students were engaging deeply in their place of school by investigating their building systems and designing proposals for improvement projects—projects that would both improve building conditions for occupants, and reduce the building's ecological footprint. Students might also leave the school building to investigate their local community. One of Angela's elementary school teachers takes her classes on walking field trips where they collect information about the availability of fresh produce in their neighborhood. They visit corner groceries, drug stores, and even restaurants. They take on challenging questions about food quality, availability, cost, and wellness in conversations with store owners, chefs, and other community members. The fresh food they grow in their school garden takes on even greater value following these community investigations. As you can see, place-based education includes the whole place—the built environment of school, the community beyond school, and the ecosystems within which schools sit. Students become local experts, knowledgeable about their communities and better prepared to engage as citizens.

Developing Citizenship for Sustainability

Citizens engage with their communities along a continuum of practice. Westheimer and Kahne (2004) presented a typology of citizenship that included

three primary categories: citizens who are responsible, citizens who participate, and citizens who work to understand and solve root causes of challenging
problems. Gallup tells us that U.S. citizens donated money to a charity, volun-
teered their time, or helped a stranger more than any other country's citizens
worldwide (English, 2011). We are a generous people. However, Gallup did
not measure Westheimer and Kahne's third category of engaged citizenship.
We describe this third category as citizenship for sustainability. These individuals are more than responsible community members who also participate in
improving their communities. They are systems thinkers who understand the
deeper connections among many societal challenges. They understand the
interdependent nature of environmental, social, and economic issues. They
believe in their capacity to operate in and influence our democratic system.
They know how to and they strive to influence the transformation of society's
systems, processes, and policy. Developing citizens who work for the common good at this deeper, more strategic level, is no easy task.

Teaching students how to apply systems thinking for understanding the
complex challenges of the 21st century is critical, but not enough for developing their capacity as citizens. Chawla and Cushing (2007) investigated
research related to developing youth who are more likely to actively care for
the environment by engaging in collective political action. Their review of literature synthesized research related to developing pro-environmental behaviors, democratic practices, personal competence, and collective competence.
Although their review was focused on precursors for strategic environmental
action and not specifically citizenship for sustainability, their description of
strategic environmental action aligns well with our conception of citizenship
for sustainability, personally responsible citizens who extend beyond their
personal spheres and work strategically for the common good. Their findings
are a clarion call for green schools.

> all four bodies of research point toward a model of education that
> not only aims to produce active citizens, but embeds democratic prin-
> ciples within the education process. According to all four fields of
> research, children and youth need to take personal ownership of the
> issues that they work on, choosing personally significant goals and
> integrating action for the common good into their sense of identity.
> They also need opportunities for direct experience, beginning with
> intimately known natural areas, and extending into participation in
> managing their school and in tackling community projects where they
> can see for themselves how local government works and feel that they
> are making meaningful contributions. In the course of these experi-
> ences, they need opportunities for discussion, analyzing public issues

together, determining shared goals, resolving conflicts and articulating strategies for overcoming challenges and achieving success. In the process, they become role models of success for each other. (Chawla & Cushing, 2007, p. 448)

Conclusion

It turns out that developing citizenship for sustainability requires the very same practices that we know support individual well-being and engagement in learning. Green school leaders that ground their practice in ecological and democratic principles cultivate the conditions in which students' well-being is high and they engage more deeply in meaningful learning. Along the way, they also contribute to improving their communities. These are the types of schools that students and teachers jump out of bed to attend; they would choose to show up each day, even if they were not required. Imagine. A restored learning ecosystem that provides vibrantly engaged learning as an ecosystem service. That is the inspiring potential of the green schools movement.

Questions for Discussion

1. Enroll in and complete the U.S. Green Building Council (USGBC) Green Classroom Professional Certificate. What green practices are common across your school's classrooms? What green practices were new to you and your school? How might greening your classrooms better engage students' love of learning?

2. Reflect on yourself as a citizen. Which of Westheimer and Kahne's three categories (responsible, participatory, and active) best describe you? What opportunities do you see for extending your citizenship practice?

3. To what extent are students in your school developing as citizens for sustainability? What opportunities do they have for developing personally responsible behaviors? For participating in class-wide, school-wide, community-wide initiatives? For influencing class, school, district, community level policies? What opportunities do you see for maximizing their development as citizens for sustainability? Select one of these opportunities, gather a core team of colleagues, community members, and students, and co-create this new initiative.

Note

1 The U.S. Green Building Council offers the Green Classroom Professional Certificate (http://www.usgbc.org/classroom/gcp) for educators who want to learn more about cultivating healthy contexts for learning.

References

Awang-Hashim, R., Kaur, A., & Noman, M. (2015). The interplay of socio-psychological factors on school engagement among early adolescents. *Journal of Adolescence, 45,* 214–224. doi:10.1016/j.adolescence.2015.10.001

Barth, M., & Michelsen, G. (2012). Learning for change: An educational contribution to sustainability science. *Sustainability Science, 8*(1), 103–119. doi:10.1007/s11625-012-0181-5

Baumeister, D., & Herzlich, T. (2015). *What bees and forests can teach you about successful leadership.* Retrieved from: http://www.inc.com/dayna-baumeister/what-can-nature-teach-us-about-social-innovation.html

Benyus, J. M. (1997). *Biomimicry.* New York: William Morrow.

Benyus, J. M. (n.d.). *A biomimicry primer.* Retrieved from: http://biomimicry.net/b38files/A_Biomimicry_Primer_Janine_Benyus.pdf

Berto, R., Pasini, M., & Barbiero, G. (2015). How does psychological restoration work in children? An exploratory study. *Journal of Child and Adolescent Behaviour, 03*(03), 200–209. doi:10.4172/2375-4494.1000200

Bransford, J., Brown, A. L., & Cocking, R. R. (Eds.). (2000). *How people learn: Brain, mind, experience, and school.* Washington, DC: National Academy Press.

Chan, T. C., Mense, E. G., Lane, K. E., & Richardson, M. D. (Eds.). (2015). *Marketing the green school: Form, function, and the future.* Hershey, PA: Information Science Reference.

Chawla, L. (2015). Benefits of nature contact for children. *Journal of Planning Literature, 30*(4), 433–452. doi:10.1177/0885412215595441

Chawla, L., & Cushing, D. F. (2007). Education for strategic environmental behavior. *Environmental Education Research, 13*(4), 437–452. doi:10.1080/13504620701581539

Demarest, A. B. (2015). *Place-based curriculum design: Exceeding standards through local investigations.* New York: Routledge.

Dodge, R., Daly, A., Huyton, J., & Sanders, L. (2012). The challenge of defining well-being. *International Journal of Wellbeing, 2*(3), 222–235. doi:10.5502/ijw.v2i3.4

Dumont, H., Istance, D., & Benavides, F. (2010). *The nature of learning: Using research to inspire practice.* Paris, France: OECD.

English, C. (2011). Civic engagement highest in developed countries. Retrieved from: http://www.gallup.com/poll/145589/civic-engagement-highest-developed-countries.aspx

Frumkin, H., Geller, R., Rubin, I. L., & Nodvin, J. (2006). *Safe and healthy school environments.* New York: Oxford University Press.

Gill, T. (2014). The benefits of children's engagement with nature: A systematic literature review. *Children Youth and Environments, 24*(2), 10–34.

Gillett-Swan, J. K., & Sargeant, J. (2014). Wellbeing as a process of accrual: Beyond subjectivity and beyond the moment. *Social Indicators Research, 121*(1), 135–148. doi:10.1007/s11205-014-0634-6

Gillis, K., & Gatersleben, B. (2015). A review of psychological literature on the health and wellbeing benefits of biophilic design. *Buildings, 5*(3), 948–963. doi:10.3390/buildings5030948

Goleman, D., Bennett, L., & Barlow, Z. (2012). *Ecoliterate: How educators are cultivating emotional, social, and ecological intelligence.* San Francisco, CA: Jossey- Bass.

Goleman, D., & Senge, P. M. (2014). *The Triple Focus: A new approach to education.* Florence, MA: More Than Sound, LLC.

Gruenewald, D. A., & Smith, G. A. (2014). *Place-based education in the global age: Local diversity.* New York: Routledge.

Hartig, T., Mitchell, R., de Vries, S., & Frumkin, H. (2014). Nature and health. *Annual Review of Public Health, 35,* 207–228. doi:10.1146/annurev-publhealth-032013-182443

Houten, G. V., Reckhow, K., Loomis, R., Cunningham, J., & Casey, S. (2012). *Enterprise assessment for the reduction of nutrient pollution in South Florida waters* (RTI Project Number 0212984.000.001). Retrieved from Research Triangle Park, NC: http://www.evergladesfoundation.org/wp-content/uploads/2012/04/Report-RTI-Study.pdf

Jennings, P. A., & Greenberg, M. T. (2009). The prosocial classroom: Teacher social and emotional competence in relation to student and classroom outcomes. *Review of Educational Research, 79*(1), 491–525. doi:10.3102/0034654308325693

Kachur, D. S., Stout, J. A., & Edwards, C. L. (2013). *Engaging teachers in classroom walkthroughs.* Alexandria, VA: ASCD.

Kagawa, F., & Selby, D. (2010). *Education and climate change.* New York: Routledge.

Kellert, S. R., Heerwagen, J. H., & Mador, M. L. (2008). *Biophilic design: The theory, science, and practice of bringing buildings to life.* Hoboken, NJ: Wiley.

Knoester, M. (2012). *Democratic education in practice.* New York: Teachers College Press.

Krapfel, P. (1999). Deepening children's participation through local ecological investigations. In G. A. Smith & D. R. Williams (Eds.), *Ecological education in action: On weaving education, culture, and the environment* (pp. 47–78). Albany, NY: State University of New York Press.

Kuo, M. (2015). How might contact with nature promote human health? Promising mechanisms and a possible central pathway. *Frontiers in Psychology, 6,* 1093. doi:10.3389/fpsyg.2015.01093

Lawson, M. A., & Lawson, H. A. (2013). New conceptual frameworks for student engagement research, policy, and practice. *Review of Educational Research, 83*(3), 432–479. doi:10.3102/0034654313480891

Lewallen, T. C., Hunt, H., Potts-Datema, W., Zaza, S., & Giles, W. (2015). The whole school, whole community, whole child model: A new approach for improving educational attainment and healthy development for students. *Journal of School Health, 85*(11), 729–739.

Lopez, R., Campbell, R., & Jennings, J. (2008). *Schoolyard improvements and standardized test scores: An ecological analysis.* Retrieved from Boston, MA: http://www.schoolyards.org/pdf/sy_improvements_test_scores.pdf

Louv, R. (2008). *Last child in the woods: Saving our children from nature deficit disorder.* Chapel Hill, NC: Algonquin Books of Chapel Hill.

Mager, U., & Nowak, P. (2012). Effects of student participation in decision making at school: A systematic review and synthesis of empirical research. *Educational Research Review, 7*(1), 38–61. doi:10.1016/j.edurev.2011.11.001

Meier, D. (1995). *The power of their ideas: Lessons for America from a small school in Harlem.* Boston, MA: Beacon Press.

Meier, D., Knoester, M., & D'Andrea, K. C. (Eds.). (2015). *Teaching in themes: An approach to schoolwide learning, creating community, and differentiating instruction.* New York: Teachers College Press.

Murphy, J. (2015). The empirical and moral foundations of the ISLLC Standards. *Journal of Educational Administration, 53*(6), 718–734. doi:10.1108/jea-08-2014-0103

Mustapa, N. D., Maliki, N. Z., & Hamzah, A. (2015). Repositioning children's developmental needs in space planning: A review of connection to nature. *Procedia—Social and Behavioral Sciences, 170,* 330–339. doi:10.1016/j.sbspro.2015.01.043

NBEA. (2015). *Professional standards for educational leaders 2015.* Retrieved from Reston, VA: http://www.ccsso.org/Documents/2015/ProfessionalStandardsfor EducationalLeaders2015forNPBEAFINAL.pdf

Russell, R., Guerry, A. D., Balvanera, P., Gould, R. K., Basurto, X., Chan, K. M. A., . . . Tam, J. (2013). Humans and nature: How knowing and experiencing nature affect well-being. *Annual Review of Environment and Resources, 38*(1), 473–502. doi:10.1146/annurev-environ-012312-110838

Seeley, T. D. (2010). *Honeybee democracy.* Princeton, NJ: Princeton University Press.

Senge, P. M., Cambron-McCabe, N., Lucas, T., Smith, B., & Dutton, J. (2012). *Schools that learn (updated and revised): A fifth discipline fieldbook for educators, parents, and everyone who cares about education.* New York: Crown Business.

Shernoff, D. J., Tonks, S. M., & Anderson, B. (2014). The impact of the learning environment on student engagement in high school classrooms. In D. J. Shernoff & J. Bempechat (Eds.), *Engaging youth in schools: Evidence-based models to guide future innovations* (pp. 166–177). New York: NSSE Yearbooks by Teachers College Record.

Sobel, D. (2004). *Place-based education: Connecting classrooms and communities.* Barrington, MA: The Orion Society.

Sobel, D. (2008). *Childhood and nature: Design principles for educators.* Portland, Maine: Stenhouse Publishers.

Strong, W. B., Malina, R. M., Blimkie, C. J., Daniels, S. R., Dishman, R. K., Gutin, B., . . . Trudeau, F. (2005). Evidence based physical activity for school-age youth. *Journal of Pediatrics, 146*(6), 732–737. doi:10.1016/j.jpeds.2005.01.055

Sukhdev, P., Wittmer, H., Schroter-Schlaack, C., Nesshover, C., Bishop, J., ten Brink, P., . . . Simmons, B. (2010). *Mainstreaming the economics of nature: A synthesis of the approach, conclusions and recommendations of TEEB.* Retrieved from

Geneva, Switzerland: http://www.teebweb.org/publication/mainstreaming-the-economics-of-nature-a-synthesis-of-the-approach-conclusions-and-recommendations-of-teeb/

Sznitman, S. R., Reisel, L., & Romer, D. (2011). The neglected role of adolescent emotional well-being in national educational achievement: Bridging the gap between education and mental health policies. *Journal of Adolescent Health, 48*(2), 135–142. doi:10.1016/j.jadohealth.2010.06.013

Thapa, A., Cohen, J., Guffey, S., & Higgins-D'Alessandro, A. (2013). A review of school climate research. *Review of Educational Research, 83*(3), 357–385. doi:10.3102/0034654313483907

Tokuhama-Espinosa, T. (2010). *The new science of teaching and learning: Using the best of mind, brain, and education science in the classroom.* New York: Teachers College Press.

Vieno, A., Perkins, D. D., Smith, T. M., & Santinello, M. (2005). Democratic school climate and sense of community in school: A multilevel analysis. *American Journal of Community Psychology, 36*(3–4), 327–341. doi:10.1007/s10464-005-8629-8

Westheimer, J., & Kahne, J. (2004). What kind of citizen? The politics of educating for democracy. *American Educational Research Journal, 41*(2), 237–269.

Wheatley, M. J. (1999). *Leadership and the new science: Discovering order in a chaotic world* (3rd ed.). San Francisco: Berrett-Koehler.

Wijkman, A., & Rockstrom, J. (2012). *Bankrupting nature: Denying our planetary boundaries.* New York: Routledge.

Williams, D. R., & Brown, J. (2011). *Learning gardens and sustainability education.* New York: Routledge.

Williams, D. R., & Dixon, P. S. (2013). Impact of garden-based learning on academic outcomes in schools: Synthesis of research between 1990 and 2010. *Review of Educational Research, 83*(2), 211–235. doi:10.3102/0034654313475824

Wilson, E. O. (1984). *Biophilia*: Cambridge, MA: Harvard University Press.

9

Innovative Teaching in Green Schools

Inequitable access to educational opportunity is, by definition, unsustainable. Anyone who aspires to teach for sustainability must be committed to the success of all students and, similarly, any educational procedure that purports to be for sustainability must first and foremost be focused on improving the learning outcomes of all children.

(Nolet, 2016, p. 11)

In Chapter 4 we explored the ways green school leaders cultivate powerful visions for whole school sustainability. These leaders, in concert with their teachers, students, parents, and community stakeholders, commit to developing the learning capacity of all their members as means to serve local and global needs in the 21st century. Green schools strive to be healthy, socio-ecological systems that engage children and adults in deep learning about how to live in more sustainable ways. Such a vision connects the daily work of school to meaningful, purposeful aims, providing a powerful motivator for teachers and their students. As green school leaders and their teachers establish instructional, curricular, and operational goals that are personally compelling and appropriately challenging, they further engender a sense of collective commitment to this vision.

Even as commitment grows, green school leaders will likely encounter teachers, who, in the face of more immediate challenges, have difficulty "see[ing] the relevance of overconsumption and global climate change or to be concerned with impacts that may seem decades in the future" (Nolet, 2009, p. 412). Teachers currently face a sense of cognitive dissonance brought on by state and federal accountability policies that reveal inequities in students' opportunities to learn and achieve. Recent implementation of the more rigorous Common Core State Standards (CCSS) and the Next Generation Science Standards (NGSS) may only increase this sense of urgency and frustration, as more challenging expectations reveal even wider gaps in students' learning. In the face of these challenges, effective principals will seek to develop their teachers and build their capacity to "acquir[e] new sets of knowledge, skills, ways of thinking, and . . . values" (Waters, Marzano, & McNulty, 2003, p. 51), confronting longstanding myths about who is and is not capable of mastering these rigorous academic standards.

Education for sustainability (EfS) and whole school approaches to delivering such education rests in a set of knowledge, skills, ways of thinking, and values that has potential to reenergize teachers and build their sense of efficacy for addressing the diverse needs of learners. As they are provided the requisite time and resources to develop and implement the interdisciplinary, learner-centered, problem- and place-based learning experiences upon which these approaches rest, they will come to realize the potential of these methods to ensure *all* their students enjoy ample opportunities to learn and achieve. In fact, it may just be their students who provide the most persuasive arguments for investing time and effort in learning these methods as they "look to their teachers for answers and assurances about a safe, healthy, and sustainable future" (Bauermeister & Diefenbacher, 2015, p. 326). Our children may likely be the ones to "show [us] how sustainability could and should be seen as an urgent social imperative and critical context for twenty-first century learning" (McClam & Diefenbacher, 2015, p. 129).

This chapter examines how teachers in green schools learn and model the sustainability-related behaviors, dispositions, and habits of mind they seek to develop in their students. First, we consider how teachers might acquire deep knowledge of principles and constructs underlying education for sustainability and whole school approaches to its delivery. We examine how sustainability-focused concepts provide teachers opportunities to engage all their students in mastering rigorous and integrated academic content, and how teachers, themselves, develop like habits of mind and practice in order to do so. We explore how green school principals develop and sustain professional communities among teachers at their schools, providing opportunities for teachers to reflect deeply and critically on their own teaching practice. We consider how these same principals reinvent structures and processes to support the work. Finally, we discover how teachers learn about the design intentions of their green facilities so they might better model green operations and maintenance routines and leverage all the features of their green, three-dimensional textbook.

Teachers in Green Schools Model a Commitment to Deep Knowledge

The Earth Charter, formally instituted at the Hague Peace Palace in 2000 and signed by 6,000 governmental agencies, non-governmental organizations (NGOs), businesses, universities, schools, and religious and youth groups, is now considered, "a global consensus statement on the core principles of sustainability" (Nolet, 2016, p. 51). The Charter speaks directly to educating children and youth in ways that "empower them to contribute actively to sustainable development" (The Earth Charter Initiative, 2015). As we discussed in Chapter 3, the United Nations' Decade of Education for Sustainable Development (UNDESD), begun in 2005, seeks large-scale changes in our educational systems aimed at promoting this sort of education. Teacher preparation and professional development are among the primary foci for UNDESD work (Wals, 2009). As you begin to examine how best to institute education for sustainability within your school, you might spend some time exploring related documents and websites as foundational to your ongoing inquiry. As you decide how best to apply the fundamental principles of the Earth Charter, and work toward UNDESD goals, you and your teachers will no doubt encounter multiple, interrelated approaches and methods to inform your work. Table 9.1 summarizes commonly utilized terms.

All these approaches underscore a focus on environmental issues and relevant content. Some extend beyond environmental concerns to include the economic and social dimensions of life on our planet. Most stress the examination of values and seek subsequent changes in behavior. They urge learning within a local context, but require the application of global perspectives. All approaches place students at the center, engaging them in active, place-based, problem-based, and community-connected learning to encourage participation and critical thinking. In most cases, academic content is presented in a rigorous, interdisciplinary fashion, informing students' efforts to solve real-world problems.

All of these approaches depend upon teachers building foundational knowledge of sustainability concepts. In Chapter 3, you were introduced to fundamental principles underlying whole school sustainability. These principles are worth sharing with your teachers. In his recent book, entitled *Educating for Sustainability: Principles and Practices for Teachers*, Victor Nolet (2016) identifies a number of Big Ideas, in the manner of Wiggins and McTighe (2005), as over-arching constructs or themes which also inform a

Table 9.1 Terms Associated with Teaching for Sustainability

Environmental Education (EE)	Engages students in study of the environment to "encourage behavior change and action" (Thomas, 2005). EE employs hands-on activities and relevant subject matter to engage students and encourage participation. EE is "a creative and dynamic process in which pupils and teachers are engaged together in a search for solutions to environmental problems" (Fien & Tilbury, 1996). (Riordan & Klein, 2010)
Education for Sustainable Development (EfSD)	Prepares learners to make informed decisions and take responsible actions aimed at environmental integrity, economic viability, and a just society. EfSD is interdisciplinary and holistic, embedded in the whole curriculum, and values based. It emphasizes open-ended, generative thinking, critical thinking, problem solving, participatory decision making and systems thinking. EfSD is based on local context but connected to global issues, is culturally responsive and learner centered. (UNESCO, 2005)
EcoJustice Education	Teaches protection of living systems and community well-being through examination and response to what degrades them. EcoJustice Education recognizes the importance of biological and cultural diversity, and the need to make decisions on behalf of all who will be most affected, including future generations and the more than human world. Recognizes and re-values diverse commons-based practices, traditions, and knowledge from cultures and communities world-wide. (Lowenstein, Martusewicz, & Voelker, 2010)
Education for Sustainability (EfS)	Seeks to equip learners to deal with the challenges that arise from the interconnectedness of environment, culture, society, and economy that typifies life in the 21st century. EfS helps learners develop new ways of thinking, collaborating, and solving problems. Learning focuses on local concerns, interpreted through larger global perspectives. EfS is interdisciplinary, holistic, and embedded across the curriculum. It is culturally responsive, and values-based. Employs a variety of methods and pedagogies, with particular attention to learner-centered strategies. (Nolet, 2016)
Whole School Sustainability	Recognizes that sustainability is relevant to all aspects of school life including formal and hidden curricula, school leadership and management as well as teacher development. Whole-school approaches encourage schools to practice what they preach. (Ferreira, Ryan, & Tilbury, 2008)

sustainability worldview (i.e., "a way of seeing and engaging in the world through the lens of sustainability," p. 10). By no means a comprehensive list of sustainability-related concepts, Nolet suggests these eight provide a minimal set, that, once understood, will "assist teachers in prioritizing content, identifying learning progressions, developing long-term plans, anticipating students preconceptions, and guiding student learning" (Nolet, 2016, p. 68). Nolet's eight Big Ideas, *equity and social justice, peace and collaboration, universal responsibility, health and resiliency, respect for limits, connecting with nature, local to global,* and *interconnectedness,* provide a point of departure for teacher learning.

Equity and justice stands at the center of a sustainability worldview. This Big Idea incorporates a number of related concepts, including social justice, economic justice, environmental justice, gender equity, food justice, climate equity, and intergenerational equity. Through the lens of equity and justice, we consider access to resources and opportunities, confront notions of privilege, and distinguish wants from needs.

Peace and collaboration, as a Big Idea, recognizes our fundamental human need for amity and security. It also underscores the environmental conditions that threaten peace. As we come to understand the interconnectedness of human and natural systems, we appreciate how peace and collaboration contribute to a healthy planet, while conflict between people and nations has deleterious effects on both the human and the natural world.

Universal responsibility holds us to account for the consequences of our decisions and actions. This Big Idea underscores our obligation to "promote the creation of a safe and just space for all forever" (2016, p. 74). Universal responsibility requires we refrain from doing harm and *more.* Here we expect our students to realize their potential as active agents in creating a sustainable future.

Health and resiliency offers students "a context for investigating the characteristics of healthy, thriving systems" (2016, p. 75). We consider questions about individual health and well-being, on the one hand, and large scale concerns such as hunger and disease, on the other. A focus on resilience encourages an asset-based stance that underscores an individual's or a system's ability to change, to weather hardship or trauma, and to continue functioning and developing. This Big Idea also allows students to examine their own capacity to adapt to life events.

A simple outdoor life science/woodshop project had Tom's ninth graders, and Tom, thinking about explicit signs of health and resilience on their school campus.

The students worked to build the birdhouses on the wall outside the classroom. Birds came here, nested, and had their babies. We even had a killdeer make a nest in the garden beds. They do a nest in the ground. We are creating and providing opportunity for new life. When you think about these large comprehensive high schools in our communities with so many problems and so many kids dropping out, every social ill is there. And yet, I thought, it's really something when you can provide new life in an adolescent environment.

Respect for limits acknowledges the Earth's finite capacity to support the survival of its inhabitants. This Big Idea calls for a transformation in the way we think about our relationships with one other, with the generations who will follow us, with other species. Students are called to question their own wants and needs as they examine the implications of consumption in relation to notions of fairness and justice.

Connecting with nature addresses the ways humans interact with the natural world. We explored this Big Idea in greater depth in Chapter 8 as we considered the critical role that contact with nature plays in children's well-being, development, and learning. As students learn in and from nature, they gain new respect for the elegance, balance, efficiency, and adaptability of natural systems. "Learning in and from nature also help learners integrate otherwise abstract theoretical concepts into a more active and personal understanding" (2016, p. 77).

Local to global captures the interdependence of our social, economic, political and natural systems worldwide. It further underscores how our local actions impact the global community; indeed, it reminds us that we are all members of this global community, for good or bad. We have returned repeatedly to this Big Idea across chapters in this book, demonstrating how education for sustainability engages students in the places they inhabit as a practical and profound means to connect them with the wider world.

Interconnectedness draws our attention to interwoven human and natural systems, i.e., social-ecological systems (Nolet, 2016). As a Big Idea, it leads students to engage in systems thinking, examining how individual elements of a system interact with one another (e.g., organisms within an ecosystem) or grappling with complex, large-scale environmental, social, and economic systems that extend globally, with reach and influence across nations and regions.

Together, these sustainability-related Big Ideas provide a "robust framework for exploration of content standards and application of critical thinking, problem solving, and systems thinking" required of students as they are assessed on the CCSS and NGSS (Nolet, 2016, p. 102).

Nolet (2016) warns that "[m]uch of what gets labeled 'education for sustainability' is poorly planned, superficial, of too short duration, incomplete, or just plain wrong—the educational equivalent of green washing" (p. 41). He challenges teachers to "develop a deep and integrated understanding of information that makes up the sustainability knowledge domain" (p. 41). Nolet's book provides a solid foundation for teachers interested and motivated to do so. He further recommends teachers explore exemplars of effectively implemented sustainability education that has resulted in positive student outcomes (Nolet, 2009), including, for example, *Ecological Literacy: Educating Our Children for a Sustainable World* (Stone & Barlow, 2005); *The Earth Charter in Action: Toward a Sustainable World* (Corcoran, Vilela, & Roerink, 2005);

Place-Based Education: Connecting Classrooms and Communities (Sobel, 2005); and *Learning Gardens and Sustainability Education: Bringing Life to Schools and Schools to Life* (Williams & Brown, 2012).

Teachers in Green Schools Model Integrated Habits of Mind and Practice

Standard 6 of the new Professional Standards for Educational Leaders (PSEL) specifically calls for school leaders to develop the professional capacity and practice of school personnel to promote each student's academic success and well-being, through, for example, recruitment, hiring, support, development, and retention of effective and caring teachers and other professional staff, forming these individuals into an educationally effective faculty. Standard 7 suggests this support and development is best provided via establishment of a professional community of teachers, encouraging a culture of engagement and commitment to a shared vision and related goals, focused on the education of the whole child. According to the standard, effective principals provide opportunities for collaborative examination of practice, collegial feedback, and collective learning. Standard 10 directs principals to grow leaders among teachers and empower them to inquiry, experiment, and innovate for continuous classroom and school improvement (National Policy Board for Educational Administration, 2015).

We already know important things about the way teachers view their work. Altering teachers' perceptions of their work is no easy task; the capacity to resist change is enormous (Goodlad, 1984). Teachers' desire for privacy and autonomy and their primary dedication to classroom matters and instructional concerns often impedes the more collaborative relationships upon which education for sustainability relies. These same relationships will be necessary as schools work to implement more rigorous learning standards. Both education for sustainability and the CCSS require an integrated approach to lesson development through which teachers build students' competence across multiple standards and disciplines simultaneously. Nolet (2016) reminds us that no "one discipline claims ownership [of education for sustainability], all disciplines share responsibility, . . . includ[ing] content from quantitative reasoning/math, inquiry/natural sciences, creativity/the arts, critical thinking and policy analysis, social studies, communication and media, literacy/language arts, spatial reasoning/geography" (pp. 8–9).

Education for sustainability's essential practice of integrating content and instruction provides a fitting context for implementing the more rigorous learning standards schools now face. These new integrated habits of practice are nuanced and, by necessity, interrelated, thus requiring time to develop and refine. Teachers wrestle with "the exquisitely fragile relationship among knowing, valuing, and doing" (Nolet, 2009, p. 429), facing fears about their individual and collective capacity to transform classroom practice in ways that increase students' engagement and spark their love for learning. There is good news for teachers, however, for sustainability, by its very nature, "creates an accessible path to help new [and seasoned] teachers link discipline and pedagogical content with real-world problems, . . . captur[ing] the contextual nature of deep learning" (Nolet, 2009, pp. 432, 429).

As we discussed in Chapter 8, students choose to engage with and learn content to the degree this content is meaningful to them. As teachers come to know their students well, they are better able to facilitate connections between academic disciplines and between new material and students' prior knowledge and individual interests. Chapter 8 underscores the importance of teachers' efforts to individualize content and connect it horizontally across content areas and contexts, as means to develop accurate frameworks of knowledge (Dumont, Istance, & Benavides, 2010).

No doubt, your teachers will call upon their current knowledge as they grapple with conceptual shifts in understanding about how students learn. These new understandings and expectations will require that teachers look across instructional units, across content areas, and across grade and school levels to build a purposeful plan for scaffolding students' learning of integrated content knowledge. Such a comprehensive view of curricular and instructional practice may push you to consider new structures and systems to facilitate the work. Excellent teaching within individual classrooms will not suffice. In order to contribute to the larger vision, teachers must plan, organize, research, and experiment together in more collaborative fashion.

Teachers in Green Schools Model Collaborative Inquiry and Problem Solving

As you seek to develop your teachers' capacity to teach for sustainability, it will be necessary to provide multiple, ongoing, job-embedded opportunities for reflective dialogue. In order for teachers to successfully adapt and refine their teaching practices, they must have opportunities to participate in what Putnam and Borko (1997, pp. 1247, 1250) call "discourse communities."

> Just as students cannot learn science by interacting with the physical world without interaction with others who know science, teachers are unlikely to transcend their current view of teaching practice without

an influx of ideas or ways of thinking about teaching, learning, and subject matter from another source. Just as students need to learn new ways of reasoning, communicating, and thinking, and to acquire dispositions of inquiry and sense-making through their participation in classroom discourse communities, teachers need to construct their complex new roles and ways of thinking about their teaching practice within the context of supportive learning communities.

These collaborative professional learning communities provide opportunities for teachers to reflect deeply and critically on their own teaching practice, on the content they teach, and on the experiences and backgrounds of the learners in their classrooms. Sharing with one another in this way supports the risk taking and struggle entailed in transforming practice. It can also help teachers impose meaning and organization on incoming information in light of their existing knowledge and beliefs (Putnam & Borko, 1997). Working with other teachers within a context of mutual respect, one that encourages productive levels of debate, challenge, and conflict, can invigorate teaching with increased intellectual stimulation, and clarify values as these become increasingly explicit and shared (Putnam & Borko, 1997).

School leaders play a vital role in providing and protecting sufficient time for teachers to meet in professional community with one another, guiding the vision and subsequent professional development goals that will be pursued during this time, and providing necessary resources to support the ongoing inquiry that is central to the work of professional communities (Louis, Marks, & Kruse, 1996; Mullen & Hutinger, 2008; Olivier & Hipp, 2006). Along with these opportunities for discussing, planning, analyzing, evaluating, and experimenting together, teachers can be further encouraged through planned and structured professional development. Much of this can and should be self-initiated and directed. As the employees having responsibility for instruction and the most direct, ongoing contact with students, teachers are a school system's primary source of organizational knowledge about means and ends (Bacharach & Conley, 1988). Wise leaders will take advantage of this source and give teachers the chance to teach each other.

Your teachers no doubt span the career continuum, with some seasoned professionals ready to jump whole hog into project-based, collaborative, place- and community-embedded teaching and learning. Beginning teachers may be less confident about their ability to facilitate and manage the uncertainty and ambiguity that comes with challenging the traditional architecture of instruction. All teachers must learn to guide student inquiry, let questions emerge, and be more comfortable with the complexity and uncertainty that results (Lowenstein et al., 2010).

> As teachers engage in challenging learning both in and out of the classroom, teachers require a sense of their own efficacy. As teachers work with students over time and see that their students are capable of engaging in the kinds of deep thinking and reasoning they never thought possible, teachers' own sense of efficacy increases. (Woolfolk Hoy, Davis, & Pape, 2006, p. 734)

Angela observed this sort of deep thinking and reasoning among middle grade students and their teachers as they pursued a science project in genetics. She connected her observation to the new learning standards being implemented across the district.

> Students get excited to learn science, or any kind of curriculum, that is relevant to their everyday lives. And, there is this wonderful synergy between this applied learning and the new CCSS standards we're attempting to implement. The learning curve is steep for teachers, but they are out there in the garden with each other and their students, diving into Mendel and fine genetics. And, they can do it in a very hands-on way, starting with the peas.

Teachers in Green Schools Model Thoughtful Interaction with the Physical Learning Environment

As teachers are better apprised of the design intentions for their green school building, they may be motivated to collaborate more, experiment more, and venture out across the landscape beyond the classroom walls. Learning the way a building works, and why, constitutes an important focus for teacher professional development.

> When a disjuncture occurs between sustainable design and curricular delivery, teachers may be under additional stress . . . Typical problem areas identified with green schools are windows too high to open or controlled by a computerized management system . . . inadequate solar shading of south-facing windows . . . temperatures sometimes too low in the winter and too high in the summer . . . These problems are most prevalent when schools are inadequately maintained or when the operation of environmental controls is not understood by teachers. (Edwards, 2006, p. 26)

As mentioned in Chapter 7, occupant training is most effectively provided through a comprehensive commissioning process, spanning from pre-design through occupancy, and even beyond (Lackney, 2005). In one of its earliest uses, commissioning was a process utilized for the testing U.S. naval ships to ensure their reliability and quality prior to deployment. Commissioning was later integrated into the language of facility professionals to describe a process for validating a building's performance in relation to operational requirements and design intent (Lackney, 2005). Within the past ten years, Lackney and colleagues coined and trademarked the term *educational commissioning* to refer to a specific context and process "through which teachers, students, and even parents and community partners are educated as to the design intent of a newly constructed school facility" (Lackney, 2005, p. 1). While similar to previous conceptions of the term, this iteration moves beyond the original idea of simply evaluating quality and fit. By involving, educating, and training occupants and stakeholders throughout the design process and through move-in and beyond, we increase the likelihood that the building will support the specific learning and teaching needs of those who inhabit it day to day. This learning results in a higher probability of successful and effective designs.

For example, designers can share the story of the design intentions, facilitating conversation among teachers regarding various design decisions. Teachers should be encouraged to ask questions and share anecdotes about ways they envision the physical space, furniture, technological resources, and outdoor learning environment supporting or hindering aspects of the educational experience. After living and working in the spaces, these commissioning activities can also include teacher reflective tours, during which teachers are invited to spend time thinking about their individual perceptions and answering questions about how the space supports learning and teaching. Finally, teachers can engage students in similar mapping activities, encouraging them to explore their own experiences in the school and charting the ways their favorite and least favorite spaces support or limit their opportunities to learn.

Educating about purpose is particularly important, because design intentions are not always obvious to building users. Teachers may not pay detailed attention to the physical learning environment and, in particular, to its impact on their own and their students' behavior and well-being. As a result, they are less prepared to benefit from purposeful design decisions and more likely to misuse or remain unaware of specific features. Too often, we adapt spaces unnecessarily and inappropriately, waste time attempting to discern how a space can be manipulated to meet specific activity requirements, and/or utilize innovative, unconventional spaces in very traditional ways.

When school building occupants are more informed about possibilities and more involved in defining parameters, acclimation to sustainable features and technologies is assured, and users are better able to envision how these can be leveraged to change the way learning takes place. As educators have opportunity to learn green buildings, "they begin to use the world of the physical environment as a teaching tool to help students understand the underlying laws and principles that govern our complex, precious universe" (Taylor, 2009, p. 3).

Green School Leaders Balance Challenge with Support

In the face of new challenges, effective leaders quell fears and maintain productive learning cultures by adjusting systems and structures that no longer adequately support the work of teachers and students (Leithwood, Louis, Anderson, & Wahlstrom, 2004). As school leaders investigate possible processes and systems to support the implementation of whole school sustainability, they are wise to direct their inquiry toward "both the classroom conditions that students experience directly and the wider organizational conditions that enable, stimulate, and support these conditions" (Leithwood & Sun, 2012, p. 413). A simultaneous focus on the technical core of learning and teaching, along with the organizational purposes, structures, and processes that influence this core, will help you, as principal, leverage the energy of your school's professional community to accomplish the necessary changes in instructional and curricular norms of practice at your school.

In a review of literature commissioned by UNESCO to gauge progress toward UNDESD goals, Tilbury (2011) identified four common learning and teaching processes driving education for sustainable development programs throughout the world. First, ongoing *processes of collaboration and dialogue* encourage active participation and engagement of multiple stakeholders, inviting intercultural exchange and learning partnerships across schools, universities, museums, businesses, governmental organizations, and community agencies and institutions. Second, *processes which engage the whole system* build energy and commitment across classrooms, between departments and grade levels, throughout school districts, and beyond to all levels of the education system, from early childhood to higher education. Educators not only question what they teach and how they teach it, but also invent new organizational structures, operational routines, and management practices to facilitate and support these new ways of schooling. As discussed throughout this book, whole-school approaches recognize that sustainability is relevant to all aspects of school life, including formal and hidden curricula, the school's leadership and management, as well as teacher development (Ferreira, Ryan, & Tilbury, 2006). Chapter 10 will introduce strategies for influencing change at all levels of the organization, along with powerful examples of U.S. Department of Education Green Ribbon Schools that are recognized for making strides toward this sort of transformation. Third, *processes of innovation* encourage transformations in academic learning, placing students within learning experiences where they themselves solve problems, clarify their values, and facilitate change. Finally, *processes of active and participatory learning* engage students in asking reflective questions, envisioning more positive futures, thinking systemically, applying what they learn in context, and exploring the tensions between tradition and innovation. From storytelling, singing, dance and outdoor play for very young children to real-life projects, action research, and interactive symposia for older children, students assume an active role in constructing their own knowledge with their teachers as facilitators and partners in learning.

The implementation of education for sustainability provides school leaders new purchase on their continuing efforts to improve instructional effectiveness at their schools. Education for sustainability requires students to stretch for higher, more complex levels of subject matter thinking. Education for sustainability requires teachers to accomplish heightened levels of integration across content area and grade levels. Education for sustainability addresses the knowledge and skills necessary for college and careers, from the primary grades on. More so than ever, school leaders' classroom level inquiry and observations and will need to address "the central intellectual ideas of the lesson, . . . pay[ing] attention to how they are being developed within the classroom's structures and practices" (Nelson & Sassi, 2000, p. 574). Teachers will need this close examination of their practice, from you and from their peers, in order to discern if they are making the grade in challenging their students to high levels of engagement with rigorous, integrated, and context-embedded curricula.

The challenges you and your teachers face will be made all the more substantial as you attempt to initiate change while in the midst of conducting your everyday business. Engaging in significant change involves a period of disequilibrium that can leave teachers and administrators anxious, uncertain, and stressed (Uline, Tschannen-Moran, & Perez, 2003), even if the changes also bring about renewed excitement and vigor. Tom reflected on his role in removing impediments to progress at his school:

> School administrators have tremendous veto power just by dragging their feet. On the other hand, if we actively engage, if we believe and communicate that this new way of learning is important for all of us, things move forward. When I approach teachers and ask, "How do we make this bigger, stronger?" I also must ask, "How can I make this easier for you to accomplish?" "What can I take away so you have time to focus?" "How can I make your job more possible?"

If we accomplish this sort of careful, thoughtful, integrated change across all levels of the educational system, the means to more sustainability-focused habits of practice will not be squeezed in or tacked on or doubled scheduled or even scheduled. There will be no danger of us routinely canceling them in the name of other more important matters. The vehicles we introduce will, instead, be genuine, taking into account who initiates, who facilitates and for whom, who participates and for what purposes.

Conclusion

Even the most skilled and knowledgeable green school leaders will not accomplish the goals set out by the UNDESD in isolation from the larger system of public education. If education for sustainability, and whole-school approaches to such learning, are to have a fair chance, it may be necessary for state and federal officials to re-think policies related to the preparation of teachers and to academic content standards for students. Sustainability-focused curriculum goals are already embedded in learning standards for students in other nations. At least 50% of United Nations member states report having policies related to education for sustainable development (Buckler & Creech, 2014). Here in the United States, states frequently cited as innovators include California, Maryland, Massachusetts, Minnesota, Oregon, Vermont, Washington, and Wisconsin (Feinstein, 2009). A 2009 University of Wisconsin-Madison study on education for sustainable development in the United States reported only two states, Vermont and Washington, having integrated the language of sustainability into formal education policy (Feinstein, 2009). These states have adopted curricular and teacher education standards with direct relevance to education for sustainability.

According to the report, a significant number of states do include education for sustainability-relevant disciplinary materials, such as environmental science and economics, in content standards for traditional academic disciplines. As a result of the U.S. Department of Education's Green Ribbon School program, many states have applied the language and ideas of education for sustainability within in their state-level green schools initiatives and competitions. However, these programs remain voluntary without corresponding adoption of formal sustainability standards or related education policies. Consideration of such policy adjustments should proceed with caution, recognizing that existing measures were enacted for specific purpose, each according to the needs and interests of students and teachers. Any change must occur within the context of "continual public dialogue about the means and ends of schooling" (Tyack & Tobin, 1994, p. 478). As Nolet (2016) reminds us, "It would make no sense for something called education for sustainability to interfere with helping all learners develop a strong foundation in basic academic skills and knowledge . . . teaching for sustainability should enhance and augment teachers' day-to-day professional practices" (p. 10).

Each area of consideration addressed across the chapters of this book takes a different bearing on a single vision for designing and leading greener, more sustainable, and democratic school communities. Each one sets a course through the province of schooling—through the mediums of communication and participation, through the people who engage, through the structures they erect, and through the tools and techniques they fashion. Evidence from green schools across the United States and around the world suggests that when methods remain rigorous and thinking keen, our actions as green school leaders can be transformative. Making schools ecologically responsive places, where teachers, students, parents, and community members actively engage in creating a more sustainable future, will not remove the burden of responsibility green school leaders carry. School administrators will continue to be held to account, as well they should be. And yet, if schools can begin to function as more sustainable, democratic communities, teachers, and their students, will begin to hold themselves more responsible for the day-to-day workings of the enterprise, freeing their administrators to truly lead. This should engender a sense of optimism and confidence in the powers of human agency, for as Dewey reminds us:

> We are not caught in a circle; we traverse a spiral in which social customs generate some consciousness of interdependencies and this consciousness is embodied in acts . . . which generate new perceptions of social [as well as ecological] ties and so on forever. (Dewey, 1922, pp. 78, emphasis added)

Questions for Discussion

1. Choose one of Nolet's sustainability-related Big Ideas. Develop a discussion prompt that will push teaching teams/grade level planning teams/professional communities to consider how this Big Idea might provide a frame of reference for exploring particular learning standards they are currently addressing. Capture the content of one such discussion.

2. Describe the structures and processes you have designed to guarantee your teachers have sufficient time to meet, engage, and learn together. What do you do to protect this time and ensure it remains focused and productive?

3. Review the Earth Charter (http://earthcharter.org/). How might a focus on the principles of the Charter influence teaching and learning at your school?

References

Bacharach, S. B., & Conley, S. (1988). Uncertainty and decision-making in teaching: Implications for managing line professionals. In T. S. Sergiovanni, & J. H. Moore (Eds.), *Schooling for tomorrow: Directing reforms to issues that count* (pp. 311–329). Boston, MA: Allyn and Bacon.

Bauermeister, M. L., & Diefenbacher, L. H. (2015). Beyond recycling: Guiding preservice teachers to understand and incorporate the deeper principles of sustainability. *Childhood Education, 91,* 5, 325–331. doi:1080/00094056.2015.1090843

Buckler, C., & Creech, H. (2014). *Shaping the future we want: UN Decade of Education for Sustainable Development (2005–2014). Final report.* Retrieved from France: http://unesdoc.unesco.org/images/0023/002303/230302e.pdf

Corcoran, P.B., Vilela, M., & Roerink, A. (2005). *The Earth Charter in action: Toward a sustainable world.* Amsterdam: KIT.

Dewey, J. (1922). *Human nature and conduct.* New York: The Modern Library.

Dumont, H., Istance, D., & Benavides, F. (2010). *The nature of learning: Using research to inspire practice.* Paris, France: OECD.

Edwards, B. W. (2006). Environmental design and educational performance. *Research in Education, 76,* 14–32.

Feinstein, N. (2009). *Education for sustainable development in the United States of America: A report submitted to the International Alliance of Leading Education Institutes.* Madison, WI: Univeristy of Wisconsin-Madison.

Ferreira, J., Ryan, L., & Tilbury, D. (2006). *Whole-school approaches to sustainability: A review of models for professional development in pre-service teacher education.* Canberra: Australian Government Department of the Environment and Heritage and the Australian Research Institute in Education for Sustainability (ARIES).

Fien, J., & Tilbury, D. (1996). *Learning for a sustainable environment: An agenda.* Paris: UNESCO. Retrieved from: http://unesdoc.unesco.org/images/0010/001056/105607e.pdf

Goodlad, J. I. (1984). *A place called school.* New York: McGraw Hill Company.

Kelly, S. S., & Williams, D. R. (2013). Teacher professional learning communities for sustainability: Supporting STEM in learning gardens in low-income schools. *Journal of Sustainability Education,* Spring: *Experiential Education, Part One,* n.p.

Lackney, J. (2005). *Educating educators to optimize their school facility for teaching and learning.* Minneapolis, MN: Design Share. Retrieved from: http://www.designshare.com/index.php/articles/educational-commissioning/

Leithwood, K., Louis, K. S., Anderson, S., & Wahlstrom, K. (2004). *How leadership influences student learning.* Minneapolis, MN: Center for Applied Research and Educational Improvement & Ontario Institute for Studies in Education.

Leithwood, K., & Sun, J. (2012). The nature and effects of transformational school leadership: A meta-analytic review of unpublished research. *Educational Administration Quarterly, 48,* 387–423.

Louis, K. S., Marks, H. M., & Kruse, S. (1996). Teachers' professional community in restructuring schools. *American Educational Research Journal, 33*, 757–798.

Lowenstein, E., Martusewicz, R., & Voelker, L. (2010). Developing teachers' capacity for ecojustice education and community-based learning. *Teacher Education Quarterly, 37*, 4, 99–118.

McClam, S., & Diefenbacher, L. (2015). Over the fence: Learning about education for sustainability with new tools and conversation. *Journal of Education for Sustainable Development, 9*(2), 126–136.

Mullen, C. A., & Hutinger, J. L. (2008). The principal's role in fostering collaborative learning communities through faculty study group development. *Theory Into Practice, 47*, 276–285.

National Policy Board for Educational Administration. (2015). *Professional standards for educational leaders 2015*. Reston, VA: NPBEA.

Nelson, B. S., & Sassi, A. (2000). Shifting approaches to supervision: The case of mathematics supervision. *Education Administration Quarterly, 36*(4), 553–584. doi:10.1177/001316100219691000

Nolet, V. (2009). Preparing sustainability-literate teachers. *Teachers College Record, 111*(2), 409–442.

Nolet, V. (2016). *Educating for sustainabilty: Principles and practices for teachers*. New York: Routledge.

Olivier, D. F., & Hipp, K. K. (2006). Leadership capacity and collective efficacy: Interacting to sustain student learning in a professional learning community. *Journal of School Leadership, 16*, 505–519.

Putnam, R. T., & Borko, H. (1997). Teacher learning: Implications of new views of cognition. In B. J. Biddle, T. L. Good, & I. F. Goodson (Eds.), *The international handbook of teachers and teaching* (pp. 1223–1296). Dordrecht, The Netherlands: Kluwer.

Riordan, M., & Klein, E. J. (2010). Environmental education in action: How expeditionary learning schools support classroom teachers in tackling issues of sustainability. *Teacher Education Quarterly, 37*, 4, 119–137.

Sobel, D. (2005). *Place-based education: Connecting classrooms and communities*. Great Barrington, MA: The Orion Society.

Stone, M. K., & Barlow, Z. (Eds.). (2005). *Ecological literacy: Educating our children for a sustainable world*. San Francisco: Sierra Club Books.

Taylor, A. (2009). *Linking architecture and education: Sustainable design of learning environments*. Albuquerque: University of New Mexico Press.

The Earth Charter Initiative. (2015). *Earth charter: Values and principles for a sustainable future*. Retrieved from: http://www.earthcharterinaction.org

Thomas, G. (2005). Facilitation in education for the environment. *Australian Journal for Environmental Education, 21*, 107–116.

Tilbury, D. (2011). *Education for sustainable development: An expert review of processes and learning*. Paris: UNESCO.

Tyack, D., & Tobin, W. (1994). The grammar of schooling: Why has it been so hard to change. *American Education Research Journal, 31*(3), 453–479.

Uline, C. L., Tschannen-Moran, M., & Perez, L. (2003). Constructive conflict: How controversy contributes to school improvement. *Teacher College Record, 105,* 782–816.

UNESCO. (2005). *United Nations Decade of Education for Sustainable Development (2005–2014). International Implementation Scheme.* Paris: UNESCO.

Wals, A. E. J. (2009). *Review of contexts and structures for education for sustainable development 2009: Learning for a sustainable world.* Paris: UNESCO.

Waters, J. T., Marzano, R. J., & McNulty, B. A. (2003). *Balanced leadership: What 30 years of research tells us about the effect of leadership on student achievement.* Aurora, CO: Mid-continent Research for Education and Learning.

Wiggins, G., & McTighe, J. (2005). *Understanding by design* (2nd ed.). Alexandria, VA: ASCD.

Williams, D. R., & Brown, J. D. (2012). *Gardens and sustainability education: Bringing life to schools and schools to life.* New York: Routledge.

Woolfolk Hoy, A., Davis, H., & Pape, S. (2006). Teachers' knowledge, beliefs, and thinking. In P. A. Alexander & P. H, Winne (Eds.), *Handbook of educational psychology* (2nd ed., pp. 715–737). Mahwah, NJ: Lawrence Erlbaum.

10

Green School Networks, Recognition Programs, and Resources

(Co-authored by Tania McKey)

We've got to decide that we want to live in a world that is sane and happy and healthy, and that everyone deserves that.

(Majora Carter, in CNN, 2008)

Education is the most powerful weapon which you can use to change the world.

(Nelson Mandela, in Strauss, 2013)

Green schools are a rapidly growing global phenomenon. Although the actual number of green schools is still a very small percentage of schools overall, these early exemplars are demonstrating that green is the way of the future. Early evaluations of green schools are finding quite positive results for students, teachers, communities, and the environment, as we have shared throughout this book. Green schools provide a high leverage strategy for addressing many 21st-century challenges, from student engagement and performance to climate change and community resilience. A recent study of green school leaders found that 99% of respondents reported improvements in student engagement and 77% reported improvements in community engagement following their greening efforts (Sterrett, Imig, & Moore, 2014). These positive learning results, as well as dollar savings, and environmental benefits are increasingly attracting attention, as evidenced by the Green Schools Alliance (GSA), EcoSchools, and the U.S. Department of Education

Green Ribbon School (ED-GRS) award program. Following a brief look at GSA and Eco-Schools initiatives, this chapter will focus on learning from the ED-GRS award winning schools.

The GSA is one example of an international coalition of schools striving to be more sustainable. GSA facilitates school-level goal setting, implementation, and evaluation, as well as sharing network-wide success stories. In a January 2016 email from GSA's executive director, Sharon Jaye reported, "Our membership grew from 3,500 schools in 2014 to 7,884 schools with members in 41 U.S. States and 53 countries." Schools join the GSA to connect with other educators who are greening their facilities, grounds, and curriculum. Membership does not indicate mastery necessarily. This rapid growth in schools that are, at a minimum, making the effort to connect with others interested in sustainability is indicative of this educational innovation spreading throughout the world. The green schools movement serves children, communities, and our planet. It is a purposeful, practical, and powerful strategy for improving schools.

Announced in January 2016, the GSA has a new District Collaborative, including 21 U.S. public school districts, eight of which are included in the list of 12 largest school districts. See the full list of member districts in Table 10.1. These 21 school districts serve 3.6 million students in 5,726 schools and have budgets totaling $53 billion. This Collaborative aims to "Leverage [their] collective purchasing power to increase access to sustainable alternatives and promote market transformation; influence local, regional and national policy decisions; contribute to the development of district-level sustainability programs for Green Schools Alliance members; and build and share best practices at a district level" (GSA, 2016, n.p.). With their collective influence, the GSA District Collaborative is sure to help make green schools mainstream practice across U.S school districts!

Eco-Schools is another international network of schools striving for sustainability. The National Wildlife Federation (NWF) has been hosting Eco-Schools in the U.S. since 2008, although the program began in Europe more than a decade earlier. As of early 2016, there were 59 countries participating in the Eco-Schools program and 735 participating schools across 45 of the United States, plus the District of Columbia. This program is a recognition program with a seven-step application process and three levels of recognition, with the highest award being the Green Flag Award. Schools first register as Eco-Schools and then work towards recognition. Maintaining the Green Flag requires renewal every two years. The application process requires documentation of activities such as having an eco-action team, conducting an environmental audit, writing an eco-action plan, evaluating progress, integrating environmental education into learning, involving the community, and developing a school-wide eco-code (NWF, 2016).

Table 10.1 School District Members of the GSA District Collaborative, as of January 2016, Listed from Largest to Smallest Student Membership

New York City Department of Education, NY
Chicago Public Schools, IL
Clark County School District, NV
Broward County Public Schools, FL
Houston Independent School District, TX
Orange County Public Schools, FL
Fairfax County Public Schools, VA
The School District of Palm Beach County, FL
The School District of Philadelphia, PA
San Diego Unified School District, CA
Denver Public Schools, CO
Austin Independent School District, TX
Virginia Beach City Public Schools, VA
San Francisco Unified School District, CA
Boston Public Schools, MA
Detroit Public Schools, MI
Oakland Unified School District, CA
District of Columbia Public Schools, Washington, DC
Fayette County Public Schools, KY
Lincoln Public Schools, NE
Kansas City Public Schools, MO

A national initiative celebrates successful green schools across the United States. The U.S. Department of Education Green Ribbon School (ED-GRS) award program has recognized nearly 300 institutions for their practice of whole school sustainability. Although the ED-GRS program recognizes K–12 schools, school districts and higher education institutions, we remain focused on the K–12 schools for this chapter. The winning school applications are publicly available and provide an outstanding pool of evidence for what whole school sustainability looks like in practice. Tania McKey, an August 2016 PhD graduate in Educational Leadership from Auburn University, is the co-author of this chapter. We draw heavily from her dissertation research to provide a detailed description of the ED-GRS award, the winners through 2015, and their exemplar practices. We end this chapter and our book with some suggestions for greening your schools.

U.S. Department of Education Green Ribbon School Award Program

The first awardees of the ED-GRS program received recognition in April 2012. Cohorts of winners are announced annually in April. The purpose of the ED-GRS award program is to "inspire schools, districts and Institutions of Higher Education (IHEs) to strive for 21st century excellence, by highlighting promising practices and resources that all can employ" (USDOE, 2015, n.p.). Three pillars comprise the ED-GRS award program: (1) reducing environmental impact and costs; (2) improving the health and wellness of schools, students and staff; and (3) providing effective environmental and sustainability education. The three pillars aim to address whole school sustainability by including both sides of the academic house, facilities and curriculum. Pillars (1) and (2) promote sustainable and healthy practices within operations and management. Pillar (3) promotes environmental and sustainability education in the curriculum. The award does not necessarily require deep levels of collaboration between facilities and curriculum leaders. Warner and Elser (2014) found very few examples of interconnected projects within the first cohort of ED-GRS award winners. Nor does the award make specific mention regarding leadership approaches, such as cultivating democratic community, for facilitating learning and change for sustainability, as we discussed in Chapter 2. However, it is an excellent starting place for schools to highlight their progress toward whole school sustainability. As Sterrett et al. (2014) reported:

> Schools really appreciate the validation, awareness, and visibility that the ED-GRS award brings. The passion and excitement in so many of the open-ended responses indicates how eager people are for this kind of recognition, and that green efforts have often been invisible and championed by unsung heroes. (pp. 13–14)

Although the U.S. Department of Education manages this national recognition program, individual state departments of education or other qualifying authorities must nominate their jurisdiction's schools for the award. Each authority may develop its own application or adapt the sample application provided by the ED-GRS award program. They also must design and implement their own application review process for selecting the schools that they then nominate for consideration at the national level. In general, schools conduct a self-study in order to complete their application. They document evidence of their practice within each of the three pillars, reducing environmental impact, improving health and wellness, and educating for sustainability. When used as intended, this self-assessment both celebrates current green practice while also highlighting opportunities for continued growth. Whether or not schools continue to grow greener after the award is entirely up to them. Presently, schools may be recognized just once for the ED-GRS award. There is no process in place for annual or repeated recognition.

The ED-GRS Award program sets out guiding rules for nominating pre-K–12 schools. They are as follows (USDOE, 2015):

◆ If nominating more than one school, the nominating authority must include at least one nominee that serves a student body with at least 40% low income students.

◆ If nominating a private school, at least one public school or district must also be nominated.

◆ No more than one in five nominees may be a private school.

Over the four years of the ED-GRS award program, twelve states (AK, ID, LA, ME, NV, ND, OK, SC, SD, TX, UT, WY) and two qualifying authorities (Puerto Rico, U.S. Virgin Islands) have yet to participate at least once. However, the lack of participation in this particular award does not necessarily mean that the educational authority lacks green school efforts. Nevada and Texas both have school districts represented in the GSA District Collaborative described earlier. Texas also has 235 schools participating in Eco-Schools, second in the U.S. only to New York's 427 participating schools. Of the other states not participating in the ED-GRS award program, South Carolina has 37, Louisiana has 17, and the rest have 10 or fewer registered Eco-Schools (NWF, 2016). The Oklahoma Green and Healthy Schools program reports 27 active green schools as of early 2016 (Oklahoma Green and Healthy Schools Program, 2016). The growing list of exemplar and active green schools, as well as national and state-level green school networks, provide a rich source of practical inspiration and guidance for those new to greening their schools. We will turn now to look more closely at the first four annual cohorts of ED-GRS award winners, nearly 300 schools.

ED-GRS Award Winners

The pool of 249 ED-GRS award winners includes a wide range of public, charter, and independent schools, of all configurations, serving a diverse student body. Our description begins with answering the question, "Where in the U.S. are ED-GRS award winners?" Table 10.2 tells us the number of winning schools per state or qualifying authority, per year. Non-state qualifying authorities that may nominate schools include Puerto Rico (PR), the Virgin Islands (VI), Department of Defense Education Activity (DoDEA), and the Bureau of Indian Education (BIE). Table 10.3 reports a summary of school funding models and percentage of winning schools serving students in poverty. Table 10.4 reports a summary of the winning school locale classifications, as reported by the applicants.

Table 10.2 ED-GRS Award Winners by State (or Nominating Authorities) in 2012, 2013, 2014, and 2015

State	2012	2013	2014	2015	Total Schools	Total Years
AL	2	3	3	3	11	4
AZ	2	0	0	4	6	2
AR	1	0	0	0	1	1
BIE[1]	1	0	0	0	1	1
CA	4	4	3	0	11	3
CO	3	1	3	1	8	4
CT	0	3	2	4	9	3
DE	0	1	0	3	4	2
DC[2]	2	3	0	3	8	3
DODEA[3]	0	0	0	2	2	1
FL	3	2	0	3	8	3
GA	3	1	2	2	8	4
HI	2	0	0	0	2	1
IL	3	0	1	1	5	3
IN	0	1	2	1	4	3
IA	0	1	0	0	1	1
KS	3	1	0	0	4	2
KY	3	3	1	2	9	4

MD	4	2	2	2	10	4
MA	0	3	1	2	6	3
MI	2	0	2	0	4	2
MN	3	3	2	4	12	4
MS	0	1	0	0	1	1
MO	2	0	0	0	2	1
MT	0	0	0	3	3	1
NE	2	1	1	2	6	4
NH	0	1	0	0	1	1
NJ	4	2	2	4	12	4
NM	0	0	1	0	1	1
NY	3	3	1	0	7	3
NC	2	0	1	0	3	2
ND	1	0	0	0	1	1
OH	2	1	3	1	7	4
OR	4	0	2	1	7	3
PA	4	3	0	0	7	2
RI	2	2	2	2	8	4
TN	0	2	0	0	2	1
VT	0	3	3	0	6	2
VA	2	2	0	4	8	3
WA	4	4	2	3	13	4
WV	2	2	2	1	7	4
WI	3	4	4	3	14	4
Total Schools	77	63	48	61	249	—
Total Authority Participation	30	29	24	25	41	—

Notes:
[1] Bureau of Indian Education
[2] Washington, DC
[3] Department of Defense Education Activity

Overall, 38 states and the District of Columbia, the BIE, and DoDEA have had at least one ED-GRS award winner during the first four years of the program. This represents a 74% participation rate across the 55 qualifying authorities. Twelve authorities have participated only once in the ED-GRS award program (AZ, BIE, DODEA, HI, IA, MS, MO, MT, NH, NM, ND, and TN). And 13 authorities have participated in all four years of the ED-GRS award program (AL, CO, GA, KY, MD, MN, NE, NJ, OH, RI, WA, WV, and WI). Six of these 13 authorities have had over ten winning schools (AL, MO, MN, NJ, WA, and WI). California has had 11 winning schools across three years of participation (2012, 2013, and 2014).

Although the total number of participating authorities has declined since the first year, there has been substantial participation for this early phase of the award program. These early award winners are the trailblazers. Even in the high stakes climate of No Child Left Behind, they have prioritized healthy schools, wellness, and environmental education such that they had a track record that qualified them for these early awards. Now that many of the trailblazers may have received the award, a continued dip in participation over the next few years may be expected. We expect that participation numbers will likely climb in the future, as school leaders, teachers, and communities continue to learn about the benefits of and adopt green school practices.

Trailblazing schools that have won the ED-GRS award exist in all different contexts from publicly funded to privately funded, from low income to

Table 10.3 Funding Source for ED-GRS Winning Schools

Type of Funding	2012 (%)	2013 (%)	2014 (%)	2015 (%)
Public and Charter	84	84	81	90
Private/Independent	15	16	19	10
Bureau of Indian Education	1	0	0	0
High Poverty	45	50	29	44

Table 10.4 Applicant Reported School Locale by Year and Percentage of ED-GRS Winning Schools

School Locale	2012 (%)	2013 (%)	2014 (%)	2015 (%)
Rural	26	16	25	26
Suburban	45	48	56	49
Urban	29	36	19	25

high income, and from rural to urban communities. The nomination rules, as described earlier, influence the distribution of winning schools across type of funding, student socio-economic status (SES) (Table 10.3), and to some extent, even locale categories (Table 10.4). The rules ensure that lower income schools (typically found in urban or rural areas, rather than suburban locales or privately funded) receive recognition. The percentage of high-poverty winning schools has varied from 50% in 2013 to 29% in 2014. The way the rules are written suggests that states where innovative practices are more common among well-funded schools may not be eligible to nominate all of their green schools until practices diffuse and take root in less funded schools as well. In the first year of the award, only 10% of the participating authorities had just one school recognized. The second year, 2013, that number jumped to 34% of participating authorities with just one school recognized. In 2014 and 2015 the percentage of authorities with just one winning school went from 29% to 24%, respectively. These nomination criteria present an excellent incentive for continuing to develop green school practices—practices that are good for children, communities, and the planet—in all types of schools.

ED-GRS Award Winning Practices

We will end our in-depth look at the ED-GRS award winners with an overview of their green school practices for each pillar. We do not have space for reporting all of their practices, so we highlight the most common. Pillar I is about reducing environmental impacts and costs. Schools reported tracking and reducing their energy usage via energy management plans, ENERGY STAR participation, retrofitted lighting, renovations, natural light, green roofs, and occupant behavior. They shifted their energy sources from non-renewables to renewable energy including solar, wind, geothermal, and biomass. Schools also reported tracking and reducing their use of water through innovative landscaping, collection and use of rainwater, retrofitting plumbing, and occupant behavior. Waste reduction through recycling was one of the most common activities in Pillar I. Composting organic waste, including school lunch waste, appears to be increasingly common among winners. Finally, addressing transpiration also reduced impacts to the environment. Most school winners reported strict "No Idling" policies for cars and buses. Many schools are encouraging safe walking and biking to school, a once common practice.

Activities in Pillar I such as "No Idling" policies, and biking/walking to school also improve the health and wellness of students and staff in schools, the focus of Pillar II. Most winning schools reporting paying close attention to their indoor air quality (IAQ) through efforts such as integrated pest management programs, green cleaning products, low volatile organic compounds (VOC) interior products, moisture/mold/mildew control, and banning pets, air fresh-eners, scented candles, and other asthma triggers. Health and fitness programs also support wellness, and the winning schools encourage their students and staff to eat well and stay active. School gardens, farm-to-school programs, and salad bars in the cafeteria play a central role in teaching students about the benefits of eating fresh vegetables and fruit. Reducing and even eliminating sugary drinks and snacks is not uncommon across the winning schools. Students in green schools participate in many different physical education programs, play outside every day, and spend significant time in nature.

Pillar III activities build on Pillars I and II by integrating environmental and sustainability education into and across the curriculum. Most winning schools report having at least one learning unit focused on their local environment. Many go far beyond this basic level to reporting innovative partnerships with specialized non-profit organizations and student-driven civic engagement projects. These publicly available applications are a wealth of information and inspiration about what schools are doing to "go green." These applications also serve as early measures of transition from mechanical models of schooling to living system models of schooling. Few schools have left behind all vestiges of the factory model, but many are well on their way to doing so. Leading this type of transformative change requires looking to nature for fresh inspiration.

Growing a Greener School for Your Children, Community, and Our Planet

If you have read this far then we hope you are convinced that whole school sustainability offers you a comprehensive pathway for improving education, communities, and our planet. If you began reading already convinced then we hope you found some new ideas and possibilities for continuing, expanding, and deepening your work! Green schools are engaging, healthy, and resource-efficient places for learning. Although this book was not meant to be a how-to guide, but rather a detailed description of the possibilities and supporting research for whole school sustainability, we are ending the book with some guidance for growing greener schools. Sustainability initiatives require deep change (Doppelt, 2010). These are not minor tweaks to the way we've always done things. Change for sustainability requires learning to work differently across all areas of the educational enterprise. The authoritarian leader and "sage on the stage" model of teaching are left behind for good and adults become co-learners alongside their students. Collective inquiry into how we might live differently fills the learning airwaves and new insights and behaviors follow. Green schools have the potential to be vibrant places of learning that truly contribute to making the world a better place. Here are a few recommendations for getting started and continuing your leadership for whole school sustainability.

Cultivating Change

Leading change is a topic that fills volumes and volumes of scholarship, best-selling books, magazines, and podcasts. Consultants offer models and formulas for making change easier in your organization. The reality is that change is challenging because every context is unique. One-size-fits-all models and formulas just don't often work in isolation of deep contextual knowledge and understanding. In this book's preface we mentioned a quote from Day and Leithwood's end-of-book reflection on effective school leadership. We revisit and expand it here:

> But we want to dig a bit deeper below the surface of our empirical evidence than do these explanations. Such digging has led us to the view that our empirical evidence about the nature of successful principal leadership can be partly explained by the basic metaphors leaders and their colleagues hold about their organizations . . . Two competing metaphors—"organizations as machines" and "organizations as living systems"—are featured in Wheatley's explanation for both organizations and leadership that differ radically in their functioning and outcomes. *The work of our successful principals strongly suggests that they thought of their organizations as living systems, not machines . . .*
>
> In sum, then, part of the explanation, an important part in our view, for the work of the successful principals included in our study is simply that they viewed their schools as something like Wheatley's "living system" or a "family" or perhaps a "learning organization" and crafted a role for themselves that was designed to nurture such a system. (Day & Leithwood, 2007, p. 200, emphasis added)

Successful school leaders effectively lead learning and change, whether for sustainability or not. Day and Leithwood's powerful insight follows decades of research into school leadership. It tells us that our root metaphors for leadership and learning are fundamental to effective practice.

Wheatley (1999) provided guidance for leading change in schools with root metaphors grounded in living systems—"We have found life to be a rich source of ideas and wisdom for how we humans can approach the challenge of creating schools or any complex system that has the capacity to grow and change yet remain purposeful and effective over time" (n.p.). We present our adaptation of Wheatley's framework here, with specific applications to leading change for whole school sustainability that derive from our experience as researchers and participants in organizational change for sustainability.

Develop Aspirational and Purposeful Networks; Cultivate Trust

Change happens through networks of connection. Without trusting networks of connection among organizational members, change initiatives fail (Daly, Moolenaar, Bolivar, & Burke, 2010; Louis, 2007). Wheatley explained that many organizations are comprised of independent individuals operating from their own private purposes and aspirations. Unfortunately, these are the organizations where cut-throat politics are the destructive norm. Schools where people are drawn from geographical attendance zones, with no opportunity for meaningful connection, may be particularly challenged by these characteristics of disconnection and competition. As Wheatley looked to living systems, she explained that they self-organize around shared interests, not disconnected and purely self-interested agendas. Thus, in order to prepare for change, leaders must engage community members in conversations about purpose and aspiration.

Parker Palmer (1998) speaks eloquently about the value of connecting with our original motivations for becoming educators. Engaging with questions of "Why am I here?" and "What brought me into education?" can be refreshing, renewing, and reassuring. Authentic conversations with colleagues about our deeper motivations typically lead right into our aspirations for making a positive difference in the world. Each individual's motivations and aspirations may vary somewhat, but organization-wide conversations lead to greater understanding and understanding leads to deeper levels of trust and trust leads to connection. Networks of connection characterized by trust provide a healthy context for change (Daly & Finnigan, 2009).

As groups connect around purpose and aspiration in meaningful ways—over conversations that take time, then shared clarity is likely to emerge (Senge, Cambron-McCabe, Lucas, Smith, & Dutton, 2012). It is impossible to define what this emergent clarity about purpose and aspiration will be for each school community. In fact, that is the major problem with boiler-plate mission statements inspired by state-level policy (discussed in Chapter 2). Imposing purpose and aspiration on a system is doomed to fail. The practice of mandating from above is derived from mechanistic assumptions that do not align with how living systems grow and change. Mechanistic practices leave people feeling disconnected, apathetic, and uninspired. Wheatley's work (1999) makes clear that living systems are not mindlessly obedient. We can't demand that a flower grow and open more quickly or that a meadow become a forest before its time. Change in nature develops and unfolds at its own pace. Instead, leaders must artfully cultivate healthy networks of connection and find pockets of readiness for change within their school communities. Change that resonates with a community will take root and grow. Listening carefully to what people find most meaningful will reveal these opportunities.

Discover What Matters Most to Your School Community; Begin There

Meaning fuels the energy and commitment for change. "Meaningful information lights up a network, and moves through it like a windswept brush fire. Meaningless information, in contrast, smolders at the gates until somebody dumps cold water on it" (Wheatley, 1999, n.p.). When deciding where to begin with whole school sustainability initiatives, find the right place for your school community. You can begin anywhere, but success depends upon beginning where the energy—what matters to the people of your community—positively supports the work. The superintendent of North Penn School District, Dr. Dietrich, provides an excellent example of this leadership practice (Kensler & Uline, 2015).

Kensler and Uline (2015) described the transition of North Penn School District (NPSD) from an energy hog to an energy star. Although Superintendent Dietrich was eager to bring sustainability related initiatives to his district, he waited for the right opportunity. He knew his community well enough to know that reducing their carbon footprint to impact climate change effects was not going to be meaningful or motivating on a large enough scale. Calls for teachers to reduce their energy usage by removing their classroom refrigerators (as one example), for the purpose of saving the planet, would most definitely fall flat. Enter the Great Recession. By 2009, the district faced dire economic conditions. Dietrich knew his community would be willing to sacrifice convenience in return for saving each other's jobs. He, along with his leadership team, crafted a district-wide process for cutting their energy usage. He made it clear that saving energy equated to saving jobs. They were inclusive, systematic, and consistent in their communications, processes, and evaluations. By 2013, NPSD was honored as an ENERGY STAR Partner of the Year, "realizing a 30% reduction in energy use across all of their facilities and saving more than $1.1 million in utility costs" (Kensler & Uline, 2015, p. 57).

Design Processes for Co-creation and Ownership; Buy-in Is Not Enough

Positional leaders have the power to decide whether or not to share power. They have the power to design processes for engagement or not. Leaders who understand their organizations as living systems know that, "People only support what they create. We must always participate in the development of those things which affect us" (Wheatley, 1999, n.p.). Therefore, wise positional leaders practice democratic principles (Chapter 3) and artfully design authentic, inclusive processes for their community members to co-create meaningful change initiatives (Senge et al., 2012). These processes inevitably take more time than sending out directives. However, we know that directives do not facilitate deep, second order change. McKinsey & Company is a global partnership for organizational research and consulting that has been operating for more than 90 years. Based on internationally representative surveys of chief executive officers (CEOs), they consistently report that nearly 70% of change initiatives fail. What about those that succeed? CEOs report broad engagement of employees in co-creating the change initiatives that succeed (Keller, Meaney, & Pung, 2010).

Compliance and buy-in are not enough for deep change to take root and grow. Processes for employee engagement serve to have two primary effects. They tap collective intelligence and they generate ownership. Collective intelligence insures that the change initiative embodies the full knowledge of the organization, not just a few minds positioned at the top of the organizational chart. Ownership insures commitment and follow-through. A tale of two recycling stories serves to illustrate this point. In one, a district-wide recycling effort was basically mandated from above. All schools received a memo requesting that they begin recycling immediately. In schools where some members had already been collecting recyclable materials and carting them home, this was a welcome change and participation was enthusiastically high. However, in schools where interest in recycling was not yet present, participation in recycling never took hold. Recycling programs in schools rely on everyone to be successful; success depends on ownership. School members, from students to administrators, have to know and choose to put their waste in the right place. Where ownership is low, people mindlessly dump their trash without care or concern.

As a contrasting story, consider the same large, urban school district a few years later. Here the new and improved recycling effort is led by a district office employee who has brought a diverse group together to co-design more effective recycling strategies. The group includes community advocates, city representatives, facilities/custodial staff, school leaders, and teachers. Through genuine stakeholder involvement, collaborative planning, many school visits, and thoughtful implementation, the district's recycling participation climbed rapidly. The implementation phase spanned across several years and allowed schools to opt into the program. This power to choose was a critical element of program success. At their request, they received training, and support for school-based recycling teams that included administrator, teacher, custodial, and student representation. Flexibility existed within an overall guiding framework and allowed teams to adapt the recycling program to their own context. Invitational processes of engagement are worth their time and effort, if your goal is deep change.

Remain Curious, Observant, and Reflective

Leading change is a complex, messy process filled with helpful, as well as challenging, surprises. Those leading the change effort must remain curious about what is working and not working. They must watch carefully, observing individuals as well as group dynamics. Wheatley (1999) explains that this observant curiosity requires that leaders be present in the moment rather than "preoccupied with our images of how we want the world to be." She continued,

> Being present in the moment doesn't mean that we act without intention or flow directionless through life without any plans. But in an unpredictable world, we would do better to look at plans and measures as processes that enable a group to discover shared interests, to clarify its intent and strengthen its connections to new people and new information. We need less reverence for the plan as an object, and much more attention to the processes we use for planning and measuring. It is attention to the process, more than the product that enables us to weave an organization as flexible and resilient as a spider's web. (Wheatley, 1999, n.p.)

Relationships, networks, meaning, trust are all fluid properties that respond to organizational processes. Effective leaders will reflect frequently on their observations and test their interpretations in conversation with others. They will rely on formal data collection, as well as personal insight, to guide their learning and necessary adjustments.

Although, fundamentally, change requires cultivating healthy learning relationships within your specific context, whole school sustainability frameworks and assessment tools partnered with an action research framework (Bryk, Gomez, Grunow, & LeMahieu, 2015; Spaulding & Falco, 2012) are essential companions for this transformational work. Dautremont-Smith (2012) identified over 80 programs and tools related to sustainability practice in schools. Here, we are particularly interested in highlighting only a few assessment tools that support whole school sustainability practice, rather than a more narrow aspect of this work (e.g. energy savings, clean air, green cleaning, etc.). Since the first ED-GRS winners were announced after the date of Dautremont-Smith's thesis, he did not include this program in his review.

When it comes to whole school sustainability the *ED-GRS award application* is an outstanding self-assessment tool for documenting your school's progress and seeing new opportunities. If your state is not yet participating in the

ED-GRS program, then you can find a sample application at: http://www2. ed.gov/programs/green-ribbon-schools/applicant.html. Participating states and their ED-GRS contacts are listed at: http://www2.ed.gov/programs/ green-ribbon-schools/state-contacts.html.

Another recent, free and easily downloadable assessment tool for whole school sustainability is available from Compass Education at: http://www. compasseducation.org/sustainability-self-assessment-tool/ (released in April 2015). The *Sustainability Self-Assessment Tool (SS-AT)* guides an extensive self-study of practices that reflect each of the four Compass Points (Nature, Economy, Society, and Well-being) along a four point continuum of none (0) to fully operationalized and integrated into practice (3). Where the ED-GRS award application asks open-ended questions related to whole school sustainability practices, the SS-AT provides more detailed guidance for assessing differing degrees of your practice.

As mentioned early in this chapter, the NWF hosts Eco-Schools USA, and schools are able to join the program for free. The program provides online guidance at http://www.nwf.org/eco-schools for greening your school in seven steps. The seven steps include establishing an eco-action team; performing an environmental review/audit; developing an eco-action plan; monitoring and evaluating progress; linking to the educational curriculum; involving the entire school and larger community; and creating an eco-code, or mission statement. These are just a few of the assessment tools available. Find an updated and thorough review of green school frameworks in Metzger (2015).

Fertilizer for Green Innovation

Williams and Brown (2011) presented another living systems framework for thinking about leadership in schools:

> Life flows through living soil. In our effort to enliven an educational discourse presently characterized by lifeless mechanistic metaphors, we have introduced living soil as a regenerative alternative framework for thinking about schools as living organisms. Considering living soil as a metaphoric foundation for education underwrites a shift toward sustainability and emphasizes our conviction that truly meaningful learning is enacted in connection with life. Learning gardens planted directly on school grounds provide a practical example of the application of living soil as root metaphor. Like seeds of change that flourish in rich fertile living soil, school gardens and other sustainability education initiatives can be most effective when integrated into an ecological vision of education modeled after living soil. (p. 199)

With a living soil metaphor in mind, we offer some outstanding fertilizer for your whole school sustainability efforts. We have, of course, opted to present organic fertilizer! These are not synthetic, quick fix fertilizers. They are rich and complex, providing access to additional information, materials, and connections.

Find the U.S. Green Building Council's *Center for Green Schools* (USGBC, the Center) at: centerforgreenschools.org. Resources abound here from basic introductory material, to exemplar case studies, to research reports, to how-to guides for practical and political action. And there's more, much more than we can fully describe here! We will highlight just a few of the programs, resources, and partnerships.

- ◆ The *Green Classroom Professional Certificate* is a two-hour online course for learning green school basics. As mentioned earlier in this book, it is a great place to begin if you are trying to build your knowledge about green school practices. It makes for excellent school-wide professional development.
- ◆ *Green Strides* (accessed via the Center website or www.greenstrides. org) is a web portal to all green and free tools, for supporting your effort towards whole school sustainability. Originally developed by the U.S. Department of Education to support schools seeking to earn the ED-GRS award, the Center now hosts and manages the portal. You are able to access resources through filters and keyword searches. There is also an extensive webinar calendar. Sign up for the newsletter to hear about new and featured resources.
- ◆ *Learning Lab*, a partnership with EcoRise Youth Innovations, Representaciones Inteligencia Sustentable, and the Center, provides a curated catalogue of standards-aligned, project-based curriculum in English and Spanish. Educators develop these materials for educators for integrating sustainability across the curriculum. Learn more at: https://learninglab.usgbc.org/.
- ◆ The *State of Our Schools* (Filardo, 2016) report and interactive website, http://centerforgreenschools.org/state-our-schools, provides a wealth of data and information about the current state of funding for public school facilities. Visit the website and search on your school district to find out how their facilities expenditures and investments relate to recommended levels.
- ◆ The Center also convenes a national network of school district sustainability professionals in the U.S. This network utilizes technology to stay in touch throughout the year and comes together annually to share success stories, challenges, and learning for whole

school sustainability. You can find out how to join by visiting the Center's website.

◆ The *Green Schools Conference & Expo* brings together students, teachers, administrators, sustainability advocates, policy makers, and business and industry leaders—everyone who has an interest in green schools—for an annual conference. This is the place to visit each year if you want to connect with other green-minded individuals who are all striving to take their green school practice to the next level.

◆ *Green Apple Day of Service* (access via the Center website or http://greenapple.org/) is an international volunteer movement focused on greening schools. In 2014, volunteers registered nearly 4,000 projects across all 50 U.S. states and 43 countries. Volunteers numbered 306,000 and raised $4.7 million to support green school efforts that serve 2.1 million students. Make your plans to participate!

Find the **Green Schools Alliance** at: www.greenschoolsalliance.org. This is an international coalition of green schools and green school leaders. Members may be school districts, schools, student clubs, and/or individual sustainability coordinators. You will find extensive resources and the ability to network with other members, both locally and globally. The Green Cup Challenge is a fun competition for reducing energy use and improving recycling/waste reduction programs. Among many other things green, they publish a free, online journal, *The Green Journal*, where faculty and staff can share their stories about greening their schools.

Find the **Center for Ecoliteracy** at: www.ecoliteracy.org. The Center for Ecoliteracy offers resources, initiatives, and professional development related to systems change for sustainability and ecological education (Goleman, Bennett, & Barlow, 2012; Stone, 2009; Stone & Barlow, 2005). Frijtof Capra, often cited here in this book (Capra, 1996, 2002; Capra & Luigi, 2014), is one of the founders of this Center. Thus, it won't be surprising to find that a living systems perspective informs all of their efforts. Their work related to improving school food for children is particularly noteworthy (Stone, Brown, Comnes, & Koulias, 2010).

Find the **Cloud Institute for Sustainability Education** at: cloudinstitute. org. The Cloud Institute provides consulting, professional development, and curriculum design related to sustainability education. As described on their website, their "EfS Framework illustrates our whole systems approach, which springs from the recognition that lasting transformation in education requires innovation at the curricular, institutional, and community levels." We certainly agree!

Find the **Green Schools National Network** at: www.greenschools nationalnetwork.org. Once there, you can download their GreenPrint™ for "Becoming a Green, Healthy and Sustainable School." This is an excellent one-pager for guiding your greening efforts. You will also find an extensive list of green school networks by state that can be helpful for connecting with other green schools in your area.

Joining this organization will provide additional benefits and a subscription to the *Green Schools Catalyst Quarterly*.

Conclusion

The purpose of this book was to introduce whole school sustainability to emerging and practicing school leaders still new to the idea of green schools, as well as stretch already practicing green school leaders to see even more opportunities for transformation. Each chapter addressed a major domain of school leadership alongside emerging practices, research, and possibilities for whole school sustainability. In this final chapter, we emphasize that leadership for sustainability is occurring in schools across the United States and the world. These trailblazing leaders, like Angela and Tom, are demonstrating that our children, our communities, and our planet benefit from joining the global movement for sustainability. Paul Hawken described this global movement of well over 1 million organizations at the time of writing his book, *Blessed Unrest* (2007). It is a living movement that has been growing unseen for decades, but its existence, organization, and effects are becoming more and more visible, more and more influential. He described the intention of this movement:

> If you examine its values, missions, goals, and principles, and I urge you to do so, you will see that at the core of all organizations are two principles, albeit unstated: first is the Golden Rule; second is the sacredness of all life, whether it be a creature, child, or culture . . . I believe this movement will prevail. I don't mean it will defeat, conquer, or create harm to someone else. Quite the opposite. I don't tender the claim in an oracular sense. I mean the thinking that informs the movements goals will reign. (pp. 186–189)

We see the green schools movement as aligned with these inclusive and generous intentions as well as critical to its success. Educators have the opportunity to raise sustainability natives, people who grow up thinking more like living systems than machines. We are inspired by the vast array of present efforts and the transformative potential of future possibilities. We hope you are too.

Questions for Discussion

1. Choose a green school framework and conduct a self-study of your school. What opportunities do you see for continuing to grow a greener school?

2. Consider a recent change initiative in your school or district. Describe it thoroughly and then compare it to the guidance for cultivating change described in this chapter. Where did your change initiative reflect living system principles? Where did it reflect more traditional or mechanical approaches to organizational change? How might you improve future change initiatives?

3. After reading this book, what are you most inspired to do? Why?

References

Bryk, A. S., Gomez, L. M., Grunow, A., & LeMahieu, P. G. (2015). *Learning to improve: How America's schools can get better at getting better*. Boston, MA: Harvard Education Press.

Capra, F. (1996). *The web of life*. New York: Anchor Books.

Capra, F. (2002). *Hidden connections*. New York: Doubleday.

Capra, F., & Luigi, L. P. (2014). *The systems view of life: A unifying vision*. Cambridge: Cambridge University Press.

CNN. (2008, June 6). Interview: Majora Carter. Retrieved from: http://www.cnn.com/2008/TECH/06/05/carterinterview/

Daly, A. J., & Finnigan, K. S. (2009). A bridge between worlds: Understanding network structure to understand change strategy. *Journal of Educational Change, 11*(2), 111–138. doi:10.1007/s10833-009-9102-5

Daly, A. J., Moolenaar, N. M., Bolivar, J. M., & Burke, P. (2010). Relationships in reform: The role of teachers' social networks. *Journal of Educational Administration, 48*(3), 359–391. doi:10.1108/09578231011041062

Dautremont-Smith, J. (2012). *School sustainability rating systems: Strengths, limitations, and future prospects*. Unpublished master's thesis, University of Michigan, Ann Arbor, MI.

Day, C., & Leithwood, K. (Eds.). (2007). *Successful principal leadership in time of change: An international perspective*. Dordrecht, The Netherlands: Springer.

Doppelt, B. (2010). *Leading change toward sustainability* (2nd ed.). Sheffield, UK: Greenleaf Publishing.

Filardo, M. (2016). *State of our schools: America's K–12 facilities 2016*. Washington, DC: 21st Century School Fund, U.S. Green Building Council, Inc., & the National Council on School Facilities.

Goleman, D., Bennett, L., & Barlow, Z. (2012). *Ecoliterate: How educators are cultivating emotional, social, and ecological intelligence*. San Francisco, CA: Jossey-Bass.

GSA. (2016). *GSA District Collaborative*. Retrieved from: http://www.greenschools alliance.org/district-collaborative

Hawken, P. (2007). *Blessed unrest: How the largest movement in the world came into being and why no one saw it coming*. New York: Penguin Group.

Keller, S., Meaney, M., & Pung, C. (2010). *What successful transformations share: McKinsey Global Survey results*. Retrieved from: http://www.mckinsey.com/insights/organization/what_successful_transformations_share_mckinsey_global_survey_results

Kensler, L. A., & Uline, C. L. (2015). The transformation of a school district from energy hog to energy star. In S. J. Gross & J. P. Shapiro (Eds.), *Democratic ethical educational leadership: Reclaiming school reform* (pp. 54–58). New York: Routledge.

Louis, K. S. (2007). Trust and improvement in schools. *Journal of Educational Change, 8*, 1–24.

Metzger, A. B. (2015). Green school frameworks. In T. C. Chan, E. G. Mense, K. E. Lane, & M. D. Richardson (Eds.), *Marketing the green school: Form, function, and the future* (pp. 1–14). Hershey, PA: IGI Global

NWF. (2016). *Calling all eco-schools*. Retrieved from: http://www.nwf.org/Eco-Schools-USA.aspx

Oklahoma Green and Healthy Schools Program. (2016). Retrieved from: http://www.okgreenschools.org/

Palmer, P. J. (1998). *The courage to teach*. San Francisco: Jossey-Bass.

Senge, P. M., Cambron-McCabe, N., Lucas, T., Smith, B., & Dutton, J. (2012). *Schools that learn (updated and revised): A fifth discipline fieldbook for educators, parents, and everyone who cares about education*. New York: Crown Business.

Spaulding, D. T., & Falco, J. (2012). *Action research for school leaders*. New York: Pearson Higher Ed.

Sterrett, W. L., Imig, S., & Moore, D. (2014). U.S. Department of Education Green Ribbon Schools: Leadership insights and implications. *Journal of Organizational Learning and Leadership, 12*(2), 2–18.

Stone, M. K. (2009). *Smart by nature: Schooling for sustainability*. Healdsburg, CA: Watershed Media.

Stone, M. K., & Barlow, Z. (2005). *Ecological literacy: Educating our children for a sustainable world*. San Francisco: Sierra Club Books.

Stone, M. K., Brown, K., Comnes, L., & Koulias, J. (2010). *Rethinking school lunch guide. Second edition*. Retrieved from Berkeley, CA: http://www.ecoliteracy.org/sites/default/files/rethinking_school_lunch_guide.pdf

Strauss, L. (2013, December 5). Nelson Mandela on the power of education. *Washington Post*. Retrieved from: https://www.washingtonpost.com/news/answer-sheet/wp/2013/12/05/nelson-mandelas-famous-quote-on-education/

USDOE. (2015). *U.S. Department of Education Green Ribbon Schools*. Retrieved from: http://www2.ed.gov/programs/green-ribbon-schools/index.html

Warner, B. P., & Elser, M. (2014). How do sustainable schools integrate sustainability education? An assessment of Certified Sustainable K–12 schools in the United States. *The Journal of Environmental Education, 46*(1), 1–22. doi:10.1080/00958964.2014.953020

Wheatley, M. (1999). *Bringing schools back to life: Schools as living systems.* Retrieved from http://www.margaretwheatley.com/articles/lifetoschools.html

Williams, D. R., & Brown, J. (2011). *Learning gardens and sustainability education.* New York: Routledge.

Index